THE BAPTIST

THE
BAPTIST

**An historical and theological
study of the Baptist identity**

Jack Hoad

Grace Publications

Grace Publications Trust
139 Grosvenor Avenue, London, N5 2NH, England
© Jack Hoad 1986
First published 1986

ISBN 0.946462.10.0

Distributed by:
EVANGELICAL PRESS
16/18 High Street, Welwyn, Hertfordshire, AL6 9EQ, England

Cover photographs
Front: Hallstatt in the Salzkammergut, Upper Austria, where biblical reform survived the Catholic Counter-Reformation, but where persecution by both Catholics and Protestants silenced Baptist testimony.

Back: The commemoration tablet on No.5 Newmarkt, Zurich, Switzerland, the meeting place of Swiss Brethren. The inscription reads: (in German) "In this house lived Konrad Grebel who, together with Felix Mantz, founded the baptist movement." (Rebuilt 1752).

Typeset by Wagstaffs Design Associates, Henlow, Bedfordshire.
Printed in Great Britain by The Bath Press, Avon.

TO MY WIFE

Acknowledgements:

The author acknowledges the encouragement and help of many colleagues in the baptist ministry, and in particular, the stimulation of the suggestions and criticisms of Revs. Stephen Dray MA BD, Rbt. J. Sheehan BA and G. Michael Thomas BA, his own pastor; the detailed checking and advice of Rev. Colin Vincent Vincent BA BD; the cooperation of Dr J. K. Davies BD ThD and Mr N. Clarkson FIB, of Grace Publications and the staff of Evangelical Press; M. F. Buhler BD pastor of La Bonne Nouvelle, Mulhouse, France, whose long years of friendship have meant so much and who first challenged the author to write this book, with Mr N. A. Cox FCA and others, chief among whom is the devoted partner of fifty years spent in the independent baptist ministry. The author takes sole responsibility for the content of the book.

Contents

Introduction

The baptist heritage is an immensely rich record of the grace of God in preserving a biblical church witness throughout the centuries of the christian era. In repeated upsurges of a revived testimony to the rugged simplicity of New Testament principles, the Lord of the churches has proclaimed against the heretical departures of those claiming to be main-line christianity. This heritage is a treasure which baptists ought not to esteem lightly but which they are in danger of losing outright in these critical times. With today's ecumenical movement gaining progressive momentum towards the evolution of a 'World Church', it is already apparent that the objective is far more than a 'unification of christian churches'. That is but the near focus. Beyond lies an enormous 'syncretistic corpus' in which all religions of all nations will be co-ordinated into a World Body. This book is written in the belief that the only credible answer to that apostate conglomerate is to be found in the world-wide spread of baptised churches holding the doctrines of grace in a simple and total submission to the Word of God. It is, in the first place, addressed to fellow baptists with the plea not to ignore our heritage at such a time as this. To do so is to cast back the mercy of God in his face and to lose hope of an effective christian witness tomorrow.

The baptist's heritage was born of the faithfulness of believers throughout the christian era, who refused to be called the children of the emperor, not being afraid of the king's commandment. They chose to suffer as the people of God rather than enjoy the world's pleasure and favour

1

by the compromise of a simple, biblical discipleship of Jesus
their Lord, (cf Hebrews 11:23). They shed their blood
rather than sacrifice the biblical principle of the sole
sufficiency of the Holy Scriptures in all matters of faith and
practice. Their blood is indeed the 'seed of the church'
bearing a harvest today against those who sell their liberty
to the state, to the system or their souls to the devil. Like
their master, his faithful followers must affirm insistently
that his 'kingdom is not of this world' (John 18:36). Rather
than compromise the simplicity of the gospel, baptists
today, in their fathers' footsteps, must be prepared to
suffer the hatred of men, even of those fellow-christians
who are willing to bow the knee to Baal. More baptist blood
has been shed through the centuries than can be reckoned
up, leading one church historian, in his lectures, to call
their story, 'The Trail of Blood'[1]. Despite their history of
faithfulness, there are many baptists today who are ready
to throw aside their heritage as a worn out garment, no
longer useful to the owner.

This baptist heritage was not born in the seventeenth
century with John Smythe of Gainsborough, whom the
historian Underwood called, 'The Father of English
Baptists' even though he made a significant contribution to
the baptist churches in England.[2] Nor did it come into
being when John Spilsbury immersed his London church
in 1643, as those of the 'Particular Baptist' tradition tend to
say. Recent decades have brought to light vast amounts of
newly available documentation on the 'Anabaptists' in
Europe, causing a radical reassessment of their place and
importance in the Reformation years. Indeed, that
reappraisal has provoked an entirely new approach to the
many separatist groups throughout the christian era, which
establishment christianity has always dubbed 'heretics'.
They can be seen as 'repeated upsurges of revived
testimony' exercising an important witness against the
apostasy into which mainline christendom so constantly
and progressively sank. Donatists, Cathari, Paulicians,
Albigenses, Waldenses and catholic mystics all demand
examination as giving evidence of being our forebears in
some real sense, as also do the effective challenges of
protesting reformers like Savonarola, Tauler and the

Lollards with their eminent leader, John Wyclif, the Morning Star of the Reformation and his remarkable Czech disciple, Jan Hus. All these showed some common characteristics and have been claimed as our baptist forefathers by some church historians, bent on establishing a kind of 'apostolic succession', or doctrine of unbroken continuity for baptist churches.[3] No space will be taken here to expound that theory, but an examination of those witnesses and their outstanding testimony at crises in christian church history must be made. Indeed the more clearly these common characteristics are identified, the stronger is the inclination to call them 'baptists', or at least, to describe them as 'baptistic' (see note on use of this descriptive).[4] In turn, the more time given to the sixteenth-century anabaptists, the more reason the student will find for counting them, not so much as '*The Reformers' Stepchildren*', as does Verduin in his book of that name, but rather to see them as the 'Fathers of the Reformation.'[5]

These general preliminary considerations will provoke at least two questions, '*What is a Baptist?*' and '*When did Baptist Churches first emerge?*' This book will seek to face these questions, primarily out of the history of these churches and their ancestry, and also by an examination of the manner in which total submission to scripture shaped baptist doctrine and practice in a distinctive manner. In doing this, it is not necessary to cover that great body of truth which, by common judgement, forms the fundamentals of the faith because the baptist is neither a heretic nor is he sectarian but wholly orthodox. He neither adds nor subtracts from revelation but is the upholder of mainstream christianity as defined in the all-sufficient Word of God. It will be necessary to look closely at those distinctive characteristics in doctrine and practice which are the product of his insistent submission to scripture in everything and this we will do. Characteristically, the doctrine of the church will concern us, with attention being given to those distinctives which set the baptist apart from both catholic and protestant. Whilst such a methodology will constitute a testimony to biblical faith and church order, as baptists understand the scriptures, and will prove profitable reading for the non-baptist believer or unbeliever, yet the real challenge of this book is to the baptist reader, multitudes of whom have no longer any message for compromised christianity into whose universal vagueness they are rapidly being absorbed. Such have lost sight of their biblical and historical heritage with its vital witness against apostasy and duty to call the churches to reform by the Word of God.

1
What is a baptist?

Cardinal Stanilaus Hosius, a Polish prelate and scholar and president of the Council of Trent, said in 1524, 'Were it not that the baptists have been grievously tormented and cut off with the knife during the past 1200 years, they would swarm in greater numbers today than all the reformers.'[1] The cardinal bishop clearly identifies 'baptists' and, in doing so, asserts their existence for twelve hundred years! The historical significance of this we shall return to in considering the question, 'When did baptists first emerge?' In the present chapter, we ask, 'What is a baptist?' to whose twelve centuries of tormented history the catholic scholar referred. Clearly he had no doubt that his contemporary sixteenth century 'anabaptists' were to be identified with those he calls 'baptists', namely, those protesting separatists of the earlier centuries of the christian era. Hosius takes us back to early in the fourth century, to the Constantinian Apostasy when the '*church*' married the '*state*' and empire. In doing so, he is implying that the protesting Donatists, of twelve centuries before the Council of Trent, were baptists. In his masterly history of that unholy alliance entitled '*The Anatomy of a Hybrid*', Professor L. Verduin states without hesitation, 'We know that at the time of the birth of the hybrid that there were already people who were called 'anabaptists'. Furthermore, Emperor Charles V received a memorandum from the Council of the Archbishopric of Cologne telling him to 'suppress the "anabaptists"[2] because they seek to introduce the community of goods... etc... even as has been the nature of the anabaptists throughout the ages, as the old Imperial Law over a thousand years

5

testifies.'[3] Three baptist characteristics already appear,
namely, they are separatists who practise anabaptism,
oppose the union of the church and state and share their
goods in community.

These separatists have always rejected the name 'anabaptists' as a name for themselves because it implied that the
state-church's 'first baptism' in infancy and unbelief, was
notwithstanding a valid christian baptism. This persistent
suggestion they vehemently denied and, on the contrary,
asserted that their baptism as believers was the true and
only valid first baptism. Their opponents claimed it a
'second baptism', accusing the baptists of rebaptising,
hence the name of 'ana-baptist'. The simplification of the
name to 'baptist' appears to have occured in Holland and
England as a result of these separatists' churches calling
themselves, 'The baptised church of Christ worshipping
at...'. The records of the early English baptist churches
show this.[4] The early English General Baptists used the
term voluntarily though they avoided its use in their
publications, e.g. in their confessions such as, *'The Faith and
Practice of Thirty Congregations gathered according to the
Primitive Pattern dated 1551.'* In this document they describe
themselves as 'The churches of God who walk in the
commands of Jesus Christ.'[5] The same is true of the
Somerset churches in their confession of 1656, for they
were content to speak of themselves as *'Several Churches of
Christ'*.[6] Throughout the Commonwealth period in Britain,
these churches were called 'baptist'. The Particular Baptist
Confession of 1677/89, and the American Philadelphia
Confession of 1742, speak of *'congregations of christians
baptised on the profession of their faith'*.[7] By the beginning of
the eighteenth century, the term 'baptist' had become
acceptable as a denominator used amongst themselves.
However, because of the two streams of such churches in
England, holding different views of the atonement, it
became useful to speak of *'General Baptists'* and *'Particular
Baptists'*. For example, the fund to aid the ministry raised in
1717 by the latter type of churches in London, was called
'The Particular Baptist Fund' and a similar fund formed by
the other group in 1725, was named,. *'The General Baptist
Fund'*.[8] So much for the name 'baptist'.

The first principle of baptist conviction is the **'Doctrine of Church'**. The baptist believes that the churches of Christ comprise only regenerate believers who have been immersed in the name of the Trinity upon the profession of their faith. Therefore they were incapable of compromise with the secular powers, such as the union of the church and state imposed upon fourth century churches by Constantine. Such union was apostasy to them. Similarly, they rejected the autocractic rules of the catholic and orthodox churches, which were born of that unholy alliance. The same principle led baptists to reject the state marriages engineered in Britain by Henry VIII and Elizabeth I, in Germany by Luther, in Switzerland by Zwingli and of the Puritans and Independents in New England in the following century in the American colonies. It was not sufficient to say that Lutheran, Zwinglian, Calvinist, Presbyterian or Anglian churches were re-formed. Their churchmanship was unbiblical and therefore unchristian. Basically, this is a major reason for those baptist churches, which adhere to their biblical heritage, separating from the modern ecumenical movement of today, and it will be the ultimate reason for their separation from the World Church of tomorrow unless it reforms by total submission to scripture. It is the biblical doctrine of the church, with an unqualified submission to scripture as the Word of God, which becomes the test of what is a baptist church.[9]

'Absolute Authority of Holy Scripture' as was implicit in all the early baptist confessions and is explicitly expressed in Chapter I of the *Second London Baptist Confession of Faith 1677/89* as follows: 'The Holy Scripture is the only sufficient, certain and infallible rule of all saving Knowledge, Faith and Obedience...therefore it pleased the Lord...to reveal himself and to declare his will unto his church...and to commit the same wholly unto writing...(#4) The Authority of Scripture...dependeth not on the testimony of any man, or Church; but wholly upon God, the Author thereof; therefore it is to be received, because it is the Word of God.' Further, (#6) 'The whole counsel of God concerning all things necessary for his own Glory, Man's salvation, Faith and Life, is either expressly set down

or necessarily contained in the 'Holy Scripture. 'To which
(#10) adds, 'The supreme judge, by which all controversies
of Religion are to be determined, and all Decrees and
Councils, opinions of ancient Writers, Doctrines of
men...are to be examined, and in whose sentence we are to
rest, can be no other but the Holy Scripture...into which
Scripture...our faith is finally resolved'.[10]

These two principles form the basis of fellowship of
every true baptist church and their faithful implementation has brought into being that 'distinctiveness' that others
denominate 'baptist' but the baptist himself sees as no more
than the characteristic of a truly christian church. Some of
the 'distinctives' he shares with other christians who in
varying degrees apply the authority of scripture to their
church life. With all those reformed christians, whose
churches are based on the Westminster or Savoy Confessions, he shares his high view of scripture and such
doctrines as the 'Universal Priesthood of all Believers.' Yet
their claim to hold this high view of scripture does not
enable them to yield some cherished traditions to its rule.
An example of this is evident in the retention by reformed
churches of the practice of infant baptism, or of sprinkling,
or of links with secular authorities despite their open
acknowledgement that these are unscriptural practices.
These matters will be examined in detail later, but are
quoted here as illustrations of the failure of 'reformed
churches' to implement their own professed submission to
Holy Scripture in everything.

The baptist will share with many whose churchmanship
reflects the 'Free Church' tradition which has been
attributed to the early baptists: liberty of conscience,
voluntary discipleship and the renunciation of coercion in
religious proselytism. Such christians will be equally
opposed to all union of church and state. Almost all, who
identify themselves as evangelical christians, will share the
baptist's commitment to preach the gospel to every
creature. The baptist's distinctives are not exclusively his. It
is his adherence to them all that is unique and constitutes
the baptist's challenge to other christians to conform to the
scriptures in everything. This is worked out more fully in
later chapters.

This bible-disciplined doctrine of church disqualifies large numbers of churches in Britain, and elsewhere, which retain the descriptive 'baptist' from being recognised as truly baptist. To be a 'baptist church', a biblical doctrine of church is essential, both in the creed held and the practice adhered to. A correct mode of baptism does not make for a correct church order. For this reason three observations arise at this point:

1. Not all churches calling themselves 'baptist' are in reality baptist churches. This is particularly true in England and those parts of the world where English influence is reflected. Even though known as baptist locally, and affiliated in some national or international grouping, many have departed from a simple biblical church order distinctive of the true baptist.

2. There are some evangelical churches, which do not call themselves baptist, but which must be recognised as such because they adhere to that requisite doctrine of church.

3. The third observation is of a different nature, namely, that not all baptist churches hold the 'doctrines of grace.' The once clear position as to the extent of the atonement no longer obtains. Many churches, which were once 'Particular Redemption Baptists,' both in Britain and America, have drifted into universalism.

Baptist churches today form collectively the largest non-catholic grouping of christian churches in the world. It is extraordinary that so little is known about their origins and distinctives in this twentieth century when communication science is so highly developed and literature of all kinds floods the world. To some extent this ignorance amongst baptist church members themselves, is the consequence of the fact that 'baptists' do not constitute a 'denomination' in the usual organisational sense of the word. Unlike other groupings of christians, which have highly developed hierarchies and centralised governments and, contrary to the appearance of things, true baptists reject denominationalism. Their emphasis is on the local company of believers as being God's basic unit. As already stated, baptists are essentially separate from all forms of establishment-christianity, eschewing all links with secular authorities. At the very most, fellowship with other like-minded churches provides all that is needed to realise the 'family-oneness' of the whole body of believers at any one time. Though present in great numbers around the globe, baptists today are little understood for what they truly represent. They have spent too long in accommodating their historical biblical characteristics to the norms of the world's other churches, striving to eliminate their inherent nonconformity.

Baptists, let it be repeated, are not in essence a denomination at all. Their 'stripes' or 'spots' may be deep-dyed but are not all found uniformly and consistently in all those families of christians called by that name. Casual observers, and editors of major encyclopaedia, conclude that it is the 'baptist mode of baptism', i.e. immersion, that marks the baptist species. The shallowness of this judgement is exposed easily. The researcher soon finds, to his surprise, that there are 'baptists', apparently of good international standing, that do not insist on immersion as the mode nor even the necessity of baptism for church membership. Serious examination, on the other hand, brings to light some defining marks which stamp the baptist for what he is, marks found in many groups of christians, not known as baptists, and who would not desire such an appellation.

One clear factor, which is emerging in this ecumenical age, is that baptists, true baptists, are uncomfortable bedfellows.[12] Their inherent nonconformity and rugged independence is liable to wreck the best laid schemes to merge into one the many strands of professed christianity in the world. Indeed, it is of the essential nature of baptists to stand apart from all hierarchical and organisational collectivity. From their earliest manisfestations, they have been a protest movement against any over-riding authority, whether secular or ecclesiastical. They stand for the simplicity of the New Testament order of local independent churches. Not that they are isolationists for they have

readily recognised like-minded churches and sought to
express their inherent responsibilities towards each other-
.They have, however, persisted in there being one only
God-appointed basic unit, the local church, with no
overlordship of any kind, other than that of Christ himself,
who is the Head of the Church. It is this, taken with the
insistence on a regenerate, believing and baptised church-
membership, which makes that primary distinctive of
baptist churches. This is the baptist doctrine of the church.
Two Dutch Reformed Church scholars, Ypeig and Der-
rmont, are quoted as saying, 'We have seen that the
baptists...may be considered as the only christian community which stood since the days of the apostles as a christian
society which has preserved pure doctrine of the gospel
through the ages'.[13]

It is instructive to look at some statements, made by
eminent baptists, in which they list the baptist's distinctive
marks. In the first place, here are **Dr G. R. Beasley-
Murray's** twelve doctrinal principles which he states are
characteristic of the 'Anabaptists of the Reformation
Period', that is the sixteenth century, which stated briefly,
are:

1. Freedom of the church from state domination;

2. Freedom to worship in the way the individual believes
   right;

3. No coercion in the churches' freedom to propagate the
   faith;

4. Faith is the individual's free response and discipleship
   is voluntary;

5. No religious act can serve as a substitute for faith; so
   that baptising the unbeliever is worthless, whether
   infant or adult;

6. Christian faith is inalienably joined to christian
   conduct. Where the latter is absent, the former is
   spurious; faith without works is dead;

7. Discipline is the continuing necessity of the church membership;

8. There is both disjunction and connection between Israel and the Church, between the Old Covenant and the New;

9. The universal priesthood of all believers; hence the equal worth of all the membership however diversely gifted;

10. The obligation to evangelise the world; Christ's commission is still binding;

11. Christian love makes believers sit loosely to material things;

12. The civil oath is strictly limited in application and is to be refused whenever it implies a demand of 'Caesar' for what belongs to God alone.

Dr Beasley-Murray gives this list in the course of writing his postscript to Verduin's book, '*The Reformers and their Stepchildren*'. [14] As these principles, widely held and acceptable in this twentieth century, are considered it will seem incredible that christians should have suffered as severely as the baptists of the sixteenth century did, and that, frequently at the hands of the reformers themselves. A careful analysis of the sufferings of the baptists today will reveal that many still suffer for these same principles. Now Dr Beasley-Murray is British and may well be reflecting the viewpoint of the baptists of his homeland, even though he was a professor at the Baptist Seminary, Rüschlikon, Switzerland at that time. It is good therefore that we look at an American baptist viewpoint.

Dr Joseph M. Stowell, pastor of First Baptist Church, Hackensack, N.J., and member of the council of the General Association of Regular Baptist Churches, provides this list of '*Baptist Distinctives*' in the published study course so entitled and dated 1965: [15]

1. Sole authority and sufficiency of the Holy Scriptures;

2. The priesthood of all believers;

3. The autonomy of the local church;

4. The lordship of Christ, the Head of the church;

5. A regenerate church membership;

6. A baptised church membership;

7. The discipline of the church and the Lord's Supper;

8. Separation of the church and state;

9. The doctrine of grace;

10. The church's mission of world-wide evangelism.

When comparing these two lists, the things in common are evidently matters concerning the doctrine of the church. This proves to be the constantly dominant note in baptist convictions, whenever and however expressed.

Those matters missing from the American list reflect the achievement of a large measure of religious liberty for all citizens of the United States of America. This liberty was secured, in large measure, by baptist endeavour as we shall discover in the following historical studies.

The surprising omission from the Englishman's list is the 'Sole Authority and Sufficiency of the Holy Scriptures' and it probably arises from the impact of reformed theology on the British churches. Whether anglican, presbyterian, congregational or baptist, all accept this principle in their creeds, even if they fail to enforce it in their faith and order. Furthermore, Dr Beasley-Murray is reflecting the issues of principle as they arose in the days of baptist persecution during the 'Reformation' years.

Dr W.T. Whitley, speaking of the British baptists of the twentieth century, says, 'Baptists are recognised as careful enquirers, a body with clear doctrines which are earnestly propagated. Their distinctive feature is the doctrine of the church...that it consists wholly of people who have pledged themselves to Christ Jesus, to live the life he desires and win and train more disciples for his service'.[16] His brief, succinct summary reflects the generalised definition of the baptist identity.

So we extract again these **two primary distinctives that characterise the baptist**, namely,

> 1. The Supremacy (or Sole Authority) and Sufficiency of Holy Scripture in all matters of faith and practice;
>   *and*
> 2. The Biblical Doctrine of the Church.

Most, if not all, of the distinctives fall under one or the other of these two heads. Indeed, in his doctrine of the church, the baptist rejects all that is not required by scripture and so the two primary principles harmonize, the second being an extension of the first.

Under the first head, the baptist insists that the christian is to be ruled absolutely by the Holy Scriptures, in his fellowship in the local church and in his personal life. The Holy Scriptures, the Word of God, remains an unchanging standard which is not modified by the times and situations. All traditions and rites, not possessing an explicit biblical base, are not required of him. This high doctrine of scripture produces the typical 'non-conformity' of the baptist. However, it is apparent immediately that the baptist is the true 'conformist' seeing that he submits to the scripture in everything. The so-called 'main-line christian' is the non-conformist because he it is who does not conform to God's Word in everything but takes to himself the freedom to determine for himself what he will obey and what he will not; or who submits to the arbitrary requirements of religious institutions which have formed their own rites and traditions in the course of their own development. The grasping of this insight is the key to an understanding of the role of the baptist throughout the christian era.

From this high view of scripture, and willing submission

to its teaching, arise some of the baptist characteristics listed above. Many seventeenth century baptists, for instance, would not use the civil oath as required in their state courts. Their reason for this was rooted in their understanding of the scripture, that is, in the ban to render to Caesar that which belongs to God.[17] Their emphasis on the right of the individual to worship God, as his own conscience dictates, was largely based on the same principle. Similarly, the separation of church and state, always a pre-eminent baptist characteristic, shares similar grounds, though the very nature of the church itself demands such separation.Baptists have adhered to the doctrine of grace taught in the scripture,attributing to God alone the glory of their salvation. Some have gone as far as did John Calvin, in his systematized doctrine of salvation, and they came to be called 'Particular (Redemption) Baptists' for that reason. Not many baptists shared the reformer's view of the covenant but instead drew a clearer line between the Old and the New Testaments.[18]

Under the second head fall all those many aspects of baptist distinction in churchly fellowship listed by the authors quoted above. The four most common aspects being:

1. The Separation of Church and State;

2. The Universal Priesthood of All Believers;

3. The Biblical Discipline of the Local Church and its Membership;

4. The Church's Regenerate Membership of Baptised Believers only.

The simplicity of the scriptural doctrine of the church insists on the autonomy of the local church and rejects all authority over it, whether civil or ecclesiastical. This eliminates the possibility of the union of church and state, all interference in church affairs by the civil authorities and all hierarchical structures among churches.

The baptist insists that the 'church is the gathered

company of regenerate persons in any locality, each of
whom has evidenced his spiritual life by a personal
repentance of sin towards God and faith in the Lord Jesus
Christ for salvation, and who has begun christian discipleship voluntarily in believer's baptism by immersion in
the name of the Trinity.' The baptist rejects the heresy of
the reformed confessions, namely, that 'the visible church
of Christ consists of all those, throughout the world, that
profess the true religion, together with their children,' to
quote the Westminster Confession. Indeed, the baptist
rejects the division of the church into '*visible*' and '*invisible*',
believing that God's basic unit is the 'local church' and that
the 'total number of the glorified saints' is the only other
proper use of the word 'church' in a biblical sense.[19]

The baptist rejects completely the so-called 'baptism of
infants' because it lacks the basic requirements of 'personal
repentance of sins, faith in Jesus Christ and a voluntary
commencement of discipleship in baptism.' Everything
required is missing and is substituted by the 'vicarious
actions of other persons,' which are outside of scripture.
Voluntary discipleship is of the essence of the biblical norm
and the lack of it invalidates completely any alleged
baptism administered. God, in his action to save sinners,
acts with each person in view and not in any vague or
general manner. He deals with individuals in their election,
redemption, calling and in bringing them to repentance
and faith. The individual is separately and personally 'born
again', comes to repentance and faith and personally takes
up his cross, being baptised, added to the church and
commences discipleship. He takes up his cross and follows
Christ, the Head of the Church.[20]

The **'Baptist Identity'** is therefore defined by this
thorough-going submission to the Word of God in
everything, with the consequent rejection of all else that has
no explicit requirement in scripture. This over-riding
principle is most plainly evident in the baptist's doctrine of
the church. It is these two principles which define the
baptist identity and are stamped on the recurring upsurges
of distinctive witness at critical moments of the churches'
history. The failure of the then contemporary churches to
respect, implement and maintain them fully gave rise to

God's gracious intervention in raising up a protesting baptist witness against that which must be seen as apostasy. Were the whole of christendom to surrender its traditions and yield totally to these 'baptist principles' of submission to scripture and the consequent doctrine of church, there would cease to be any separate baptist witness. Where scripture rules there can be no marriage to the state, no shared rule with the magistracy, no subservience of the local church to denominational structures or officialdom, no use of force of any kind to compel faith, no unwilling or unconscious 'baptisms' and no compromise with erroneous bodies. The single, clear task of the churches would be addressed without any hindrance arising from either the churches themselves, or 'their spheres of influence', and the world would be evangelised. The whole generation of believers would appear watchfully alert as it awaited the coming of the Lord from heaven and the glorious consummation of the age.

It is the failure of whole generations of christians to be willing to subject themslves to scripture in any such way, and to be willing to gather themselves as simple, local churches to worship God, and serve him with the Gospel in the world, that has occasioned the need for the recurring baptist testimony of the past. To the study of this questioin of the history of the emergence of baptists we next address ourselves.

2
When did baptists first emerge?

There are some who assert categorically that all first century churches were 'baptist'. This seemingly arrogant claim might well be permissible in the sense that the faith and order of those churches plainly witnessed to their entire submission to those biblical distinctives which today are called 'baptist'. Charles Haddon Spurgeon took his stand for such a view, saying, 'We have an unbroken line up to the apostles themselves. We have always existed from the days of Christ, and our principles, sometimes veiled and forgotten, like a river which travels underground for a season, have always had honest and holy adherents.'[1] He returns to this subject later, saying, 'Long before Protestants were heard of...anabaptists were protesting for the 'One Lord, one faith, one baptism.'[2]

As stated in our *Introduction*, many American baptists claim John, the Forerunner of Jesus Christ, as the first 'baptist' and trace their beginnings from him. In doing so, they advance a continuity which claims to trace their churches' history through various separatist movements, such as the Montanists, Novatianists, Donatists, Cathari, Paulicians, Petrobrussians, Waldenses and Anabaptists, down to the baptist churches of today. This presents a dogma approaching the classical catholic doctrine of 'apostolic succession'. The reader will find the case presented in '*A History of the Baptists*' by Dr J. T. Christian, which is an official publication of the Southern Baptist Convention of America dated 1922,[3] or in the published lectures of Dr J. M. Carroll, a Texan Baptist, to which reference was made in the *Introduction*,[4] More recently, this case has been argued in '*The Baptist Heritage*' by J. M. Halliday, published in 1974, which book gives an extensive bibliography on the subject.[5]

A contrary view is found in Thomas Armitage's '*The History of Baptists*' 1890. In the introductory chapter, he says, 'Little perception is required to discover the fallacy of visible apostolic succession in the ministry; but visible **church** succession is precisely as fallacious and for exactly the same reasons... Such evidence cannot be traced by any church on earth, and would be utterly worthless if it could, because real legitimacy of christianity must be found in the New Testament and nowhere else'.[6]

This theory has not made much headway in the United Kingdom. Recent English historians have tended to ridicule the hypothesis, as does Dr A. C. Underwood in his '*History of the English Baptists*',[7] or to ignore it entirely, as does Dr H. Wheeler Robinson in his '*Life and Faith of the Baptists*'[8] and Dr W. T. Whitley in his '*History of British Baptists*',[9] Such writers tend to date the commencement of baptist churches from the Reformation, and in Britain, from the return to London of a small group of John Smythe's émigré church in Amsterdam under the pastoral care of Thomas Helwys in 1612.

It is much easier to find the baptist's ancestry among the later Waldenses and Anabaptists but we must not ignore the fact that the unsympathetic catholic prelate, Cardinal Stanilaus Hosius, said in 1524 that 'the baptists have been tormented...during the past twelve hundred years.' His unprejudiced judgement substantiates the continuous 'baptist' presence and protest throughout the centuries from Constantine's day, that is, from the fourth century onward.[10] Verduin states that the anabaptist movement of the sixteenth century was a 'resurgence, a reiteration, a restatement precipitated by Luther's Theses but essentially older than 1517.'[11]

From Pentecost and New Testament apostolic times, the christian churches, wherever established, bear the same biblical and simple characteristics which were to mark out those churches later described as 'baptist'. Those early churches were called 'christian', a descriptive much to be preferred,[12] The reformation of today's churches by the scriptures to conform to the same primitive submission to God's Word in everything, accompanied by the shedding of all else, would again make possible its use, honestly and with great joy to believers. It was the 'church of Christ' which was redeemed at Calvary and it will be the 'church of Christ' which will be glorified with him eternally. Who could desire a better name?[13]

This chapter must note those marks in mainline christianity which are characteristic expressions of apostasy against which those early baptist christians raised their protest. Whilst there is little to mar the first century of christianity, soon afterwards the urge to protect its genius, by hedging it around with a hierarchical authority and structure, was apparent.

Authoritarianism was the first departure from New Testament simplicity. The 'spiritual' eldership of the churches took to themselves an overruling authority that is absent from the scriptures. From this developed a structured hierarchy.

Baptismal regeneration was the next departure. The ordinance of believers' baptism was made to become the instrument of salvation instead of a witness to it, so placing in the priest's (!) hand the communication of grace.

Infant-baptism inevitably followed. It was the natural outcome of making baptism the means of salvation. Parents felt the need to baptise their newborn infants immediately lest they died unsaved. It is not possible to establish beyond doubt whether this was a conscious conformity to pagan rites of initiation then prevalent but that is what infant baptism achieved.

The union of church and state achieved under the Emperor Constantine in the fourth century with the connivance of the church's perverted hierarchy, bound christianity to the secular world. The opportunism of the Emperor opened the gates for the 'church' to be identified with the nation and made citizenship and church membership to be coextensive and ultimately identical.

The coercion of consciences and the denial of Freedom to Worship according to an individual's own convictions, followed. This was the sacralist's substitute for christian evangelism, the winning by force of conforming citizens rather than converted christians. Inevitably, its corollary was the persecution of non-conforming christian believers and the forceful suppression of their churches.

The baptistic movements of protest, which arose during the first fifteen centuries of the christian era, invariably set the standards of the Word of God over against the innovations and heresies of institutionalised religion. Those upsurges of protest rebuked constantly and rejected everything not explicit in the scriptures. There emerged among these movements distinctive marks of a 'baptistic' nature in the pre-Reformation period by which the Holy Spirit witnessed against the apostasising trends in catholic christianity of both the east and the west. These can be summarised as follows:

1. **The requirement of evidence of regeneracy prior to church membership**. This has been noted in the Ancient British churches, Montanists, Donatists, Petrobrussians and Waldenses. The anabaptists of the sixteenth century adhered to this principle tenaciously.

2. **The requirement of faith before baptism**. It was insisted upon by the same groupings. It ruled out in practice the baptism of infants. Tauler, the catholic reformer of Strassburg, preached this requirement and was excommunicated for it. The Friends of God, The Brethren of the Common Life, the Swiss Brethren and the anabaptists all demanded it, as did most of the Pre-Reformation Waldenses.

3. **The universal priesthood of all believers** was taught by the Donatists and Paulicians, the latter also strictly enforced the quality of ministry of all. The Waldenses and the Anabaptists held to this position, including the administration of the ordinances by those not ordained to the ministry of the Word.

4. **The necessity of a godly life to validate christian profession** was the most prominent protestation of all the separatists which we have considered because of the blatant failure of catholicism, both east and west. Catholic priests and bishops were constantly being rebuked for their godlessness and immorality. The Anabaptists made the same protest against Luther because of his seeming sterile teaching of 'Justification by Faith Alone' which implied that 'Good Works' were not necessary at all. Both parties agreed that works did not provide any part of the basis of salvation but the Anabaptists insisted that 'faith without works was dead', with the apostle James, whose divinely-inspired letter Luther once called an 'epistle of straw'!

5. **The sufficiency of the Holy Scriptures for faith and practice** was generally held by all the separatist groups. They stood by the Word of God as the final court of appeal and insisted that nothing should be demanded of the believer which is not explicitly found in the scriptures.

6. **The obligation of the churches to preach the gospel everywhere.** This missionary commitment is a prime baptist principle and was evidenced in a variable degree among the early separatists but was characteristic of the Albigenses, Waldenses and Anabaptists particularly.

Wyclif taught all these principles, though he did not translate them into practice. The same is true of Hus, except that he did not insist on faith before baptism. The Czech Hussites thrived on baptist doctrine without the vital element which would have made them baptist churches in the fullest sense.

Those baptist type protests of the separatists of earlier generations stir the sympathy of twentieth century evangelicals and rightly so. The stands then made were bravely made, against all odds, regardless of the cost to the protester and they were made against errors which we can see as apostasy from our perspective better than those

involved in the issues of those times. Yet we must remind
ourselves that several of these protest movements were
guilty of espousing grave errors themselves. Catholic
historians have dominated church recording and have
given us perverted pictures of these 'heretics', as they call
them, over-emphasising the faults of the persecuted
christians. Some of those faults were grave. Catholic
historians have highlighted deviations from the doctrine of
the Godhead, particularly of the Person of Jesus Christ.
Doubtless, the catholic church did this to mitigate the force
of the protests of the separatists against the widespread
evils in the catholic institutions. Indeed, they took every
opportunity to destroy the separatists' literature, causing
totally false pictures of those striving for a biblical church.
Making a full allowance for the failures of those early
baptistic witnesses for the truth, we conclude that the Holy
Spirit has continually raised up a bibilical witness against
apostasy and to a surprising extent these upsurges have
borne a common testimony, majoring on those principles
of faith and order which are characteristically baptist, or
what is even more important, the marks of true apostolic
christianity.

3
Early baptist ancestry

From the Apostles to Constantine

The reader will be familiar with the first century christian churches and their story recorded in the New Testament. Let Robert D. Linder assess their characteristics in the recent *Lion Handbook of Christian History*. He says, 'The hallmarks of apostolic christianity were simplicity, community, evangelism and love'.[1] The deterioration of christianity thereafter can be seen by fastening attention on those four factors and watching them being eroded steadily throughout the early centuries of our era. Equally well, the presence, or otherwise, of those hallmarks will test adequately the biblicity of those repeated upsurges of evangelical protest which mark the early separatists to whose story we now address ourselves.

Before doing this, it will help greatly to note that the departure of the early churches from their initial New Testament character was not a sudden apostasy but a 'slow drift away from its living spontaneity and simplicity to preserving the genius of the christian movement by enclosing it in an elaborate hierarchical system. In attempting this, they transformed it into an inflexible, architectured order of vast uniformity, very startlingly unlike the New Testament original', as G. O. Griffith says. His little known work provides an excellent analysis of the pre-Constantine centuries of the early church, the study of which well repays its reader.[2] He further says that the replacement of apostles by bishops gradually led to a hierarchical order with regional bishops, through those of the cities, then metropolitans and, at the top, those of Jerusalem, Antioch, Alexandria and Rome. It was a

25

'natural step' for the latter to become the 'father-in-chief'. In this way, he says, the Roman Imperial Empire was reproduced in the structure of the churches. He summarizes helpfully the drift under the following four heads:

1. Simplicity and spontaneity replaced by despotic institutionalism;
2. Salvation by faith was replaced by a standard mechanical rite;
3. Sacraments became magical mysteries;
4. Life in Christ was replaced by submission to priestly authority.

In this, the vital, organic life of the New Testament churches was replaced by an organisation in which christianity became a 'system' and the imposition of its domain the only 'evangelisation' it knew.[3] As this process progressed and baptism, the sign of regeneracy, became its means, the supper became sacrifice and the presbyter a priest and 'The Church,' no longer 'the churches,' is prepared as an Old Testament bride for marriage to the Empire and no more is the 'Bride adorned for her Husband'. Again, quoting Griffith, 'the early stream of evangelical faith passed out of sight and became an underflow, now and then, gushing upward in various movements of protest — upbursts in which earthy elements mingled with the pure springs'.[4]

The gospel had reached all provinces of the Roman Empire, from Britain to the Persian Gulf, from the Danube to the Lybian Desert, by 180AD. Justin Martyr wrote that there was no race, Greek or Barbarian, that either wandered or dwelt in tents, which did not offer praise to the Crucified. In his '*Apology to the Emperor*', Tertullian wrote, 'We are but of yesterday, yet we have filled your empire, your cities, your corporate towns, your assemblies, your very camps, your tribes, your companies, your palace, your senate, your forum; your temples alone are left to you. So great are our numbers that we might successfully contend with you in open warfare; but were we only to withdraw ourselves from you, and remove by common consent to some remote corner of the globe, our secession from you would be sufficient to accomplish your destruction and avenge our cause'.[5]

Among the christians at the close of the apostolic period, there were five leaders known to us by their writings, Barnabas, Clement, Hermas, Ignatius and Polycarp. All these lived during the lifetime of the apostles. Clement was pastor at Rome 91-100AD. He was an administrator and left to us his *'Epistle to the Corinthians'* in which he rebukes the church for abusing its elders. Hermas wrote an absurd work called *'The Shepherd'*. Ignatius , the venerable pastor at Antioch, was martyred in Rome by Trajan in front of 80,000 spectators. Polycarp, the disciple of John of the Apocalypse and pastor at Smyrna (modern Izmir on Turkey's Aegean coast) lived a consistent, godly life and was burned at the stake at the age of 90 in 166AD. Almost his dying words were, 'Eighty and six years have I served my King and Saviour and he never did me any wrong. How can I blaspheme him now?'[6] Shortly afterwards, Neander writes of the simple church order practised by the elders, chosen from amongst themselves.[7] Both he and the Lutheran historian, Mosheim speak of the independency of the individual churches and of their loving care for each other, treating one another as equals.[8] This reflects the New Testament standards and the hallmarks we have already set. It was in the following generation that destructive errors crept into churches. Useless ceremonies were added to baptism, such as anointing the candidate with oil after immersion, giving milk and honey to symbolise his spiritual food, the milk of the Word, and the making of baptism the means of regeneration. Decline in godly standards of conduct of christian leaders also set in at this time. Hippolytus, the godly bishop of Pontus by Rome, is frequently heard rebuking the bishop of Rome and his clerical circle for worldly living.[9] Protesting voices were to be heard again and again throughout the succeeding centuries of the christian era, just as G. O. Griffith said in the passage quoted above.[10]

As has been noted, the declension of the early churches of the pre-Constantine period was a slow drift away from Paul's 'simplicity in Christ'.[11] It moved the emphasis back to a legalistic concentration on external ritual, 'away from grace to the works of the law',[12] The transformation of the christianity, which could 'turn the world upside down', into a manageable organisation made possible its marriage to the state which was the undoing of its witness and the occasion of its malaise for centuries to come. Constantine accomplished the apostasy of christianity in two stages, first by the recognition of it as a religion among others permitted to be practised through the Empire. In this stage, persecution of christians was halted and the right to propagate itself given. Again, the transition of 'the churches' to the 'The Church' stands out. The final step was the adoption by the State of this apostate ecclesiastical organisation as an imperial institution. The apostolic age of the christian churches was at an end. From this fourth century calamity, the interests and decisions of the Empire would determine their life and course. Even when the Empire was forgotten, other national powers would sponsor 'The Church' and control its life and work. As we shall find later, even the reformed churches of the sixteenth century and, even more surprisingly, the independent puritans of the seventeeth century, would perpetuate this enervating heresy of the submission of church to state,[13]

Turning away from the Middle East to consider the birth of christianity in Britain, we must notice firstly the **Ancient British or Welsh churches**, commonly known as the Celtic church. The Romans invaded Britain in 56BC in the reign of the Celtic king, Cassibellan.[14] Failing to master the Welsh, they made peace and lived among them, intermarrying so that many Celts visited Rome in those mixed race families. Among them, some who went to Rome in 63AD, appear to have lived in Caesar's household and became christians, possibly under the ministry of Paul, who was at Rome at that time. It has been claimed that these, and other converted Welsh people, carried the gospel back to their homeland in the hills and valleys of Wales. Indeed Paul speaks of such christians in 2 Timothy 4:21 and makes the general observation in Philippians 4:22.'All the saints salute you, chiefly they that are of Caesar's household',[15] Archbishop Usher names those saints as '**Pomponia**, the wife of Aulius Plautus, the first governor of Britain, and **Claudia Ruffina**, the daughter of Caractercus, the British king held prisoner in Rome and whose husband was **Pudens**, a believer in Christ',[16] Dr John Gill, minister of the Southwark baptist church, now called the Metropolitan Tabernacle, in his commentary on Genesis 10:2 states that 'the Welsh people descended from

Gomer, son of Japhet, from whom all the Gallic nations came', and in support he quotes Josephus, Pliny and Herodotus.[17] Tertullian also added to the traditions concerning the entry of christianity into Britain.[18] Paul is credited with bringing the gospel to this land during his freedom between his first and second Roman imprisonments.[19] Joseph of Arimathea is said to have lived and preached Christ in a wicker chapel at Glastonbury.[20] Much use has been made of these early traditions but little hard evidence exists for their support. Both the Anglo-Canadian Dr Cramp and the American Dr Armitage, victorian baptist historians, dismiss them out of hand.[21] However, this much has been granted by the eminent historian, Professor G. M. Trevelyan, that of the three benefits which the Romans left in Britain, the first was Welsh christianity which, he says, survived among the Welsh when every other Roman institution disappeared.[22]

Faganus and Damicanus, two Welsh born christian ministers, were sent from Rome to preach the gospel to their fellow-countrymen in 180AD and a Welsh king is said to have embraced the faith. The christian religion spread throughout the land from Anglesey to Thanet.[23] In 300AD, Welsh christians suffered great persecution during the reign of Diocletian. Alban is said to have been the first British martyr. Others also died for their faith, such as, Aaron and Julius of Caerleon in 285AD and persecution continued until Constantine gave status to christianity throughout the Empire. The Welsh baptist historian, J. Davis claims that Constantine was born of a Welsh mother, Ellen of Gloucester, who became known universally as the benefactor of christendom, building many church buildings, including that of the Nativity at Bethlehem, and to whom sainthood was duly accorded... Saint Helena![24] However, evidence is sparse and Schaff-Herzog, for instance, calls the Lucius story 'fabulous.' When all these traditions and hazy records are collated and perhaps deposed as history, the hard historical fact remains that there were well-organised christian churches in Britain by the fourth century. At the Synod of Arles in 316AD, three bishops, an elder and a deacon from York, Lincoln, Caerleon and Colchester were present and a representation is also documented at the Synod of Rimimi in 359AD.[25]

Returning to the eastern Mediterranean arena, we

discover separatists in Phrygia in 158AD, known as
Montanists[26] Their founder, from whom they are named,
was Montanus who 'spoke with tongues' when he was
converted and began to prophesy declaring that the Holy
Spirit was speaking through him. They demanded a return
to primitive piety in the light of the near return of Jesus
Christ. They pleaded for a high standard of holy living,
advocating fasting, celibacy and community of goods and
they were characteristically 'puritans'.[27] Not all separatists,
who have been called Montanists, derived their origin from
Montanus or came from the Phrygian movement. Broadbent says, 'Montanists constantly pressed for definite
evidences of christianity in the lives of all applicants for
church membership'.[28] Neander goes even further in
highlighting their 'baptistic' characteristics when he says
that they demanded conscious personal faith for baptism.
Montanists were 'charismatic' christians in the contemporary use of that word. They held a high view of marriage as a
christian ordinance and were practical 'millenialists', living
in the expectation of the early return of the Lord.[29] Their
most famous member was Tertullian, who was born of
wealthy pagan parents in Carthage, North Africa, in the
middle of the second century. He was well read in
philosphy and history, says Latourette,[30] knew Greek well,
and practised law in Rome. Converted early, he spent most
of the rest of his life in his native city, becoming an elder of
the church there. He was the first to write extensively on
christian subjects in Latin, his style being vigorous,
systematic and aggressively polemical, not unlike Calvin
with whom he shared a common legal background. Among
his voluminous works, that on 'baptism' will be quoted
later.[31] His specification of the seven deadly sins as being
'idolatry, blasphemy, murder, adultery, fornication, false-
witness and fraud' is frequently quoted.[32]

Novatianists were a third century group of separatists
making a strong protest against the same moral laxity and
the weak, almost non-existent disciplinary standards in the
churches, which had aroused the Montanists a little earlier.
Their leader was Novatian who was a presbyter in the
church at Rome and a capable theologian of impeccable
orthodoxy. Appointed a bishop, he ordained new bishops

for the separatist churches which responded to his call for godly living. Novatianists flourished in North Africa and in Constantinople and Rome, until their suppression in the fifth century, after which they met as underground gatherings. Ultimately, they were reabsorbed into the catholic churches.[33]

From Constantine to the Conqueror

The unholy union of church and state under Constantine provoked further apostasy in the christian churches, removed the biblical separation of believers from the world and progressively secularized christianity. Inevitably the Holy Spirit's testimony against this evil was expressed in the testimony of a new wave of protest. The **Donatists** were the strongest and most widespread of the early christian separatist church movements, arising initially in North Africa in 311AD as a witness against laxity in morals of the clergy and the lack of discipline in the churches. It was not long before their protest acquired a further dimension and they refused to surrender their local churches' independency when Constantine united church and state. They viewed all clerics working for the 'union' as evil priests, working hand in glove with the 'kings of this earth', and who, by their conduct, declared that there is 'no king but Caesar.' They viewed the church as a small body of the saved surrounded by the unregenerate mass. When Rome's soldiers were sent to suppress them, they were not surprised nor were easily put down. Mosheim says that they had over four hundred bishops or pastors in Africa alone.[34] The Donatists resisted Constantine and his subservient church and the first christian blood shed by fellow christians occurred in a disgraceful contest among themselves.

Donatus, whose name attached to these separatists, was appointed bishop of Carthage under Theodosius (379-395AD) whose successor in office, Honorius (395-432) issued an edict in 415AD forbidding the Donatists to meet on pain of death, reducing them to extreme poverty and obliging their leaders to flee into the deserts. Their bishop,

Petelian refused to entertain any difference between those persecutions staged by pagan governments and those in his own time suffered at the hands of a supposedly christian regime.[35]

In considering whether these Donatists bore any of the marks of being 'baptist', the following four characteristics should be considered: They believed in the separation of church and state, a regenerate church membership, in the necessity for a moral, godly life in all christians, especially the ministers of the churches, and they appear to have practised re-baptism, as their critics called it, by immersing all new converts despite their having been 'baptised' as infants. The accusations made against them, and the war waged for their extinction, indicate clearly that most of those convictions were stubbornly held. Diogenes, a fourth century contemporary of the early Donatists, said that 'They believe that christians are separate from the rest of men... they dwell in hellenic or barbaric cities, as each man's lot is, following the customs of the country in dress and food and the rest of life; the manner of the conduct which they display is wonderful and confessedly beyond belief... they live on earth but their citizenship is in heaven'.[36] When Theodosius ordered that all men should be called 'catholic christians' and the rest be reproached as 'heretic', the Donatists refused to conform and insisted on calling themselves simply 'christians'. They would not use the word 'catholic', not even in the Apostles' Creed, just as their sixteenth century successors, the anabaptists, were to refuse to do in their day.[37] As a movement, Donatism was put down but wave after wave of dissent against medieval sacralism revived its testimony right down to Luther's day.[38] As Augustine of Hippo sneered at the Donatists, calling them 'spotless saints', so did the reformer despise the anabaptist in his day with similar jibes.[39]

The **Paulicians** arose in the south of Armenia about 650AD as a virile group of churches practising a primitive form of christianity and calling themselves simply 'christians', just as the Donatists had done.[40] Their leader was Constantine-Silvanus, who was set on fire by reading the Gospels and the Letters of Paul. So large a place did the teachings of Paul occupy among them, that they were called by that apostle's name.[41] Some of them were 'Dualists', that is, they held that this world of sin and the flesh is a creation of an evil power, the 'imperfect God' of the Old Testament, whilst the spirit and souls of men are the work of the 'good God'.[42] They rejected infant baptism and, taking Jesus as their model, they were baptised at the age of thirty in a river.[43] They also rejected Mary-worship, prayers to the saints, candles, icons, incense and all material symbols.[44] They taught that Jesus derived nothing material from being born of Mary, as the sixteenth century Hoffmanites and early English General Baptists were to do.[45] They proved themselves good citizens and soldiers. One emperor moved colonies of Paulicians into Bulgaria,[46] rather like the Stuarts moved Scottish presbyterians into Ireland, in order to establish good husbandry and moral citizenship. There were other migrations into the Balkans where they came to be called **'Bogils'**[47] There is reason for believing that the **Cathari** or **Puritans** may have had their origin from among the Bogils,[48] The Cathari prospered in northern Italy, southern France and northern Spain in the twelfth century. Their emphasis was that constantly observed feature of all the previous separatist movements we have considered, the need for a godly life before the world to validate any christian profession, particularly that of the leaders. Like their predecessors, they were often 'Dualist' as to creation and God, but they went further in rejecting the Roman church and its orders entirely. They were ardent missionaries and extended their influence into northern Europe.[49] They were also called **'Albigenses'** from the name of their centre at Albi in southern France. They published scriptures in several vernacular translations.[50]

Returning to Britain, where 'The Church' had become the favourite of the state, as throughout the Empire, and that church adopting rites and practices of pagan origin as it adapted itself to its new role, the Celtic christians resolutely adhered to their simple biblical forms. Gildas preached against the degeneracy of the age, demanding holy living, in which he was supported by Dyfrig and Dynawt. The latter was principal of Bangor College and chief debater with Augustine of Canterbury when he came from Pope Gregory to impose Roman conformity by force in 596AD. Teilo, Padarn, Pawlin, Daniel, Cadog and Dewi were others whose names are preserved. Dr Richard Davis, Bishop of Monmouth, said, 'there was a vast difference between the christianity of the ancient British churches and the mockery introduced by Augustine'. The Britons kept their christianity largely pure, without admixture of human traditions, just as they received it from the disciples of Jesus and from the church of Rome when she was pure, strictly enforcing the Word of God in their churches.[51]

However, as so often happened with christian churches striving to withstand the apostasising pressure of Rome, they themselves fell into error whilst strenuously opposing the errors of the catholic church. Two hundred years earlier, the British monk Pelagius had vigourously rebuked the loose living tolerated by the Roman church. In the course of pleading for the exercise of man's will in resisting immorality, and choosing and living a godly life, he asserted that man's will was free to do so if he would. Progressing from there, he declared that man was not 'born in sin', that is born guilty before God of the original sin of his forefather, Adam. This roused the opposition of Augustine of Hippo, who in his 'Confessions' had expressed the contrary view. Pelagius protested that 'man had sufficient free will to perform his duty to God and should exert himself to do so,'[52] This 'Pelagian heresy' arose frequently in the successive upsurges of evangelical protest against immorality which repeatedly marred christian witness and this same blot is to be found on some of the sixteenth century anabaptist movements.[53]

The action of Augustine of Canterbury, begun in 596AD, almost extinguished the old British churches and stamped a tight Roman, or western catholic grip on christianity in this land. Thereafter little of interest for the student of baptist history arises until that critical period date 1066AD

From 1066 to Jan Hus.

When William of Normandy conquered England, it was necessary for his Archbishop Lanfranc to publish a treatise against 'Waldensian' views which had permeated the country.[54] One hundred years later, in 1166 a group of German peasants, led by Gerhardt of Mainz, refused to conform to Roman teaching in respect of purgatory, which they denied existed, nor would they baptise their infants or attend Mass. They were condemned as 'heretics' at Oxford, branded on their foreheads, stripped naked to the waist, ferociously beaten and driven out into the snow-covered countryside to perish.[55] The public were forbidden to aid them in any way on pain of death. Such **'Bible-men'**, as they were often called, roamed the country reading and preaching the Word of God to any who would hear. In the reign of Henry II, a group of Waldensian believers settled at Darenth in Kent. In Edwards III's time, colonies of such 'Bible-men' established themselves in the county of Norfolk. Indeed, there is evidence of such groups of simple christians gathering for worship in many parts of East Anglia and in the south-east prior to the Reformation, but this brings us to the time of John Wyclif and his Lollard preachers prematurely and at this point the story of baptist witness in Britain must be set aside until later and an account be given of 'baptist' testimony on the mainland of Europe down to Wyclif's time. Throughout that period, as Latourette says, 'small groups of believers broke from the catholic church, in part or in entirety, in protest against what they held to be too great leniency of the latter towards moral lapses, especially apostasy.[56] Among these were the Albigenses, of whom we have already spoken, the Petrobrussians, Henricians, Arnoldists, Waldenses and some outstanding individual witnesses to truth.

The **Petrobrussians**, or followers of **Peter of Bruys**, arose about 1115AD and practised an ascetic way of life, rejected infant-baptism, re-baptising those who joined them upon a profession of faith, and for this reason, were called 'anabaptists'. They also rejected all the rites and ceremonies of the church of Rome and destroyed altars and many church buildings.[57] Peter of Bruys was a prominent teacher within the Roman communion and is described as 'an able and diligent preacher who for twenty years braved all dangers, travelled throughout Dauphiny, Provence, Languedoc and Gascony, that is throughout southern France, drawing multitudes from the superstitions in which they had been reared and bringing them back to the teaching of the Bible. He was burned at St. Gilles, near Nîmes, in 1126. He taught that none should be baptised until they attained to the full use of their reason; that it was useless to build churches, as God accepts sincere worship wherever it is offered; that crucifixes should not be venerated; that at the Supper the bread and wine are not changed into the body and blood of Christ, but are but symbols commemorative of his death; and that the prayers and good works of the living cannot benefit the dead.'[58]

The **Henricians** were followers of Henri of Lausanne who despite his name, was born in Paris. He was a monk of Cluny in deacon's orders, whose striking appearance, powerful voice and great gift of oratory compelled attention. His convincing expositions of the scriptures, with his zeal and his devotion, turned many to repentance and faith, among whom were notorious sinners whose changed lives validated their conversions. Peter and Henri, with their followers, were so successful with their evangelism that the regular catholic churches were emptied and an urgent appeal was made to Bernard of Clairvaux, probably the strongest man in Europe at that time, to intervene and suppress these movements. Henri escaped for a time but was ultimately arrested by the clergy and imprisoned. He either died in prison, or was put to death quietly to avoid public riots about 1140AD.[59]

The **Arnoldists**, or disciples of Arnold of Brescia, were roughly contemporary with the Frenchmen, Peter and Henri. Arnold was an Italian, born in the city of northern Italy which gave him his name. Ordained as a priest, he practised a life of purity and poverty, gathering around him a community of canons-regular striving for the reformation of the catholic churches. Arnold attacked the bishops for their cupidity, dishonest gains and irregularity of life urging them to renounce all ambition for political or physical power and all property. He was executed by hanging in 1155AD at the instance of Bernard of Clairvaux who obtained his condemnation at the Council of Sens in 1140AD.[60] Bernard was not always true to his reputed saintly character which his hymns have given him! The three groups of separatists, the followers of Peter, Henri and Arnold, are often confused with the Cathari, whose campaign for reform of the church across southern France has been mentioned previously. Not being dualists but totally orthodox on the doctrine of the Godhead, they ought not to be called 'heretics' by church historians. Their ministries were characteristically 'baptist' in that they pressed for reform of the churches by the Word of God, which they preached faithfully to the masses in the vernacular with considerable success.[61]

The Waldenses, or Vaudois, outnumbered the separatist groups mentioned above and were different in that they provided real and lasting church fellowship for their large congregations. Their name may have been derived from the 'Valleys' (vaux) where they dwelt, or from one of their leaders, **Peter Waldo** (Valdez). Companies of believers had remained apart from the east and west apostasies of so-called 'Orthodox' and 'Catholic' churches, maintaining a simple form of bible-based worship and had endeavoured to hold fast to primitive christianity. Constantly persecuted, they found little shelter except in the high valleys of the Alps and Taurus mountains. In no sense were they 'reformers' of the catholic churches, as were most of the other separatists. They were churches in their own right independent of Rome and Constantinople. Marco Aurelio Rorenco, an Italian catholic writer in 1630 said that the Waldenses 'are so ancient as to afford no absolute certainty as to the precise time of their origin, but that in the ninth and tenth centuries they were not a new sect.' Claudius of Turin was a Waldensian who plainly taught 'Justification by Faith'.[62] Moreland's *History of the Evangelical Churches of the Piedmont Valleys* gives a copy of an extant Confession of Faith dated 1120 containing fourteen articles showing them to be totally orthodox in doctrine.[63] When they made representations to the catholic princes of Savoy and to Francis, king of France, as well as when later they negotiated with the Genevan reformers for intercommunion, they always claimed the continuity of their congregations and teachings from the apostles, saying, 'from the very days of the apostles we have ever been consistent respecting the faith.'[64] On the return of the Waldenses to their valleys in 1689, their leader said that their religion was as primitive as their name is venerable as their adversaries had always attested.[65] Many Waldensians joined the main reformed movement under the persuasion of Farel and Beza. Unlike their earlier Confession, that of 1655 is clearly calvinistic. More recently, they have emigrated in large numbers to South America where they now have more adherents than in their native Italy.[66]

Peter Waldo was a wealthy merchant of Lyons, probably born a little before 1150AD and converted in 1176. When seeking spiritual peace, he was given the words of Jesus in Matthew 19:21, 'If thou wilt be perfect, go and sell that thou hast and give it to the poor.' Waldo did that literally. Selling his possessions, he provided adequately for his wife and family, paid all his debts and distributed the rest to the destitute. He lived by begging bread and gave himself to the study of the scriptures in his native French. Afterwards, dressed simply and carrying no purse, he preached the gospel in city and countryside, just as Jesus had commanded. He attracted many followers, who were called, '**The Poor Men of Lyons**'. In 1174, the Pope excommunicated them in an attempt to silence their acutely embarrassing witness. Believing that 'they ought to obey God rather than man', they continued to preach, quoting whole passages of memorised scriptures in the vernacular, just as the Lollards were to do in England. They taught that Christ alone was the Head of the Church, that the mass was without biblical warrant and that all believers had equal access to God at all times and places, not just in churches. They observed the Supper but taught that a lay person could administer it.[67]

The Poor Men of Lyons spread rapidly and were soon to be found in Spain, Italy, Germany and Bohemia, as well as throughout their native France. They rejected the rites and rituals of Rome, saying that any believer could preach, pray, lead the Supper and hear confessions. They prayed extemporaneously except for the use of the Lord's Prayer and the Grace. They were bitterly persecuted between 1150 and 1250AD, finding refuge in the high Alps and the Piedmont valleys where they can still be found.[68]

A remarkable movement of catholic mystics must not be overlooked entirely because some bore striking resemblances to the anabaptists who were to follow in the succeeding centuries.[69] **Johannes Tauler** (1291-1361) was a native of Strassburg and later a prominent priest in the city, noted for practical godliness, Christlike sympathy and self-sacrificing ministry to the dying during the Black Death. Whilst most other clergy fled from the diseased community, he remained to tend the sick. His sermons were widely read and he was called the 'Protestant before Protestantism' because of his emphasis on the simple gospel of God's all-sufficient grace and the need for a godly life.[70] His followers were known as '**The Friends of God**' or, as in the Netherlands, '**The Brethren of the Common Life**'. **Thomas à Kempis** (c1379-1471), whose simple manual of pious living entitled, *'The Imitation of Christ'* is still in print today, was one of these godly preachers. Tauler taught that those who trusted in the church and its rites would find no peace for their souls unless the Word of the Heavenly Father should inwardly renew and make a new creation of them.[71] Tauler's sermons were instrumental in bringing Luther to grasp the inwardness of true religion and that saving faith was the gift of God. Luther said of Tauler's writings, 'I have nowhere found a sounder or more evangelical theology.'[72]

John Wyclif (1320-84) was born at Spresswell, on the Yorkshire-Durham border.[73] His family were of Saxon extraction and lived in that district from the Norman Conquest up to the seventeenth century and remained roman catholics throughout. John was educated at Oxford University, receiving Master of Arts and Doctor of Divinity degrees and became Master of Baliol. He was one of the greatest scholars of his day, a many-sided man far in advance of his age, a prophet and a powerful personality. He displayed warm patriotism, a glowing zeal for the dignity of the crown, for the honour and well being of his countrymen and for the rights and constitutional liberty of the people.[74] In 1366, Wyclif stood against the Pope on the separation of church and state. As a Member of Parliament, he was party to, and some say, the prime mover in, the dismissal of clerics from political office under the crown. He wrote many tracts against the claims of Rome and her English neophytes.[75] He declared that the Pope

was fallible and insisted that he ought to be seen to be the
humble disciple of the meek and lowly Jesus. Wyclif argued
constantly for the supremacy and sufficiency of scripture
as the sole guide and standard of truth and conduct.[76] He
exposed the unscriptural and base character of most
preaching in his own day, saying. 'This practice comes from
nothing less than the pride of man, every one seeking his
own honour, every one preaching only himself and not
Jesus Christ (cf 2 Corinthians 4:5).' He added, 'such is a
dead word and not the Word of eternal life.'[77] In all his
arguments, he employs the scriptures as the sole standard
of truth.[79] Wyclif trained a corps of intinerant preachers to
read and preach the unadorned Word of God. The
Archbishop of Canterbury condemned this missionary
enterprise as heretical but Wyclif redoubled his efforts
both from Oxford and, after enforced retirement, from
Lutterworth. His preachers were called 'Lollards', a term of
reproach, meaning 'weeds' as distinct from 'wheat', Wyclif
commanded his preachers to 'Cry aloud and spare not, the
sin of the people is great but the sin of the prelates is
greatest...' (cf Isaiah 58:1).[80]

'I am inclined to believe that Wyclif was a baptist'. says
Dr J. M. Crosby in his excellent first *'History of the Baptists'*
and others have come to the same conclusion. Crosby gives
this reason, 'some men of great note and learning in the
Church of Rome have left it on record that Wyclif denied
infant-baptism.' He supports his case with quotations,
adding the names of some protestant writers as well, such
as, Jan van Braght and Henry D'Anvers. However, his
conclusion rests on weak foundations and Wyclif remained
a catholic until his death even though he so often expressed
his convictions in 'baptist' terms. He laboured ceaselessly
for the reform of the church in England and gave his
countrymen the Bible in their own tongue.[81] He demanded
regeneration, repentance and faith for real church
membership and almost reached Luther's position on
Justification by Faith. He was typically 'baptist' in demanding a life consistent with rightness with God, backed by
good works, bearing evidence to the reality of the
christian's profession. Similarly he was 'baptist' in demanding the separation of church and state, and in his doctrine

of church, simple worship and rule of scripture. Though pre-dating Calvin by twenty years, he was Pauline in the doctrine of grace and sovereignty of God.[82] Wyclif, the 'Morning Star of the Reformation' died 31 December 1384.[83]

This pre-Reformation chapter cannot close without reference to the remarkable **Hussite movement** in central Europe, chiefly in Bohemia, now part of Czechoslavakia. Waldensian preachers penetrated Bohemia but it is their own **Jan Hus** to whom its people owe their most effective reform witness. The personal piety and commitment to the gospel of the devout and godly Bohemian Princess Anne bore much fruit in both Britain and her native land. Marrying the English king, Richard II, she came under the influence of John Wyclif and was responsible for spreading his teaching and literature, especially the scriptures, thoughout both nations.

Jan Hus (1373-1415) was born of peasant stock in Husinecz from which place he derived his patronym. A scholar in arts and divinity, he became Rector of Prague University in 1402. He began preaching reform in the catholic city in line with Wyclif's teaching, and gained immense popularity through his fiery, fearless sermons in the common tongue. Immediately Archbishop Zbneck of Prague sought to silence Hus and stamp out all Wycliffite activity in the land. Hus protested and was excommunicated forthwith. Although his popularity grew, yet he was persuaded by King Wenceslaus to retire to the country. Two hundred of the English reformer's books were publicly burnt in Prague on 13 July 1409. Hus continued to preach with indefatigable zeal, making full use of the forbidden writings. Ultimately, he was persuaded to attend the Council in Constance to defend his position and the king gave him a royal safe conduct guaranteeing his return home. Despite the regal promise, Hus was seized by his ecclesiastical enemies, condemned and burnt at the stake on 6 July 1415 in Constance. His Bohemian colleague, **Jerome of Prague** (c1375-1416), who had studied for a year (1398) at Oxford under Wyclif, was executed the next year. The accusation against them was that 'they preached Waldensian and Wycliffite heresies', so giving official catholic evidence for the 'near-baptist' nature of their witness.[84]

After his death, the Hussite movement split into two parties. The Taborites repudiated all church practices for which express biblical warrant was not found. The Ultraquists allowed all practices not expressly forbidden, a division that still troubles the churches today! In some sense Hus was less 'baptistic' than Wyclif but his life and work bore clear hallmarks of biblical christianity. Though the Taborites represented his views more closely, it was the other faction that triumphed unhappily on the battlefield of Lipan in 1434. The Taborite remnants, were absorbed into a new fellowship known as **Unitas Fratrum**, the spiritual ancestors of the **Bohemian** and **Moravian Brethren** who adopted anabaptist pacificism. For a time the Hussite churches enjoyed religious freedom and liberty of conscience. However, a civil war in 1620, was won by catholic noblemen and the old faith was re-imposed within a year. The greater part of Bohemians and Moravians emigrated to the north and east, carrying their biblical faith with them and so fortified the growth and development of the anabaptist movement throughout Germany and eastern Europe.[85]

4
The baptist's Anabaptist ancestry – 1

The hundred years before Luther was pregnant with upsurges of protest demanding the reformation of the churches by Bible studying groups throughout Europe. Vernacular translations of the scriptures and the invention of the printing press had let the Word of God loose among the common people. The fires of the martyrs had intensified the yearning for God's shining forth to dispel the darkness in which the continent had been too long. One hundred and twenty years from the burning of Jan Hus in Constance, Martin Luther posted his Ninety-five Theses on the door of the castle church in Wittenberg and the sun broke through. A mighty reformation took place at one time in Germany, Austria and Switzerland with parallel strands in Spain, Italy and France. With the five-hundredth anniversary of Luther's birth so fresh in our minds, (1983), with its plethora of republished materials, it is not necessary to detail his life and reforming ministry. However, some understanding of it is essential to a proper evaluation of the witness of the evangelical anabaptists, to which attention is now given, first to Germany and then to Switzerland, with comment on Britain and other countries to follow.

Anabaptist groups were already meeting, preaching and missioning throughout Europe when Luther was born at Eisleben in 1483. Anabaptist translations of scripture were in circulation in Germany long before Luther's version appeared.[1] Young Martin was brought up in the Roman faith, as he himself said, 'I believed in heaven and hell, angels and saints, the devil and demons; and I stood in terror of Jesus Christ, as the awful judge; I believed in Mary as the

43

gentle intercessor and the apostles as mediators... I was taught
the Lord's Prayer, the Ten Commandments and the Creed; I
conformed to the catholic church in everything.' By way of
latin school and Erfurt University, he graduated and later
took his doctorate at Wittenberg. After six months in law
school, he quit and entered the Augustinian monastery and
was ordained a priest 1506. Thereafter his life revolved
around Wittenberg University where for thirty years he
lectured students twice a week.[2] The story of his conversion is
well known, as also is his coming to the doctrines of
predestination and justification by faith alone. This latter was
to be his primary gift to the Reformation and also his greatest
problem when dealing with anabaptists. Luther so emphasised the corollary, namely, 'not by works', as if to rule out all
need of good works to accompany and to validate salvation.
The anabaptists, on the other hand, affirmed that a man's
faith must be accompanied by good works and only then was
his profession of faith valid and saving, just as James enforces
in his espistle.[3]

Luther was soon in trouble with the catholic church and its
traditional system based on works, which problem needs no
attention here. The crisis came with the posting of the
Ninety-five Theses and the challenge to public debate
accompanying it.[4] It is said that he had no intention of
breaking with Rome at that time but he had overlooked the
previous century of exposure to the Bible by reading and
preaching, which had 'made the tinder dry' and in no time
the German Empire was ablaze. The sequences of catholic
endeavours to silence him is not our concern now though it
should be noted that, at the Diets of Augsburg 1518 and
Leipzig 1519, he was accused of 'preaching the teaching of
Jan Hus', the martyr of Bohemia. Luther argued in court that
'Hus was biblical and evangelical' and identified himself with
much that the anabaptists stood for.[5] Luther's insistence
upon the Union of State and Church set him in positive
opposition to them in spite of that. So that we look at the
conflict between Luther and the anabaptists asking ourselves,
'How could it be that this godly reformer should so fiercely,
and with such cruelty, strive to suppress the biblical witness of
his brothers in Christ?' Perhaps the answer to that question
will reveal the reason for the Lutheran churches of the

twentieth century being in the state they are today. When Luther had established his 'reformed churches' he retained the bond between Church and State and thereafter, Luther the Reformer became the implacable enemy of the anabaptist churches and preachers persecuting them ferociously. If the former question is asked again. 'Why should such a godly reformer treat his brothers in Christ so...?' It must be said that Zwingli, Calvin and Cranmer were no different! Their defenders have found no better reply than that they were 'children of their times'. The solemn truth is that all these godly reformers failed to submit wholly to the Word of God but temporised with the civil governments of their day and compromised the truth in so doing. Doubtless the reasons for the reformed churches of today having lost spiritual authority and for the Catholic Counter Reformation to have gained such extraordinary success then, recapturing two-thirds of Europe, are the same. The Reformers, like the Catholics, put their trust in princes and not the Word of God.

A summary of truths, recovered by Luther at the Reformation, as given by the Lutheran historian Mosheim reads:[6]

1. Supremacy of the Bible as God's Word and man's final authority;

2. Justification by faith alone;

3. Freedom of individual to worship God as his own conscience dictates;

4. Christ is Head of the Church and has no vicar on earth;

5. Priesthood of all believers, each having equal access to God;

6. The Bondage of the Will because of Original Sin;

7. God's Grace in Temptation;

8. Liberty of Marriage for Ministers;

9. Wisdom of God in Providence.

The majority of these truths had been highlighted in
some of the previous upsurges of biblical reformism of
earlier centuries, as has already been noted. From an
anabaptist point of view, Luther failed to implement the
first premise, 'The Supremacy of the Word', and that is
their chief complaint against him. To the second point,
they demanded the addition of 'the Necessity of Good
Works accompanying Salvation as the Validation of a
Saving Faith.' The anabaptist understanding of the
'Headship of Christ' ruled out all union with, or submission
to, the State. This Luther failed to do as his success had
seemingly depended so much on the support of the
'Protestant Princes'. He could not bring himself to demand
the Church's utter independence without risking everything. Some anabaptists taught that the whole world's
original sin was covered at Calvary and so they did not
agree with Luther on the 'Will'.[7]

The principal problems that the anabaptists had with
Luther were in those areas not listed above, as follows:

1. The Doctrine of the Church:
    a. Luther remained catholic and did not reform;
    b. Luther's churches admitted members by its adminis-
        tration of baptism and confirmation; thus remaining
        catholic and did not reform;
    c. Luther retained the hereditary concept giving chil-
        dren of christian parents a preferential or covenantal
        standing before God; thus remaining catholic and did
        not reform;

2. Luther rejected the strict discipline of church members
    as practised by the anabaptists on literal New Testament
    lines;

3. Luther retained the pagan ritual of infant baptism, not
    requiring the prior faith of the baptised person;

4. Luther retained the catholic doctrine of the real
    presence of Christ in the mass as an essential reality only
    slightly reforming it;

5. Luther retained the Roman doctrine of the Union of Church and State.

In all these points the anabaptists of the sixteenth century insisted that the scripture demanded a contrary stance and that complete reformation of doctrine and practice by the scriptures was needed as, for instance,[8]

1.   a. The church in the New Testament was local, independent and comprised regenerate baptised believers only;
   b. Admission to the church was by evident regeneration, repentance and faith confessed in believers' baptism;
   c. All men, including the children of believers, were sinners before God equally and needed salvation equally;

2. Baptism without prior faith was no christian ordinance;

3. Strict church discipline of all members was necessary to maintain a godly witness;

4. The bread and wine at the Supper were symbolic only, of Christ's presence

5. The church should not render to Caesar that which was for God alone.

So ferociously did both catholic and reformer persecute the anabaptists, sometimes uniting their efforts in doing so, that the effective witness of biblically disciplined christians was almost eliminated by the close of the sixteenth century throughout the German States. Luther stayed with his old catholic views, condemning baptists fiercely for their radicalism often using violent and unchristian language. Occasionally his conscience smote him as it bore witness to the biblical correctness of the anabaptists. In 1526, for instance, he conceded that 'such as intend to be serious christians and confess the gospel in word and deed, should enrol their names and gather together in some house to pray, read and baptise, receive the Lord's Supper and practise other christian rites. In this church order, those who did not behave as christians might be known and chastened, reformed, or excluded according to the scripture Matthew 18:15.'[9] That was exactly what the anabaptists were demanding. Luther could not see his inconsistency and historians have failed to explain why this was so. Whilst advocating the very principles that the anabaptists sought to apply, he called them, 'demons possessed by worse than demons'. Philip Melanchthon, preaching Luther's funeral sermon, said, 'On account of the great evil of that depraved time, God gave a rough physician...', adding, 'I wish that Luther had barked and bitten without snarling.'[10]

Until this point, the anabaptists in Germany have been referred to as a generalised group but that is not fair to them, or to Luther. The diversity that prevailed among them can be best illustrated for our purpose by looking at some of their outstanding preachers and leaders and noting the diverse emphases in their teaching as well as in their character and conduct.

Johannes (Hans) Denck (c 1500-1527) was called 'The Pope of the Anabaptists' by the reformer Bucer, but by those that knew him more intimately, 'The Apostle of Love', on account of his irenic disposition.[11] Let him reveal himself in his own words, 'It gives my heart pain that I stand in disunity with many men whom I cannot help but consider my brothers, because they pray to the same God, to whom I pray, and they give honour to the Father for the same reason that I honour him, because he sent his son, the Saviour of the World. Therefore, as God wills and so much as in me is, I will not have my brother as an opponent, and my father as a judge, but in the meantime will attempt to reconcile all my adversaries with me.'[12] Almost all church historians are establishment figures and tend to suppress this side of the anabaptists, who were predominantly pacifist, irenic and brotherly and very far removed from the enthusiasts and fanatics of the Münster tragedy as is chalk removed from cheese.

Denck was born in Upper Bavaria of an educated burgher family, educated in Ingolstadt University, where he mastered the classical languages, and as a recognised scholar, he joined the Erasmus circle in Basel as a proof reader and editor. Like Luther, he was greatly influenced by the catholic mystic and reformer, Tauler. His conversion was under Hubmaier's ministry and he it was that baptised him at Augsburg in 1526, after banishment from Nuremburg, where he had been headmaster of St Sebald's school for two years. Denck attacked Luther's theology as 'only partly reformed', showing him to be unwilling to submit to the scriptures unreservedly.[13] Wagensell, in his 'History of Augsburg', speaking of the baptists in that city in 1527 says, 'None was baptised who had not attained to years of discretion and that candidates were wholly immersed'.[14] The Catholic historian Sender, says that the Augsburg baptists met in the gardens of three adjacent houses, sometimes more than 1100 people both rich and poor being present, and many were baptised. He also says, that the ladies wore trousers when they were baptised, which garments were kept for the purpose in the houses. It is interesting to recall that in the London Confession of 1644, there is a note to Article 40 requiring the administrator and the candidates to wear convenient garments with all modesty.[15]

Denck found refuge for a time with Conrad Grebel, Felix Mantz and the Swiss Brethren in Zürich, whose story is found in the next chapter. Driven from Zürich, Denck found refuge in St Gallen, in NE Switzerland, where he gradually identified himself with the Swiss Brothers and with anabaptist doctrine. His scholarship and great gifts were realised quickly and his ministry as an anabaptist missionary was greatly blessed, though so short. He died at under thirty years after having written numerous works and exercised a teaching role in several churches. He founded the baptist churches of Augsburg and Worms. His attitude to the sacraments revealed his mysticism. His doctrine of grace included belief that the atonement was sufficient for all, dealing with all mankind's original sin, unlike his colleague, Hubmaier who stood with the reformers and their classical augustinianism. Keller says that Denck was one of the most distinguished men of his time. Unstinted praise was accorded to Denck by his opponents who testified to his exemplary life as well as to his remarkable talents.[16]

   Michael Sattler (1490-1527) was born at Stauffen, near Freiburg in SW Germany, about 1490. He had a monastery education and obtained a knowledge of both Hebrew and Greek. Like Luther, he was reading the Pauline epistles when scripture brought him to Christ and his new-found evangelical faith compelled him to leave both monastery and the Roman church. Initially, Sattler embraced Lutheran doctrine. Driven out of his native land by persecution, he turned to Zürich in 1525 where he became an anabaptist through the ministry of William Reublin, a pastor there. Missionary minded towards his own people, he became an itinerant preacher throughout SW Germany, forming a church at Horb, which became an important anabaptist centre.[17] His influence among the baptists of the Black Forest area was immense. He preached at an international anabaptist conference at Schleitheim, a village near Schaffhausen, on 24 February 1527, presenting to the gathered believers a careful statement of biblical faith and order for new testament churches, which received acceptance. It became known as the **Schleitheim Confession of Faith** and was widely used as the basic statement of faith of the sixteenth century anabaptists. Early German and Swiss anabaptists owe their doctrinal and organisational stability to this confession.[18]

   Sattler, with others, was arrested at the close of the conference and, anticipating his condemnation, he wrote a moving letter to his beloved congregation in Horb. Abounding in scripture, it emphasises love to all men and is free from all bitterness. It opens with a truly trinitarian salutation showing his orthodoxy. Estep gives a detailed summary of this remarkable document.[19] The sentence passed on him was fiendish. It ordered Sattler to be 'committed to the executioner... who shall cut out his tongue, then forge him to a wagon, and then, with glowing tongs, twice tear pieces of flesh from his body; then on the way to the place of execution, five times more to repeat the same and then burn his body to powder as an arch-heretic.' His last words were, 'Father I commend my spirit into your hands.' Three others were executed with him. His brave and faithful wife, who resisted every attempt to make her recant, was drowned eight days later in the River Neckar. Sattler's heroic martyrdom became a symbol of anabaptist fidelity.[20] A Lutheran pastor and scholar says, 'Sattler's character lies clear before us. He was not an highly educated divine, and not an intellectual, but his entire life was noble and pure, true and unadulterated.'[21] Our baptist forefathers paid an horrific price for their love of the Word of God and their total submission to it. One-sided church historians have largely suppressed the utter godliness and the heroic discipleship of those sixteenth century saints, in their endeavours to exalt the reformers, whose denominations still reflect their semi-reformed characteristics; the anglicans and the lutherans. Sattler's life and ministry has proved foundational to the growth of the contemporary baptist movement. In telling the '*Story of the Anabaptists*', Estep gives a whole chapter to Michael Sattler and entitles it, '*A Superlative Witness.*'[22]

Thomas Müntzer (1488-1525) became a spiritual warrior for the peasants in their war against their oppressive feudal rulers. He belonged to the 'Magisterial Reform' party rather than to the anabaptists, among whom he is frequently and wrongly included. His character stands in sharp contrast to the two anabaptist leaders in South Germany whom we have already considered briefly. They were noted for their irenic, godly lives. He is described as 'a fiery fanatic, possessed of a demoniac spirit which finally hurled him into the leadership of the rebellious peasants of Middle Germany.' Müntzer belonged to the Lutherans throughout his career, despite his association with certain anabaptists. He was born in Stolberg, in the Herz mountains, in 1488. Having a priestly education, he became Provost of Fröhse, near Halle. He lost his faith in God and his confidence in the validity of Christ's gospel, though later he began to think himself the 'chosen

instrument of God.' With Storch, he was one of the
Zwichau prophets and an eloquent interpreter of the
Reformation movement in a radical way. Believing in
direct revelation, in visions, dreams and spirit possession,
and abandoning the sacraments, he identified himself with
the 'Spiritualists' and not with the 'anabaptists.' He stirred
up trouble among the Hussite radicals in Prague when he
was there and was an acute embarrassment to the German
reformers, to whose party he belonged. They invariably
described him as a fanatical anabaptist which was untrue.
He preached the imminent return of Christ and out-
pouring of the Holy Spirit with the enthusiasm of a
twentieth century charismastic. Müntzer was involved in
the Münster episode and in the Peasants' War and met his
death after escaping from the battlefield of Mülhausen,
being captured, tried and put to death. Although he
recanted and reverted to the Roman catholic faith, he was
still beheaded in 1525.[23]

Having referred to the tragedy of the Münster episode, it
is necessary to notice it in passing. Though the insurrec-
tionists included some fanatical anabaptists, yet it was not
an anabaptist action but rather a part of the revolt of the
common people against their feudal oppressors at a time
when religious reform was in progress. At that period, both
catholic and lutheran authorities lumped together all
political and religious rebellion as the work of anabaptists.
Since history has been recorded by catholic and lutheran
writers holding such an unfair generalisation, the tragedy
at Münster, as well as many other happenings, have been
labelled anabaptist.

Münster in Westphalia was a member city of the
Hanseatic League, the seat of a bishop and it enjoyed some
degree of independence. The city declared itself lutheran
and evicted its bishop. **Bernard Rothman** began preaching
justification by faith but went on to criticise the lutheran
retention of infant baptism as unbiblical and refused to
baptise infants. In a public debate, Rothman was deemed to
have defeated his catholic and lutheran opponents and the
news spread that the city had declared itself anabaptist.

The rebellious followers of **Melchior Hoffman** flocked to
this city. Hoffman held spiritualistic views akin to Müntzer,
claimed to be a prophet foretelling the coming of Christ in
1533. He predicted that after his death, he would return
with Christ and set up New Jerusalem in Strassburg. The
year passed with him still in prison! Jan Matthys, a Münster
baker, convinced that he was a prophet, then stated that
Münster and not Strassburg, was to be the site of the
heavenly city. Other Dutch enthusiasts joined him in the
city in anticipation and declared it to be an independent
christian state. The worst elements of both lutheran and
anabaptist fanatics joined in an effort to make it an utterly
free city. In 1533, the Roman catholic bishop laid seige to it,
with both catholic and lutheran armies, and captured it.
Matthys perished in a sortie and other leaders were killed.
The lutherans promptly labelled the tragedy 'anabaptist'
which resulted in all anabaptists being given an unsavoury
name which has persisted. In fact, as had been shown, the
rebellion was only supported in part by anabaptists and
those not of the true anabaptists in the Denck or Sattler
mould. Perhaps this is a suitable point to return to the study
of the traditional anabaptists and take for our next
example one who was an outstanding leader in the early
days of the movement.[24]

Balthasar Hubmaier (1486-1528) is of special interest to
twentieth century baptists because of his closer theological
and practical relationship to the reformers Luther and
Zwingli. There has been a revival in the recent few decades
of the calvinistic doctrine of salvation which characterised
the main stream of the contemporary baptist movement
known as 'Particular Baptist' for its adherance to a precise
atonement. Hubmaier pre-dated Calvin but had they been
contemporaries, they would have had much in common.
Hubmaier was systematic, conservative and strictly biblical.
He would have rejected Calvin's links with the civil
authorities, as indeed, he rejected those established by both
Luther and Zwingli but he would have had a greater
understanding of that relationship than most of his
anabaptist brothers. Hubmaier was the radicals'outstand-

ing theologian and as such was greatly feared by the 'magisterial reformers', Zwingli sinking to very low levels in his endeavours to silence Hubmaier. An excellent assessment of Hubmaier's life and ministry is to be found in the account given by Torsten Bergsten.[25]

Hubmaier was born in 1486 in Bavaria, close by Augsburg, and was educated in the universities of Freiburg-im-Breisgau and Augsburg. At 19 years of age, he was lecturing in Old and New Testaments and at 23 was professor in theology and elected Rector of Augsburg University in 1510. Acknowledged by all as a brilliant scholar, a master of biblical languages and an able debater, he received priest's orders from the Bishop of Constance. Moving on to Ingolstadt University, he was granted a doctor's degree and made Professor of Theology there as well as vicar of the city's largest church. He then moved to Regensburg as cathedral preacher. Whilst here, still a loyal catholic, he was shocked by the excesses allowed on pilgrimages[26] and withdrew to a quieter living in the town church of the beautiful walled city of Waldshut on the Rhine. This city was relatively independent and here he felt free to begin reforming church life for a short while. He was recalled to Regensburg, where Lutheranism had established itself and he built up the reformed church in the city. He rapidly became totally Lutheran. He returned to Waldshut to convert the people there to the reformed faith.[27] The town council declared for the reformation and ejected its catholic authorities. Hubmaier's catholic masters viewed him as an enemy of the old faith and commenced a compaign to silence him. Hubmaier and Waldshut's council leaned towards Zürich and the Swiss reformers more than to Luther and opened communion with them. Hubmaier became the most powerful preacher among the new reform movement. His expositions of the Pauline Epistles were used for the establishing of many evangelical churches in the Black Forest and among the NE Swiss cantons, reaching as far east as St Gallen and the Austrian Tyrol.

Hubmaier and Zwingli, the leading Swiss reformer, drew close together and came to an agreement that it was not biblical to baptise unbelieving infants until they had been instructed in the faith, a position that Zwingli reneged on later. Hubmaier took part in many open debates on theological matters in Zürich. Zwingli and he agreed also that the Lord's Supper was only a memorial and that the cup should be given to the laity. At this time Hubmaier met Conrad Grebel and the leaders of the Swiss Anabaptist Brethren who were pushing the reformation to the full lengths of the scriptures. Meanwhile, the Reformation was well established in Waldshut.[28] Technically the township was within the Austrian Empire whose catholic leaders ordered the people of Waldshut to hand over their pastor and revert to the catholic faith. When that town was attacked Hubmaier escaped to Schaffhausen, which still gave full religious freedom to its citizens.[29] In this Swiss city, the reformer Dr Johann Hofmeister laboured as a disciple of Zwingli. Here Hubmaier began publishing a stream of polemical and expository works. He argued against the reformers, when Luther and Zwingli said 'anabaptists should be as heretics' insisting firmly that a 'heretic is one who teaches contrary to the Holy Scriptures, rather than one who denied church tradition and rites'. He argued strenuously for equal liberty of expression for those who differed from himself, a typically baptist principle. His work on toleration has been held as the finest apologetic treatise on it during that century.[30] He also wrote against Papal authority, declaring that no cleric possessed any authority of office other than the bare Word of God, saying, 'The Holy Scriptures alone comprise the court of highest appeal'. He further insisted that 'The gift of the Holy Spirit was vital to right judgement' adding, 'only those who are familiar with the Scriptures and are taught by the Spirit can be judges in religious matters'.[31] Whilst this heavy pressure to seize Hubmaier was being made by catholic Austria, supported by the majority of the Swiss Cantons, that is, the catholic cantons, Hubmaier grew in stature as a theological and spiritual leader and one of the finest preachers of the time.[32]

From 1525, Hubmaier began to draw closer to Conrad Grebel and the Swiss baptists in the controversy over baptism which they had with Zwingli who had gone back on his former agreement. Hubmaier was baptised by Wilhelm

Reublin on Easter Saturday, 15 April 1525 at Waldshut[34]
and his open commitment to the baptist cause dated from
then, as did his increasing disagreements with his former
friend, Zwingli. The two drifted apart and Zwingli viewed
Hubmaier as an enemy from that time. Hubmaier's
writings provided the principal voice for the anabaptists,
shaping their church faith and practice. Indeed, Hubmaier's influence has been traced in the Schleitheim
Confession of two years prior to his baptism. He differed
from many of the more radical anabaptists, in that he
retained a solemn regard for the civil powers; and he
allowed church members to take part in the public and
social life of his township. He sympathised openly with the
oppressed and poverty-stricken peasants even when they
took up arms against their overlords. His enemies claimed
that it was he who wrote the *'Twelve Articles of the Peasants'*
and other documents used in the revolt. Indeed, his
arch-enemy, Fabri, gives this as the legal grounds for
Hubmaier's martyrdom at Vienna in 1528. In his involvement in such political matters, Hubmaier stood apart from
the main-stream anabaptists to the end. The story of
Waldshut and its fall to the catholic Austrians on 5
December 1525 and Hubmaier's flight, is well told by
Bergsten.[35]

During this second fugitive period, Hubmaier travelled
extensively, preaching and counselling throughout
Switzerland, Southern Germany and the Tyrol. It was
Zürich, Zwingli's protestant city, which first arrested him.[36]
Zwingli's determination to silence his former friend and
colleague lay behind it. Hubmaier was tortured and
recanted whilst in extreme physical weakness. Bergsten
says, 'the utterance was not that of a free man speaking his
convictions but of a prisoner bowing to outward
pressure'.[37] Hubmaier was confined in the damp dungeon
of the Wasserturm, standing out in the River Limmat, and
was tortured as Zwingli acknowledged. When released, he
again became a wandering preacher with a price on his
head. He eventually settled in Nikolsberg, on the frontier
between Moldavia and Austria, between Vienna and Brnö.
Being a free city, it could afford some liberty to Hubmaier
to renew his work as an anabaptist preacher and writer,

whilst enjoying fellowship with the Bohemian Brethren. He quickly became the leader of the Moravian anabaptist reformation and established a church of baptised believers which included the Lord of Liechtenstein, who gave Hubmaier both protection and encouragement and installed a printing press for his use. Many came from farther afield to be baptised, even from Vienna. It is said that he baptised 2,000 believers in Nikolsberg at this time and that there were 12,000 anabaptists in the city. Here he wrote '*A Manual of Church Doctrine*', '*A Form for Water Baptism*' and '*A Form for the Lord's Supper*.' providing a standing foundation for the anabaptist churches of german-speaking countries.[38] On account of the extensive regulative literature which he provided, he can be called '**The Architect of the Modern Baptist Movement**'. More can be learned of the sixteenth century anabaptist movement from his life and work than from that of any other of his contemporaries.

Hubmaier has been given a place of honour in baptist scholarship and he is regarded as the most important anabaptist leader of his century. There is also a readiness to recognise in him a spiritual brother who displayed in all essentials the major principles of the English baptist movement of the following century. Bergsten provides abundant support for this conclusion, quoting from Newman, Vedder, Payne, Zeman and Estep.[39]

Sometime between 24 June and 22 July 1527, Hubmaier was taken prisoner and sent to Vienna where he was tortured fiendishly. He was burned at the stake on 10 March 1528 and his faithful wife was drowned in the Danube eight days later.[40] Sadly the baptist churches in Moravia, which he founded, shrank after his death and only pacifist anabaptist work remained there. The catholic counter reformation decimated the evangelical witness in Austria and almost all of southern Germany, which remain catholic to modern times. However, Hubmaier's works on '*Baptism*, '*Church Order*, '*Lord's Supper*', '*Discipline*' and '*Freedom of the Will*' greatly influenced baptist and mennonite churches for a considerable time.[41] Just outside the west town gate of the old walled town of Waldshut, in the newer residential district, there stands a memorial baptist church building to commemorate this greatly used man of God, one of the greatest leaders of the anabaptist reformation of the sixteenth century. The memorial tablet bears the legend, 'For the proclamation of the gospel of Jesus Christ and the commemoration of Dr Balthasar Hubmaier, the theologian and martyr of the baptists, burnt 1528 in Vienna, this chapel was built in 1953 by the support of baptists in the United States and in fourteen European countries. Truth is Eternal.'[42] [43]

Andreas Carlstadt, or Andreas Bodenstein as was his actual name, came to be known by the name of his birthplace, Carlstadt, where he was born about 1480. He studied at Erfurt and Cologne Universities and came to Wittenburg as a professor, becoming a colleague of Luther and sharing in his reforms. Whilst Luther was hiding in the Wartburg castle, Carlstadt took over the reformation ministry in Wittenberg but proved much more radical than his master. Carlstadt denied the real presence of Christ in the Supper, gave the Cup to the laity, advocated the priesthood of all believers, insisting that none was superior on account of ordination as a priest. He permitted the removal and destruction of relics and images. On his return, Luther denounced Carlstadt and immediately reinstated catholic practices. By this, the half-measures typical of Luther as contrasted against the fuller reformation of the anabaptists, are plainly demonstrated. Carlstadt withdrew to his nearby village parish and reshaped its church life on baptist lines. Luther then had him banished and eventually Carlstadt settled in Basel where he effectively contributed to the furtherance of reform. He expounded his eucharistic theology so successfully that he gained the support of the Basel, Strassburg and Zürich reformers. Undoubtedly he won over Hubmaier to his symbolic understanding of the ordinance and he, in turn, influenced Zwingli, occasioning the lasting rift between the German and Swiss reformers.[44]

Johannes (Hans) Hut (1495-1527) was born of peasant stock in Luther's homeland about 1495 and was a bookbinder and book salesman by trade, travelling between the towns of Middle Germany, including Erfurt and Wittenburg, which brought him into contact with many of the reformers. Meeting Müntzer in Mülhausen,he acquired some of the latter's eschatological views of the near approach of the last day. He was baptised as a believer by Denck in Augsburg and joined the anabaptist cause there on 26 May 1526. His temperament was so different from Denck, his pastor. Hut was fiery and an impassioned missionary preacher, whose compass of theology was bound up with the Great Commission of Matthew 28:18,19,20. Preaching the doctrines of Christ's second coming and the Judgement of God with the inevitability of suffering for all believers; he taught that the true christian should embrace martyrdom willingly. His ministry was most fruitful and some notable persons were brought to faith in Christ and into the radical missionary movement in Austria, of which he was the leader. He attended the 'Martyrs' Synod' at Augsburg in August 1527, over which Denck presided, after which he gave himself primarily to missionary preaching. Hut, with several colleagues, was seized a month later, tortured and left for dead on a straw pallet in a prison tower where he was accidentally burnt to death. Despite this, his charred body was taken into the courthouse and condemned to be burnt, which macabre ritual was duly executed. The spread of the gospel throughout Austria was extraordinary and the numbers of anabaptists put to death terrible. Sadly this wonderful movement was almost extinguished in the counter-reformation which followed.[45]

Jacob Hutter (c 1490-1536) was a Tyrolean anabaptist whose leadership was greatly used to help the Moravian Brethren resolve their many problems as they gathered in their communities, ordering their lives by Acts 2:44,45. Hutter patterned their lives in brotherhoods, noted for honest, hard work and model citizenship and they were much sought after by landlords as profitable and reliable stewards. These brotherhoods developed a strong, spiritual witness and their pattern of church-communities

spread into the German States, both west and north, and
into Hungary and Poland too. These Hutterite Communities, as they came to be called, enjoyed a measure of
toleration and a high degree of prosperity, and seemed to
many suffering anabaptist groups like living in the
Promised Land.[46] These were the most stable of all the
anabaptist groups. Their young were well educated and
prepared for a useful life. Biblical standards were applied
across the whole of the community and family life. In 1575,
there was a membership of 30,000 baptised persons.[47] The
Moravian Brethren became widely spread throughout
Europe and proved a great stimulus for the evangelical
revivals of later years. These anabaptist churches were
blessed with remarkably able leaders, of whom we have had
room to consider so few. However, some space must be
given to that remarkable administrator and teacher,
Pilgram Marpeck, whom the reformers feared more than
the contemporary enthusiasts, spiritualists and prophets
like Hans Hut, Caspar Schwenckfeld and Melchior
Hoffmann.

Pilgram Marpeck(1495-1556) is claimed by Estep as the
most influential theologian among the south German
anabaptists,[48] which is the more remarkable as he was not
trained as such. He followed Hubmaier in doctrine, was an
assiduous Bible student and gifted with ease of speech to
the unlearned. Born in the silver mining town of
Rattenberg, in the Austrian Tyrol, about 1495, of a good
family, he was educated in latin school and graduated in
civil engineering. He became the City Engineer in his
native town and an honoured citizen until his conversion in
1527 when he joined the local anabaptist church. This
baptist community was largely among the miners. He had
been instructed to suppress this rebel spirit among them
but instead they led him to Christ and into baptised
fellowship. This cost Marpeck his job and all his possessions
on 28 January 1528, whereupon he sought refuge among
the anabaptists in Strassburg and became their leader when
Reublin left. Strassburg was an imperial free city practising
liberty of conscience and so a haven for those persecuted

for conscience sake and it became a baptist stronghold much to the embarrassment of Bucer, the leading reformer there.[49] Marpeck endeared himself to the City authorities as an engineer, building aqueducts and a timber waterway-slide to bring wood from the Black Forest to the City's docks, extending its prosperity considerably. Bucer despised Marpeck, saying 'he is nothing but a stubborn heretic...' but that Marpeck and his wife were 'of fine irreproachable character'.[50]

Marpeck took part in public debates and published several important works. His *'Confession of Faith'*, based on the Athanasian Creed in its order, published 1531-32 was translated into English by Wenger in 1938 and establishes the worthiness of Marpeck as a sixteenth century theologian. Kiwiet says that Marpeck was 'the only one who has given the Free Church movement a thorough theology.'[51] He wrote on *Baptism* and the *Lord's Supper*, published a mammoth *Concordance to the Bible* in German (1550) and condemned Münsterite fanaticism. He was expelled from Strassburg after the Third Debate with Bucer 18 January 1532. Out of regard to his high esteem in the city, he was given three weeks to dispose of his possessions and the opportunity to move out quietly, which he did with great dignity. He settled in Augsburg becoming a City Engineer once again and became one of its highly esteemed citizens despite his public identification with the anabaptist community. He died there in December 1556, still in public office.

Marpeck struck clearly a typical anabaptist note by distinguishing between the applicability of the Old Testament and the New, though accepting the full inspiration of both. He stated that the Old Testament was not normative for the christian's discipleship. The failure to make this distinction, he said, was the cause of the fundamental error of the Pope, Luther, Zwingli, the excesses of the Peasants' War and the grievous Münsterite debacle. He illustrated the point by saying, 'The Old Testament is as different from the New as the foundation is from the house built upon it.'[52] Williams sums up Marpeck's life's work as being 'the chief organiser of normative (i.e. non-communistic and non-spiritualistic) anabaptism for the whole of the

High German zone from Metz to Austerlitz, in the course
of the twenty-five years between his debates with Bucer and
his death in 1556.'The large space that he gives to Marpeck
in his monumental classic,'The Radical Reformation', bears
out that conclusion.[53]

5
The baptist's Anabaptist ancestry – 2

The Swiss Brethren

The first truly reformed baptist church in Switzerland was formed on 21 January 1525, in the home of **Felix Manz** at Zollikon, just outside Zürich, on the NE shore of the lake. **Conrad Grebel**, a layman, baptised **George Blaurock** and was then himself baptised along with six others; that is baptised as believers in accordance with New Testament practice. The little band of disciples gathered around the Lord's Table, sharing both the bread and the wine, and the first Swiss Baptist Church that century was formed. By their actions they declared their childhood christening not to be baptism as they were at that time not only infants but unregenerate. They dared to proclaim that only those could be baptised who themselves freely confessed their repentance towards God and their personal faith in the crucified and risen Lord Jesus Christ as their sole ground of salvation, and, furthermore, only those could form a truly christian church. They had dared to take this stand immediately after two successive Tuesdays of debate with Zwingli and Bullinger before the City Council. Though public opinion deemed the baptists to have won the debate, the City Council immediately published a decree that all who should fail to have their infants baptised within eight days would be exiled. The formation of that little baptist church at Zollikon took place on the first day of their expulsion.[1] Most of these men died for their faithfulness to God's Word at the hands of the reformers or catholics during the next few years. Soon the Swiss cantons were aglow with the preaching of the full New Testament gospel and the confession in baptism of a newly found faith but the temporising, protestant reformers began a vigorous persecution of this work of the Spirit. To see the beginning of this baptist reform movement in Switzerland it is necessary to turn back the clock a few years and to recall that Waldensian and Hussite gospellers had been at work for a century or more.[2]

At the beginning of the sixteenth century, catholic priests at Einselden, east of Zürich had been studying the scriptures together and thereby progressively testing their beliefs with growing concern. Their appetite had been quickened by the publication of Erasmus' Greek New Testament at Basel in 1516. Among these was Ulrich Zwingli who was born at Wildhaus in the Toggenberg seven weeks after the birth of Luther in 1484. Zwingli was destined to become the eminent Swiss reformer. He became a priest in 1516 at the Great Minster in Einselden, the pilgrimage centre of the Black Madonna. Three years later he was appointed to the cathedral (Grosmunster) in Zürich, where there were greater opportunities to expound the Bible because the city was virtually independent.[3] Here he established bible study groups and also encouraged the learning of the original languages. Among those sharing in these groups were some of his former friends from Einselden days, including Felix Manz from Zollikon and George CaJacob (better known as Blaurock) and a son of a city councillor, an erudite scholar named Conrad Grebel; also Leo Jud, Conrad Haetzer and Wilhelm Reublin. The last two became prominent anabaptists and Jud a close colleague and successor of Zwingli. The house where Grebel and Manz lived at No 5 Neumarkt in Zürich exists to this day and bears a memorial to that fact.[4] This central city home was the frequent meeting place of the brothers.

In 1523, Zwingli declared against monastic vows, clerical celibacy, intercession of the saints, purgatory, mass and salvation by good works. He preached salvation by faith and the city council of Zürich supported him. He also introduced a simple form of worship in German.[5] There followed extensive discussion and public debates about infant baptism and Zwingli began to waver. It will be recalled that he had enjoyed close fellowship with the south German reformer, **Balthasar Hubmaier**, who had helped Zwingli develop his reformed theology including an agreement that 'children should not be baptised before they are instructed in the faith'.[6] At this point Wilhelm Reublin, a friend of Zwingli and member of the reformer's study groups and now a pastor in the city, began preaching openly against infant baptism. Zwingli made the fatal error of appealing to the City Council to determine the theological issue. This it did forthwith, declaring against the baptists and against further reformation by the scriptures. Zwingli was immediately tied to the coat-tails of the magisterium and committed to a Church-State union which blighted his former reforming zeal and then turned him against his colleagues who refused to follow his compromising leadership and soon the full force of the civil law was brought against them with Zwingli's concurrence. Hubmaier's fate has been told already[8.] and Zwingli the persecutor emerged. Grebel was imprisoned and died there; Manz and his wife were drowned in the River Limmat and others were driven as fugitives from the city.[9] This monstrous evil of christian crushing christian lasted several decades in Switzerland, the land of liberty!

With Zwingli's new reformed church married to the State and leaning on the City Council for spiritual guidance, as well as using the Civil Courts to maintain its opposition to the baptists, the breach between him and the Swiss Brethren was complete. Like Luther, Zwingli carried through his reformation only as far as he deemed practical by political judgement and no longer was he ruled by the Word of God alone. Under the influence of Reublin and Broetli, two anabaptist pastors in Zürich, several fathers refused to have their children baptised despite the City Council's severe decree to that effect. Nonconforming pastors were imprisoned and parents heavily fined. Furthermore, all meetings of the Swiss Brethren or anabaptists were ordered to cease.[10] It was at this juncture that the brothers gathered together in the family home of Manz at Zollikon and, after much prayer, formed the separated baptised church of believers to which the opening paragraph of this chapter referred. The newly formed church's members pledged themselves as true disciples of Jesus Christ, to live separated from the world, to preach the gospel and hold the faith.[11] They went from house to house preaching Christ and baptising throughout the canton of Zürich and beyond. At Schaffhausen, Grebel baptised **Wolfgang Ulimann**, a former monk, by immersion in the River Rhine in February 1525 and from that time immersion was practised instead of affusion.[12] Ulimann and others went to St Gallen and commenced evangelism there and soon a sizeable church was formed of more than five hundred baptised believers, all immersed in the nearby River Sitter.[13] Returning to his home town of Grünningen, Grebel preached for four months with remarkable success until his arrest with George Blaurock and a sentence of a long term of imprisonment.. They escaped and preached throught NE Switzerland and the Oberland, where Grebel fell a victim of the plague and died.[14]

Felix Manz (1498-1527), a citizen of Zürich has been mentioned frequently. He was a former priest of the group which studied with Zwingli and he was fluent in the biblical languages and possessed a remarkable knowledge of the scriptures. He participated in the public debates in Zürich during the early years of the Swiss reformation. At first he stood with Zwingli but when the latter turned away from the principle of the total sufficiency of scripture and bowed to the City Council in spiritual matters, then Manz opposed him vigorously. It is said that Manz surpassed all his colleagues in eloquence and popularity. He persevered in preaching and baptising even though hunted and frequently imprisoned. Estep says, 'Hardly a prison in the vicinity of Manz's labours escaped being honoured by his presence.'[15] Under 30 years of age, he was put to death by drowning on 5 January 1527 with Zwingli's full involvement. All the way to the waterside,. he witnessed to the crowds and to those accompanying him. He was trussed up like a turkey and tossed from a boat into the River Limmat. Zwingli said, 'Let him who talks about going under water...

Go under!' We may well ask how a godly man could treat his brother in Christ in such a satanic manner.[16] Manz sang as he sank, 'Into your hands, O Lord, I commend my spirit.'[17] He left a few writings and a hymn still sung in Mennonite circles. *'Now with gladness will I sing My heart delights in God.'*[18] Another of this group of Swiss baptists was...

George Blaurock (1491-1529) who was born near Chur in the Graubunden canton. His family name was probably 'Jacob', but he became known as 'Blaurock', meaning 'Blue Coat', after being pointed out by that description at a public debate in Zürich.[19] He has been mentioned as a colleague of Grebel and Manz during those momentous years of reform in that city. He had been educated at the University of Leipzig and ordained a priest, becoming a vicar at Trins in his home district.[20] When Blaurock arrived in Zürich, he was already a reformed man, almost certainly convinced of believers' baptism and he was married. He was described as a 'tall, powerful figure with fiery eyes, black hair and a small bald spot.' He was an effective and aggressive debater and known as 'Stark Jorg', the title of the standard biography.[21] Alongside Grebel and Manz he laboured earnestly for the biblical faith and practice and preached Christ passionately. He was known as the '**Hercules of the Anabaptists**, excelling the others in the vast extent of his ministry. He was the first of the group to demand baptism as a believer, completely rejecting his childhood's rite. He was arrested with Manz and Grebel and thrown into prison with twenty-one others. On the day that Manz was drowned, Blaurock was stripped to the waist and beaten with rods through the city streets and sent out of town. He was not a Züricher, therefore the City Council could not sentence him to death. He went first to Bern, and renewed his former zealous ministry there. Indeed Zwingli came to the city to debate with him there. Expelled from Bern, he went on to Biel (Bienne) where there was already an anabaptist church, the fruit of his own early labours but here he was treated in the same way. He went back to Bern and then through almost the whole of the Swiss cantons preaching Christ and baptising and forming churches. He was arrested in the Grisons and expelled from all Swiss cantons, so he turned eastwards into the Tyrol. He found a baptist church in the Adige valley whose pastor **Michael Kürchener** had recently been burnt at the stake. He took immediate pastoral charge of the little flock fearlessly and also undertook evangelistic tours throughout Austria. Multitudes came to Christ, were baptised and formed into churches. Arrested again in Innsbruck in August 1529, he was cruelly tortured by the catholic authorities and condemned to be burned at the stake at Gufidaun. He went to his death earnestly preaching the gospel and exhorting bystanders to read the scriptures. The beautiful valedictory letter which he wrote to his church whilst waiting death in prison, together with other writings and two hymns, remain to give a lasting insight into the inner life of this saint who walked closely with his God and feared no man. These are all to be found in the '*Martyrs' Mirror*'and the two hymns are in the Anabaptist Ausbund Hymnal.[22]

From the death of Manz and Grebel and the banishment of Blaurock, the momentum of the anabaptist movement in the Swiss cantons was lost. Persecution was sharp and enforced with all the powers of civil governments in all those cantons, whether catholic or reformed. The Swiss Brethren were scattered abroad, some to South Germany to join their brothers there among whom Hubmaier, Reublin, Sattler, Denck and others had laboured. Others went into Moravia and joined the communities there and even emigrating with them to Poland, North Germany and the Netherlands.[23] The anabaptist message and the potent witness of their impeccable lives made a lasting impact everywhere. 'Then the disciples went out and preached everywhere and the Lord worked with them and confirmed his word by the signs that accompanied it'.[24]

Wilhelm Reublin, whose birth and death dates are unknown, was a native of Rottenberg and educated in the University of Freiberg. Of his early years little is known until he became a priest at St Martin's and the people's priest and preacher at the Cathedral of St Alban's in Basel, where he was so popular that he commanded congregations of 4,000. This evidence of remarkable gifts stands in contrast to Zwingli's dismissal of Reublin as 'simple of mind, foolishly bold, garrulous and unwise'.[25] He preached against masses for the dead, fastings and relic worship, progressively proclaiming reformed doctrine. He replaced a relic in the cathedral by a copy of the Word of God, declaring that if anything religious was worthy of worship, then it was the scriptures.[26] He was banished from Basel 27 June 1522 and moved into the Zürich area, into Zwingli's circle of reforming priests, being the first of them to marry, and settled at Wytikon as reformed pastor and took Zollikon under his care.[27] He was the first of the Zürich group to preach against infant baptism in 1524. He took part in the First Baptismal Disputation of 10 & 17 January 1525 and began to preach the separation of baptism and state citizenship. Under Zwingli's established church in Zürich, an annual oath of allegiance was required from every citizen, with evidence of having been baptised and regularly taken communion, in order to continue his status as such. Reublin was expelled from the city 21 January 1525 and moved to Schaffhausen where he preached, strove for the conversion of the Burgomaster and took part in the famous anabaptist conference at nearby Schleitheim when the celebrated Confession was promulgated.[28] He was the joint leader of it with Sattler.

Reublin baptised Hubmaier and sixty believers at Waldshut at Easter 1525 and, escaping capture, he reached Strassburg in 1526 to join the already substantial anabaptist community there.[29] Here he participated in public debate but was expelled as a recalcitrant anabaptist 22 October 1528, refusing to conform to the paedobaptist concensus enforced there. Reublin was warned not to return on threat of drowning.[30] It appears that the city reformers took strong objection to his insistence that personal faith was necessary before baptism. Whilst at Strassburg Reublin visited Horb during 1527, preaching and encouraging the substantial anabaptist community there which was sending out missionaries and expanding its influence.[31] Eventually, the catholic authorities imposed a clamp down on these radicals and on the protestants also. They enforced life-long penance for restoration to the 'Church' as the alternative to severe physical penalties or death.[32] Reublin did not stay there but travelled further east into Moravia and joined with the Hutterite communities there, ministering to them and striving to heal the breaches among them. He gathered a church of three hundred at Eslingen but this was dispersed by armed force.[33] How he spent his last days is not clear though it is known he returned to Rottenberg seeking to recover his lost estates there and then lived in both Zürich and Basel a quiet life with his wife.[34]

In considering the development of the anabaptist churches and their testimony in this and the previous chapter, we have looked at the magisterial reformation of the protestant reformers, Luther and Zwingli. They are referred to in that way because of their failure to separate church and state, their willing submission to the civil authorities in spiritual matters and their use of the civil powers of the magistrates to impose physical penalties on those convicted of religious errors. This has been necessary in order to understand the contrast between their 'half-way reform' and the insistence of the anabaptists on complete submission to scripture in all matters of faith and practice. It is for the same reason that a brief background reference to Calvin, the Genevan magisterial reformer, must be made here.

Jean Calvin (1509-64) was born at Noyon, 100kms south of Paris and educated at the Sorbonne at the same time as Ignatius Loyala and Francis Xavier.[35] Turning his back on the church, he went to Orleans and studied law, coming under humanist influence there. He had a sudden conversion and joined a group of keen protestants in Paris, doubtless studying the writings of Luther and Erasmus. His life in detail is freely available and an excellent biography by his compatriot, François Wendel, is in print in an English translation. Summarising, Calvin wrote his '*Institutes of the Christian Religion*' whilst a refugee in Geneva. This work, by its clarity, comprehensivity and logical plan provides the 'most inclusive and systematic presentation of the christian faith as held by the protestants which has thus far appeared'. His doctrine of the church was closer to that of Wyclif, Hus and the anabaptists than it was to that of either Luther or Zwingli. But Calvin differed from the anabaptists in that he retained the augustinian heresy of the 'Wheat and Tares' in which it was asserted that no church membership could be pure, that is entirely regenerate on earth, since Christ had stated that it would be a mixture of good and bad until the end of the world. The anabaptists rejected this heresy outright. They insisted that Christ had stated clearly that 'The field is the world' and had not in any way referred to it being the church. (Matthew 13:38). Calvin provided for the choice of ministers by the church members, although he placed the final say and authority in the hands of the civil powers, perpetuating in his system the unholy marriage of the church and the state.[36] Though he and Farel tried to make Geneva a 'Church-State', they were banished from the city by its civilian rulers! In 1541, Calvin returned to Geneva, labouring there until his death in 1564, throughout which period he was the dominant figure in the city. Luther and Calvin shared large areas of agreement in doctrine, such as, the sovereignty of God, the retention of the historic catholic creeds, reverence for the scripture as the Word of God, believing in predestination and salvation by faith through grace, but they disagreed over the nature of the presence of Christ in the Lord's Supper. Calvin in this matter was nearer to Luther than he was to Zwingli which means that he was farther from the anabaptists than was Zwingli.[37] Exercising his ministry later than Zwingli, he was not faced with the initial dynamic upsurge for total reform that occurred in Zürich. Anabaptism was already a broken force, having been largely suppressed by the civil powers in all Swiss cantons excepting Bern. The protestant reformers had turned away from such total reform by the Word of God. Calvin sought by all means at his disposal, including the use of the civil powers, to persecute, suppress and exterminate the baptists wherever he found them. Most readers will know the story of the martyrdom of Servetus, the Spanish anabaptist, but perhaps know little about the victim.

Michael Servetus (1514-53) was born of a Spanish aristocractic family in Navarre and received a university education at Valladolid, Toulouse and Paris. He was converted early in his life and became an earnest enthusiast for the total reform of the church by the Word of God. He graduated in law, medicine and theology and practised in all three. A brilliant scholar, he wrote one of the most successful medical works in his day which remained a classic for at least a hundred years. Servetus was not well received in reformed circles because he developed anti-trinitarian views. In 1548, he read some of Calvin's works and decided to go to Geneva and share with that writer some of his own convictions. Calvin immediately named the Spaniard as a 'heretic' and determined to silence him. Writing to Farel, Calvin had said, 'I will not suffer him to get out alive'.[38] So Calvin provided the catholic inquisitor at Lyons in France, where Servetus was then living, with theological incriminatory documentation and the court there sentenced him to be burned but the prisoner escaped! The court then carried out the sentence using an effigy instead![39]

Servetus appears to have been distinctly naive and very trusting in his fellow christians, as he then travelled immediately to Switzerland. There he was denounced by Calvin and put on trial for blasphemy and heresy in Geneva. Found guilty of anti-trinitarianism and anabaptism, the Spanish baptist was led to the stake by Farel and burnt on 28 October 1553.[40] The proof of Calvin's involvement is found in both Williams and Estep. Calvin's harsh action did more to propagate Servetus' heresies than did the latter's whole life. Unitarianism spread rapidly and widely, particularly in Italy where it infected almost all the evangelical churches, whether Waldensian, Calvinist or anabaptist. The calvinist lawyer and theologian, Matthew Grimaldi (1506-64), like many others, declared that the execution of Servetus was an indelible blot on the reformation and because of it Italy turned away from Calvin.[41]

The mention of Spain and Italy points up to the inadequate account of the radical reformation in those countries which lack of space imposes on this book. There was considerable spiritual awakening in Spain during the fifteenth and sixteenth centuries and the twin brothers Valdés were prominent in it. The **Valdés brothers** were initially humanist catholics, followers of Erasmus. **Alphonse** became a reformer within the administration of the state but early was disillusioned with his hope of biblical revision of government and died early of the plague in 1532. His brother, **Juan Valdés** (1500-41), was educated in law and theology and published several writings to promote a spiritual reformation, one of which occasioned him to be attainted of heresy and he escaped from Spain to Italy taking with him some of the extraordinary ideas of his university colleague, Michael Servetus.[42] The Spanish Inquisition, which had condemned Valdés's writings, was set up by Ferdinand and Isabella in 1478 to stamp out reform. The catholic monarchs based their action on the astonishing exegesis by Augustine of Luke 14:23, 'Compel them to come in!' and of John 15:6, 'cast forth and burned'. This reveals the typical misuse of the bible in order to suppress believers in their biblical reform of that time.[43]

In referring to Italy the name of that godly preacher, **Girolamo Savonarola** (1452-1498) cannot be omitted. His mighty reform of Florence, in the face of the immensely powerful and wicked Medicis, by a wonderfully effective and popular ministry lifted the city from a sink of iniquity to an orderly community where christians gathered freely around the Word of God. He also proclaimed against the worldliness and evil living of the Pope and his clerics with such success that the Papal chair determined on his murder. History records that 'the devil excommunicated the saint' and on 23 May 1498, Savonarola was hanged and his body burned in the very city where his holy life and biblical ministry had been so honouring to God. Great man of God though he was, he cannot be claimed as a baptist.[44]

Italy and Calvin come face to face again in Poland where both anabaptists and calvinists had carried reformation into the heart of that catholic country. The former were mostly Hutterite brethren from the Austrian provinces and neighbouring lands. In time it was the calvinists who triumphed and for a while secured a voice in the national government. Dutch baptists had also penetrated the coastal lands of Prussia, Lithuania and Poland and established churches. The king of Lithuania gave reasonable liberty to his subjects and 'free churches' prospered under his liberal rule. With the amalgamation of the kingdoms, this freedom also extended initially to Poland as well. Vilnius (Vilna now in USSR) became an anabaptist centre of considerable proportions. As has been noted, there had been a tendency for some anabaptists to lean towards an Arian view of Christ and this appeared in Poland at this time causing sharp friction between them and the calvinists. The anabaptists also came to convictions rejecting infant baptism completely and adopting immersion for believers only and the two groups of churches reacted on each other producing a large secession from the so-called Major Reformed Church of Poland. The seceders were known as the Minor Church of Poland which became unitarian and adopted both modes of baptism. Some traditional anabaptists remained true to the Word and gathered separately for a time. Outstanding among the Polish Minor church and its foremost promoter of its unitarianism was undoubtedly Faustus Socinus whose name was stamped on his distinctive heresy.[45]

Faustus Socinius (1539-1604) was born in Sienna, Italy and his family name was really Sozini. He developed a Christology that stated Christ was divine by reason of office but not by nature. He published a work expounding this teaching whilst among the calvinists at Basel in 1578, called *'Jesu Christo Dervatore'*. After his arrival in Poland, he quickly identified himself with the Minor church and progressed to be a leader among them, shaping them into his own unitarian form. By this time he had also embraced some anabaptist views including that on baptism of believers only but he was indifferent as to the mode. His controversies with the calvinists led to a new Socinianism coming into being as the characteristic of the Polish Minor Church. This has marked Polish evangelicalism ever since and fellowship between them and the Dutch Mennonite churches led to its introduction in Holland and onwards into Britain among the 'General Baptist' churches to whom reference has yet to be made. The persecution by Cranmer of the 'Dutch Baptist' churches of Kent and Essex, as he called them, was based upon the charge of blasphemy concerning the Person of Christ. Ultimately, the General Baptist churches were to lapse totally into unitarianism and cease to be recognised as baptists.[46]

Peter Riedermann (1506-1556) was pre-eminent among the second generation of anabaptists and has been called the Second Founder of the Hutterite Brethren. He was born in 1506 at Hirschberg in Silesia, today Poland's southern province and was a cobbler by trade. Little is known of his youth or his conversion which must have been early on. He was ordained an anabaptist minister of the Word in 1529 at Linz on the Danube where there was already an established anabaptist church. He was sent to Gmunden on the Traunsee in upper Austria to preach the gospel and a church was founded there. He himself was put into prison for three years during which time he wrote the first edition of his *Statement of the Christian Faith* which he called, *'Rechenschaft'* from 1 Peter 3:15... 'Always be prepared... to give the reason' (Gk *logos* tr. German *Rechenschaft*), which reveals a mature understanding of the scriptures and of Hubmaier's writings. On his release he went to Linz and became an effective preacher of the gospel there. The Linz elders sent him as a missionary to preach in Upper Austria, Tyrol and Franconia and once again he was put into prison in Nürnberg. On release he again itinerated, evangelising and founding churches in Austria, Swabia and Württemberg. For a third time he was imprisoned but was latterly given the freedom of Castle Wolkersdorf on parole, during which time he wrote his second edition of the *Rechenschaft*, which was immediately accepted by the Hutterite communities as the definitive statement of their faith and practice. On release, he returned to the Moravian Hutterite communities and became their spiritual leader in which capacity he served until his death in the Protzko commune December 1556. Characteristically, anabaptist Riedermann's Statement was firmly trinitarian and demanded evidence of regeneration and faith before baptism and church membership. Strict church discipline was demanded and admission to the Lord's Supper dependent upon a consistent life. The Church was to be completely separated from the World and congregationally ruled under Christ their Head. This was foundational for all free churches thereafter. Good works, he said, did not save but they were necessary to validate saving faith.[47]

The Anabaptists in the Netherlands

The largest body of anabaptists on the continent of Europe, which survived persecution by catholics and protestants alike during the sixteenth century, came to be called Mennonites after their leader, Menno Simons.[48]

Menno Simons (1496-1561) was born in Witmarsum in the province of Freisland in 1498. He was educated for the priesthood, with a good knowledge of Greek and Latin, and ordained at Utrecht in 1524.[49] At first a typical worldly cleric, within a year he was studying the New Testament seriously with deep inward concern which was stirred by witnessing the beheading of an anabaptist for being 'twice baptised.'[50] A little later three hundred anabaptists were killed at nearby Bolsward, including Menno's own brother. Humbly he bowed before God and was converted.[51] He tells us, 'My heart trembled within me. I prayed to God with sighs and tears that he would give me, a sorrowing sinner, the gift of his grace, create within me a clean heart and graciously, through the merits of the crimson blood of Christ, forgive my unclean walk and frivolous way of life, and bestow on me wisdom, Spirit, courage, a manly spirit, so that I might preach his exalted and adorable name and holy Word of purity'. He continues, '... taught of the Holy Spirit until I of my own choice declared war on the world, the flesh and the devil... willingly submitting myself to the heavy cross of my Lord Jesus Christ that I might inherit the

promised kingdom.'[52] For nine months he preached Christ
in the village church, exposing the error of the mass and
infant baptism, concerning which he rejected not only
catholic teaching but that of both Luther and Zwingli. On
30 January 1536, he resigned his living and left the catholic
priesthood. He was baptised and re-ordained by **Obbe
Philips**, becoming a refugee anabaptist missionary in a
catholic land.[53] He sought to pastor the baptist church in
Gröningen but a price of a hundred golden gulden was put
on his head and this made his ministry difficult. He
itinerated through Germany, Denmark and the Baltic
coast, everywhere founding churches. He wrote and
published voluminous works and began to lean towards
that view of the incarnation in which Christ, though born in
Mary, did not take his flesh of Mary. In this he differed
from the Swiss and South German anabaptists.[54] He spent
but a few years in his native land and made his home in
Holstein where he died in 1581, much discouraged by the
divisions among his followers over church discipline.[55]

Church discipline became a live issue in the Mennonite
churches. All practised the 'Ban', that is the exclusion from
fellowship of disorderly members, but they differed on the
detailed application of it. In many ways, Menno did not
play a large part in the radical reformation but his
followers, who multiplied in numbers, did so. They
suffered acutely for their faithfulness. Braght's '*Book of
Martyrs*' 1660 (the Dutch equivalent to Foxe's Book of
Martyrs) records their sufferings. In the story '*Story of the
Mennonites*' by C. S. Smith, an interesting account of their
history is found, tracing them through the Baltic States into
Russia and then, by emigration in 1711, to Pennsylvania,
giving them a homeland in the United States and later in
Canada where they still abound.[56] Their teaching has
always stressed the necessity of a godly life bearing a good
testimony to the world, so characteristic of their founder
and the anabaptists generally.

The British Anabaptists

Anabaptist influences had long been evident in Britain as
has been seen firstly, in the Celtic churches and their near

demise through Augustine of Canterbury's treacherous massacre about 600 AD. When Willian of Normandy conquered Britain, he found it necessary for his Archbishop Lanfranc to publish a treatise against 'Waldensian heresies' which he said permeated the land.[57] In 1166, a group of German christians, led by Gerhardt, an educated man from Mainz, who taught that the scriptures were totally normative for christian life and witness, came to Oxford. Though of exemplary character, they disturbed the church authorities there because they refused to believe in purgatory, to bring their infants for baptism or to attend mass. Indeed, they taught only what was to be found in the Word of God and preached the gospel as they spread around the district. They were condemned as heretics when they refused to recant and do penance. Stripped to the waist, scourged and branded on their foreheads, they were driven out from the city into the snow-covered countryside to perish. On pain of death, no one was permitted to give them any help.[58] It has been dramatised ably by Emily Holt in her very readable novel, *One Snowy Night*. Such 'Bible-men', as they were often called, roamed around Britain publicly reading and preaching the Word of God. Later, in Henry II's reign, a company of Waldensian believers settled in Darenth in Kent; whilst during Edward III's reign, colonies of 'Bible-men' were active in Norfolk. Bishop Gray's Register, in Cambridge University Library, records the arraignment before him of believers from that city, and from Swaffham in Norfolk, who confessed to meeting in conventicles.[59]

It was at just that time John Wyclif, with his strongly baptistic Lollard preachers, made their impact and laid the foundation for reformation of the churches throughout Britain. It is interesting to note the remains of a baptistry, possibly of Lollard origin, was revealed in 1841 when digging on the site of Hill Cliffe baptist chapel, Cheshire, was being done.[60] William Tyndale (c1450-1536) gave further impetus to reform by the publication of his excellent translation of the scriptures into English. He was expelled from Britain as a heretic and found refuge in Belgium to pursue his work. Some parts of the Old Testament still remained to be completed when he was burnt at the stake in Vilvorde, at the instance of the English king. He cannot be claimed as a baptist despite his commitment to much for which they stand.[61]

It is customary to credit Henry VIII, and his Archbishop Cranmer (1489-1556) with England's reformation, the first politically and the latter, ecclesiastically.[62] In a very real sense they obstructed reform, preventing it from proceeding more than half-way. Indeed, they must be exposed as bitter enemies and persecutors of our forefathers who were striving for a complete submission to the Word of God in everything.[63] In September 1538, Melancthon wrote to Henry VIII advising the monarch to 'beware of anabaptists.' The king ordered Cranmer to 'search for and examine anabaptists... and to destroy all books of that detestable sect.' The word 'examine' had a sinister meaning in those days, being a synonym for use of torture. The next month, a law was made forbidding printing and publishing of all anabaptist books and ordering all 're-baptised' persons to leave the country [64] Sixteen men and fifteen women were banished in 1540. When they landed in Holland, they were pursued and persecuted as anabaptists and put to death. Three others had died for their baptist faith two years previously, two being burnt at Smithfield and one at Colchester; whilst several others suffered during that period. Anne Askew, a most godly woman with baptist links, was imprisoned in the Tower, racked and tortured and then burnt at the stake in 1546.[65] When making an amnesty for some 'heretics' in his kingdom, Henry specifically excluded the baptists. In doing so, he defined their tenets as follows: 'They practice adult baptism, refuse to bear civil office or swear oaths, believe in the celestial flesh of Christ and insist on all things being common.' In this, Henry provides ample evidence of the anabaptist origin of these 'heretics' in England and of their close ties with the Dutch baptists who also held the 'Hoffmanite' concept that Christ derived his human flesh, not from Mary, but from heaven. Between 1540 and 1546 twenty anabaptists were put to death in England and thirty who fled to the Netherlands for refuge were slaughtered in Delft.[66]

During the following reign of the boy-king, Edward VI,

and at the instance of Archbishop Cranmer, several Kentish baptists were put to death. **Joan Boucher**, also known as Joan of Kent was one of them. She was a gentlewoman who had access to the king's court to which she carried copies of Tyndale's New Testament in English, encouraging many to read the Word of God. She belonged to a baptist church at Faversham in Kent, whose pastor was Henry Hart. Three other ministers of this church, and its sister fellowship at Bocking in Essex, with sixty church members, were taken prisoner. It was a large church for those days![67] The cross-examination of Joan reveals that she held to the Hoffmanite idea concerning the 'celestial flesh of Christ' which would link her to the Dutch baptists or Mennonite believers whose leader, Menno Simons, held that same view. It was at this time that Bishop Hooper complained that 'Kent and Sussex are hotbeds of anabaptist activity' and the bishops, Thomas Ridley and Hugh Latimer, themselves to be Marian martyrs later, were given the task of stamping them out.[68] Edward VI took strong measures to establish the reformed religion in England. All his father's catholic legislation was repealed, images were removed from churches and the cup at the Lord's Supper was given to the laity.[69] A protestant prayer book was published, revised by Cranmer in 1552, making it the standard work.[70] Cranmer also published the '*Forty-two Articles of Religion*' in the following year. Cranmer was no friend of the anabaptists which had spread from Kent and Essex throughout the country. He stood for the Union of the Church and the State, with the monarch as the head of the church. His doctrine was as near catholic as was Luther's and more so in some respects. He held tenaciously to hierarchical government of the church, with Petrine succession, and to infant baptism without prior faith or regeneration. He demonstrated his antipathy by hounding our fathers out of the country and putting some to death, as we have seen. Though he protested his sympathy with Luther, he also expelled Lutherans and Zwinglians from England.[71]

Edward died and catholic Mary I came to the throne and immediately restored the orthodox roman faith. She imprisoned Cranmer and ultimately burnt him despite his several recantations.[72] The story of the baptists in England cannot be separated from the history of protestant misfortune during her reign. The greater part of the Marian martyrs came from places where anabaptist witness was most evident, which tends to indicate the baptist background of many of them. The martyrs of Beccles and John Noyes of Laxfield were certainly Suffolk baptists. It is interesting to find commemorative plaques fixed to the baptist chapels in those towns. During catholic Mary's reign, just under three hundred believers were burnt at the stake but this was few compared to those who suffered for Christ in the Netherlands during the same period. She died in 1558 and her half-sister, Elizabeth I, gained the throne.

Elizabeth I gives little evidence of having been a real christian, despite the effulgent praise heaped on her memory by the translators of the Authorised Version of the Bible of 1611. Rome's denial of her mother's marriage to Henry VIII, made it vital for her to be a 'Protestant' politically and an 'English woman' patriotically.[73] She displaced the Pope and all allegiance to Rome and took to herself the thoroughly unbiblical and grandiose title, 'The Supreme Governor of the Church in England.' She revised Edward's Prayer Book to make it more palatable to her own high-churchmanship (and to the catholics) and imposed 'The Act of Uniformity 1559' making all gatherings for worship to conform compulsorarily to the new service book. By 1563, the Elizabethan settlement was accomplished, despite Rome's threats on the one hand and the pressures from those at home demanding a full submission to the Word of God in everything. These latter were called 'puritans', a name first used for anabaptists (cathari).[74] If the study of the reformation in Britain were the subject matter, John Knox and Scotland would follow here.

Instead, we must return to our baptist fathers. For them there was no respite in England; whether the monarch was catholic or protestant, they were abused, persecuted and put to death, just as was happening on the continental mainland. Elizabeth's archbishop, Matthew Parker, said that 'The realm is overrun with anabaptists' and his colleague, Bishop Jewel, added 'We found a large crop of anabaptists springing up overnight like mushrooms'.[75]

The Act of Uniformity 1559 decreed that 'all anabaptists must conform to the Church of England on pain of imprisonment and forfeiture of goods'. An ecclesiastical commission was set up forthwith to register, and to bring to trial, all tainted with baptist views. Despite this, anabaptist refugees from the continent still poured into England.[76] In 1575, a baptist church of Flemish baptists, worshipping in Aldersgate, London, were arrested.[77] Two were burnt, two were freed and fourteen were banished from the country. In 1571, there were 3,925 baptists in Norwich alone! Three years later seventeen were deported. By 1587, baptists formed the greater part of the town's citizens.[78]

Dissenters of a paedobaptist persuasion, that is independent believers who still held to infant baptism and a covenant theology, but who shared in a great measure the convictions of the baptists, appeared in large numbers in Elizabeth's reign. Many were harshly treated in the courts, just as if they were baptists. Many fled to the Netherlands where they set up 'free churches' of which some remained paedobaptist and some became baptist. When James VI of Scotland became James I of England on Elizabeth's death, Puritans, Presbyterians and the exiled free churches tried to secure religious toleration from the new monarch without success. The anglican bishops of the 'Establishment' persuaded him otherwise and intolerance and repression prevailed. Yet more dissenters escaped to Holland, among whom was a Lincolnshire cleric, named John Smythe (1567-1612), who favoured the baptist position and had cared for an assembly at Gainsborough in that county.[79] He became pastor of an émigré church at Leiden. The anglican polemicist, William Wall, writes 'They began baptising in their own way. John Smythe, being more wicked than the others, baptised himself and then baptised the others and from this the English anabaptists have successively received their new administration of baptism'.[80] This church reformed their mode of baptism and introduced immersion as being the true biblical form. Some members of this émigré fellowship returned to London in 1612 in Spitalfields outside the walls of the City of London gathering as the first baptist church on British soil (as some say),[81] Their leader and pastor was

Thomas Helwys, the 'Father of the English General Baptists' whose story starts the next chapter.[82]

6
The baptist in England until 1689

The presence of baptist type dissent in England during the
reign of the Tudor monarchs, Henry VIII, Edward VI,
Mary I and Elizabeth has been outlined in the last chapter.
The birth of today's Baptist movement undoubtedly
derives something from these ancestors though most
historians of the recent past have preferred to dissociate it
from anything prior to the dawn of the seventeenth
century. Such an example is found in the recent careful
study of '*The English Baptists of the Seventeenth Century*', by Dr
Barry White, probably the leading baptist church historian
in contemporary Britain. He says, 'After the accession of
Elizabeth I, all traces of an English radical movement,
which could be accurately described in any sense 'anabaptist', seem quickly to have disappeared although, in 1575,
some Dutch anabaptists were executed in London'.[1]
Though he goes on to acknowledge that, 'The disappear-
ance of the earlier English radical movement, just on the
eve of the appearance of the separatists, and the similarities
between both concepts of the 'gathered church' suggest a
link...' he proceeds to give three reasons for his earlier
negative conclusion.[2] In fairness, he does then quote Dr E.
A. Payne saying, 'That one strong current of air came from
the Anabaptist movement in the previous century, I am
convinced'.[3] Quoting his own edition of the '*Association
Records of Particular Baptists in England, Wales and Ireland
1660*', Dr White states the case against'... the influence of
anabaptism upon both General and Particular baptists
origins' and summarises in these words, 'no significant
influence could be found'.[4] The evidence which may lead

85

the reader to the contrary conclusion is not insignificant.[5]

The persecution by the Tudors of all forms of dissent had led to setting up of English dissenting churches in the Netherlands and both puritan paedobaptist and baptised churches were to be found there as the fifteenth century reached its close. That there was contact between them is true but also there were sharp differences. The congregation pastored by **John Smyth** was very close to the Mennonite churches there and when it had reached a conviction that baptism should be given to believers only and that by immersion, it sought acceptance by the Dutch assemblies. Actually, John Smyth baptised himself for want of such help and then immersed his own congregation. This led to some division in his church over his readiness to join the Mennonite community and, presumably, to accommodate to all their teaching.[6] His colleague and fellow elder, **Thomas Helwys** could not take this step and seceded to form a separate baptised church at Leiden. This is the church which came to London in 1612 and formed the first General Baptist church in England. To tell the story adequately, it is helpful to sketch biographically this remarkable man who was certainly a pioneer of the contemporary baptist movement in Britain.

Thomas Helwys (c1550-c1616), whose birth and death dates have not been discovered with certainty, came of country gentlefolk with a family seat at Broxtow Hall, near Northampton. He was educated for the legal profession in Gray's Inn, London. He gained a sympathy for the separatist group led by John Smythe at Gainsborough and eventually fled with him to the Netherlands, leaving his own wife and family behind. Mrs Helwys was imprisoned at York by the ecclesiastical authorities, because Broxtow Hall had been used as a meeting place for 'dissenters' and 'she must have been party to her husband's escape'.[7]

In the Netherlands, the separatist group enjoyed the fellowship of baptists and came to share their convictions. Helwys separated from Smythe, being unwilling to embrace Mennonite principles and discipline. Concerned for the lack of spiritual leadership among baptists in England, he returned to his native country with his church and set up in London in 1612 what Underwood calls 'the first baptist church on English soil'. The church brought with it the arminian theology[8] of the Dutch baptists and it was doubtless the first church to be clearly known as 'General Baptist.' It rejected the reformed doctrine of a precise atonement for the elect only, but held that it was 'general', that is, for all mankind. In rejecting the doctrine of 'Particular Redemption', Helwys published a book entitled, '*A Short and Plain Proof by the Word of God that God's Decree is not the Cause of any Man's Sin or Condemnation; and that All Men are Redeemed by Christ; as also, That No Infants are Condemned*'. In this long title he sums up his doctrine of a general redemption.[9] Those baptists holding the reformed doctrine were not yet in being in Britain but they were to be called 'Particular Baptists' in due course.

On points other than the extent of the atonement and the anabaptist doctrine of the church, Helwys rejected the 'Dutch Baptist' beliefs concerning 'Christ's flesh being celestial and not of Mary', the forbidding of the oaths, the apostolic succession of church leaders and their refusal to enter military or civil service. He set new standards for the English baptist churches but this does not justify the contention that they were an entirely new breed. Whitley, for instance, says that the baptists are 'to be sharply distinguished from the continental anabaptists.'[10] The new *Schaff-Herzog Encyclopeadia of Religious Knowledge* declares on the other hand, 'The General Baptists were developed from the Mennonites'.[11] The later history of the General Baptists reveals many reversions to Dutch Baptist characteristics, particularly in their drift back into unitarianism.[12]

It was not unrealistic for Dr Underwood to view Helwys' church as a new generation of baptists in Britain.[13] Certainly baptists owe a great debt to the courage of this man of God who dared to return to King James's London at a time when religious persecution of dissent was renewed. He was braver still to address to the autocractic monarch his book entitled '*The Mystery of Iniquity*' in which he charges the king with having no right before God to rule the 'Church of England.' Here is the dedication, 'Hear, O king, and despise not the counsel of the poor and let their complaints come before thee. The king is mortal and not God; therefore hath no power over the immortal souls of his subjects to make laws and ordinances for them and to set spiritual lords over them. If the king hath authority to make spiritual laws and lords, then he is an immortal God and not mortal man. O King, be not seduced by deceivers to sin against God whom thou oughtest to obey, nor against thy poor subjects who ought and will obey thee in all things with body, life and goods, or else let their lives be taken from the earth. God save the king!'[14] He was immediately clapped into Newgate prison and died there sometime before 1616 [15]

Another strand of anabaptist churchmanship was woven in Holland, that called 'Familism' and founded by a German merchant, **Henry Niclaes** who settled in Amsterdam. Often known as the 'Family of Love', his followers became an international fellowship spreading throughout the Netherlands, France and England. They were communistic like the Hutterite Brethren and pacifists and, like the Paulicians and the disciples of Servetus, received baptism as did Jesus, at the age of thirty. They held a spiritualist concept of the sacraments and prepared the way for the Quakers into which movement the English elements were ultimately absorbed. They were exposed to Polish émigré Socinians in Holland and adopted their unitarianism largely.[16]

Another English separatist movement arose during the last two decades of the sixteenth century which threatened to swallow up the early baptist communities. **Robert Browne** (1550-1663) was born in Tolethorpe, Rutlandshire, graduated at Corpus Christi College, Cambridge, in 1572 and engaged for a while in teaching. He came under the influence of Thomas Cartwright, who held anabaptist views according to John Whitgift, Archbishop of Canterbury. Brown's theology was unlike that of the anabaptists because he held the equality of the Old and New Testaments as normative for the christian life, in line with Puritan teaching. Brown's followers came to be known as 'Brownists' and were the forerunners of the Independents, later called Congregationalists. Like their predecessors, the baptists, they held to the autonomy of the local church. Browne spent some time in Middleburg in the Netherlands and was doubtless affected by baptist teaching there. He taught an ecclesiastical polity which was essentially baptist as far as it went; for instance, no union of Church and State, a regenerate church membership and a self-governing local church, but he retained infant-baptism. In 1583, he reneged on his independency and re-joined the Church of England, becoming ordained in 1591, being a parish priest in Northamptonshire until his death in prison in 1633.[17] However, Brownism was not to die with him. Assemblies of Independent churches sprung up throughout Britain and they shared the Puritanism of their founder and also a strong reformed or calvinist theology. This becomes relevant to the present study as we shall now see.[18]

A strongly calvinistic independent church arose in London, the story of which is told in the *'Kiffin Manuscript'* 'There was gathered a congregation of protestant dissenters of the independent persuasion in London in 1616, of which **Mr Henry Jacob** was the first pastor. He was succeeded by Mr John Lanthrop. In this society several persons, finding the congregation kept not their first principles of separation, and being convinced that baptism was not to be administered to infants but only to such as professed faith in Christ, desired that they might be dismissed from that communion and allowed to form a distinct congregation, in order as was most agreeable to their sentiments.' Their desire was willingly granted and the distinct church formed on 12 September 1633. Believing that their former baptism as infants was not valid, they received a new baptism as believers, probably by sprinkling but certainly not by immersion! Their minister was **John Spilsbury** (1593-c1668) and the church roll lists 'twenty men and women and diverse others.'(!) A further secession from the mother church took place in 1638, when **William Kiffin** (1616-1701) and others joined the Spilsbury church. A full account of the formation of this first of the English Particular Baptist churches is found in Dr Ernest Kevan's book, *'London's Oldest Baptist Church.'* It states that at its foundation seven members of the church were actually in prison at the Gatehouse. That church is now 353 years old and still continues in Church Hill, Walthamstow, in East London. Its first meeting place was at

Old Gravel Lane, Wapping, also in East London.[19] Similar churches sprang up in many places and some were created by division in order to plant new fellowships in more districts as was the case with the formation of Beechen Grove church, Watford.

The Spilsbury church was exercised about the mode of baptism, that it ought to be by immersion, and hearing that there was in the Netherlands an ancient baptist church which practised it, they sent their elder, **Richard Blount**, to be instructed in that mode and be immersed himself. This was done in the Dutch baptist church of which John Batte was the teacher and Blount returned home and immersed his fellow elder, Samuel Blacklock, and they two baptised the remaining members, fifty-three in number. They were probably the first immersed believers' church in England.[20]

During the first forty years, the baptists were continuously under the necessity of issuing confessions of faith in order to clear themselves from slander and libel. Two such were published in 1644 and 1646 by the '*Seven London Baptist Churches.*' The first of these was based on the earlier confession of 1596, published in Amsterdam by the refugee churches there, making a further link with the anabaptist past.[21]

With the outbreak of the Civil War (1642-1649), toleration was given in practice to most dissenters and formally by Act of Parliament 4 March 1647. During the war many baptists served with honour among the Parliamentary forces. When it was over, and the Stuart king was replaced by Parliamentary Government under the leadership of Oliver Cromwell, many baptists were admitted to parish church benefices. **John Tombs** (1603-76), an Oxford graduate, became vicar of Leominster from 1649 to 1662 when he was one of those evicted from their churches at the restoration of the monarchy. Tombs was one of Cromwell's Triers and himself founded six or seven baptist churches in the West Country. Richard Baxter, himself no friend of the baptists, described Tombs as 'the chief of the anabaptists, the greatest and most learned writer against infant baptism'. It is an interesting comment, not only for the good reference it gives for Tomb's character, but also because it validates the then current opinion that the English Particular Baptist churches had a real anabaptist ancestry.[22]

During the Commonwealth Period, under Cromwell's leadership, religious freedom was afforded to all. Many anglican clergy adopted baptist views and formed baptist churches becoming their pastors. Such was **Francis Cornwall**, a Cambridge graduate, who became pastor of the General Baptist church at Marden, Kent.[23] He was instrumental in the conversion of **Christopher Blackwell**, the rector of nearby Staplehurst, who founded a baptist church in Smarden, Kent and then went to Ireland where he boldly proclaimed his baptist convictions, expounding the scriptures from the pulpit of Dublin Cathedral and as Provost of Trinity College in the same city.[24]

The story of the baptist churches of the seventeenth century is largely that of three remarkable men all of whose names began with the letter 'K' ...Kiffin, Keach and Knollys.

William Kiffin (1616-1701) was one of the wealthiest merchants in London and a baptist. His standing in society and his christian character gave him enormous influence with the king and the government, so that he was able to save the lives and property of many persecuted baptists. Macauley says of him, 'Great as was the authority of John Bunyan with the baptists, that of William Kiffin was greater'.[25] Kiffin took part in the much publicised debate with Rev. William Featley in 1642, an account of which the latter published entitled, *'The Dippers Dipt — the anabaptists ducked and plunged over head and ears'*.[26] More interesting is the statement Featley made to Parliament, saying, Baptists preach, print and practise their heretical impieties openly; they hold their conventicles weekly in our chief cities and suburbs thereof; they flock in great multitudes to their Jordans and both sexes enter the river and are dipped. They defile our rivers with their impure washings and our pulpits with their false prophecies and fanatical enthusiams, so the presses groan under the load of their blasphemies'.[27] Such was the voice of the Establishment in 1642.

The spiritual exercises of this eminent servant of God are well told in some detail in the 'Life of Kiffin' by the historian Joseph Ivimey.[28] He was awakened to his need of Christ in his teens under the influence of the ministry of John Goodman and began to attend regular meetings with a group of christian apprentices in London which led him into a better understanding of the scriptures. He left the Church of England and first joined the Independent church under Mr Lathrop's ministry but joined the group from that church which seceded to form the first Particular Baptist church of which Mr Spilsbury was the pastor.[29] Two years later, in 1640, he left that church to form a new church in Devonshire Square of which he was chosen pastor and held that office until his death in 1701.[30] The difference between Spilsbury and him concerned the admission of unbaptised ministers to preach in a baptised church.[31]

William Kiffin's wealth was acquired through trade with the Dutch and he became a prominent figure in society known for his integrity of character. In the stormy times for baptists under the restored Stuart monarchy of Charles II, Kiffin used his influence to protect the lives of many persecuted christians.[32] The king became greatly indebted to Kiffin and this gave the baptist merchant strong influence at Court. Kiffin was made an alderman of the City of London, a Lord Lieutenant and a magistrate but he seldom filled up these offices. On one occasion, the story is told, Charles II requested a loan of forty thousand pounds from Kiffin. Knowing the propensity of the king not to pay his debts, Kiffin offered a gift of ten thousand pounds and saved himself thirty thousand![33] He was seen as the leading baptist of his day by many. His co-operation with Keach and Knollys over many years provided the backbone for the developing strength of British baptists including the convening of the 1689 assembly which published its London Confession of Faith which was to become the reference point in doctrine for baptists throughout the world. He was for sixty years pastor of the Devonshire Square church though very active as a merchant banker; and so had to depend upon ministerial assistants.[34]

Benjamin Keach (1640-1704) was the youngest of the three remarkable 'K' baptists of the seventeenth century. He was a Buckinghamshire tailor who became the minister of the Winslow Baptist church having been baptised at 15 years of age and begun preaching when 18 years.[35] He wrote a remarkable primer called 'A Child's Instructor' which quickly got him into trouble with the local anglican magistrates who sentenced him to a fine and exposure in the pillory in the market place in 1664 but this defeated their intention by giving Keach more publicity.[36] In 1668 he was ordained minister of the Southwark baptist church with the laying on of hands, an ordinance which was to be prominent in his ministry.[37] His son Elias introduced it to the Philadelphia churches who incorporated it in their American Confession of Faith of 1743.[38] Keach also was responsible for the introduction of hymn-singing in worship services and this also was written into the Philadelphia Confession. The reaction was strong opposition at first when a hymn was introduced into the Lord's Supper in 1673 at the Horsleydown chapel. Six years later the church agreed to sing at its special thanksgiving services and this limitation lasted until 1693 when it was accepted for all worship services. However, there was a secession in 1673 and a church was formed in the Old Kent Road where singing was not known until 1739.[39] He wrote 43 works of which his 'Parables and Metaphors of Scripture' is probably best known and has been republished recently by Kregel in America. His hymnbook was probably the first of its kind and he produced an allegory entitled 'War with the Devil' in 1673 which went to 22 editions and was well ahead of Bunyan's 'Pilgrim's Progress'.[40] It is interesting to read that when he was ill in 1689, Hanserd Knollys visited him and, kneeling at his bedside, prayed that the Lord would add the years that he added to Hezekiah! When the prayer was ended Knollys announced to his friend, 'Brother Keach I shall be in heaven before you!' Indeed, this was so! Knollys only lived two more years, whilst Keach went on for fourteen. He was buried in his beloved chapel at Winslow.[41]

Hanserd Knollys (1599-1691) was born at Chalkwell, the son of a Lincolnshire rector, and was educated at St. Catherines College, Cambridge, ordained to the Church of England priesthood and made incumbent of the parish church at Humberstone 1631. A Puritan by conviction, he resigned his living and became a dissenting minister in London. In 1638, he was imprisoned in Boston (Lincs.) for unlicensed preaching but was allowed by his warder to escape and he immediately fled the country with his wife and family, landing in Boston, New England. He formed a baptist type church in New Hampshire at Dover (then in Maine) which he left in 1641 for New York but was persecuted there and sailed for England. The church group left New York and settled in New Jersey where they formed a baptist church still extant. So strong was their influence at that time that the town was called 'Anabaptist City'. He gives his reasons for leaving the Church of England as being the 'use of the cross in baptism, the baptism of unregenerate persons such as infants and the admission to the Lord's Table of immoral persons'.

These points indicate his move towards a fully baptist position.[43] In London, he formed a baptist church in Great St. Helen's in Bishopsgate where a congregation of 1000 persons regularly attended. Prior to this he had enjoyed membership in Mr Jessey's church but left it on baptist grounds. Shortly afterwards Knollys baptised his former pastor Jessey by immersion as a believer. Knollys financed himself first by running a successful grammar school in London and later by participating in trade with Holland into which Mr Kiffin probably initiated him. Knollys published Greek, Hebrew and Latin grammars and an 'Exposition of the Revelation'. Politically he objected to Cromwell's pretensions towards kingship and sympathised with the Fifth Monarchy men.[43] Revolutionary ideas simmered in his heart during the restoration of the Stuart monarchy. He lived to see the Glorious Revolution of 1688. He participated as a convenor in the Particular Baptist assemblies and took part with Kiffin and Keach in many baptist endeavours, including the preparing and publishing of the London Particular Baptist Confession of 1689. He was influential in Keach's conversion to a calvinistic position. In some ways he was overshadowed by the other two prominent baptists, Keach and Kiffin but these three dominated the scene for almost a century.[44]

Retracing our steps a little, we return to the beginnings of the seventeenth century. With James I, the Scot, on the throne of England, Elizabeth's establishment standard bible published and Helwys and his General Baptists, worshipping in Spitalfields, a new era was born that would prove formative for the baptist movement of our times. Persecution was renewed and dissent stamped on so severely that the separatist congregations had to go underground, gathering under penal restraints. What future was there for those earnest christians who tenaciously clung to their conviction that 'the bible held all the genuine principles of reformation but carried them to their legitimate conclusions.'? What future was there for those who believed that the bible contained the true religion and who therefore 'rejected everything in the worship of God that was not found in the sacred oracles.'?[45]

A prominent General Baptist citizen of London and merchant tailor of Threadneedle Street, London, **Edward Barber**, in Newgate prison for his public opposition to tithes and infant baptism, dares to write in 1641 that 'no man ought to be forced in the matter of religion, the gospel being spiritual and requires spiritual worshippers like to itself; which cannot be made so but by the Word and the Spirit of God, which breathe where and when it lists and not where and when men's laws and statutes please, which may make hypocrites but not true christians'.[46] Despite the heavy hand of the Establishment, dissent prospered under persecution, as is so frequently the case. Baptist churches of both types, General and Particular, sprang up all over the country and by 1644 there were seven major particular baptist churches in London. Baptist churches with a fresh distinctive, having a conservative regard for the Jewish sabbath, appeared also, just as they had on the continent a century earlier and were called Seventh Day Baptists.

Baptists began to hammer out their confessions with a diligent submission to scripture. They debated large areas of difference such as the laying on of hands by the churches' elders on believers at their baptisms that they might receive the Holy Spirit. The Generals tended to insist on the practice, basing their case on the scriptural examples. However, some of the Particulars also adhered to it, for example, **Benjamin** Keach who was ordained to the Southwark church with 'the laying on of hands' and who was later to commend the practice to the American churches through the instrumentality of his son, Elias. Somewhat later on, baptised believers, who had not had hands laid on them at their baptisms, were not permitted to sit at the Lord's Supper in some churches.[47]

During this same period, the General baptists evolved a three tier order of ministry, and in doing so differed from the Particular baptists who adhered more closely to the Genevan reformers' doctrine of equality in the ministry. Both recognised elders and deacons as being charged respectively with the spiritual and practical care of the local church's membership. The Generals held that there was an 'apostolic' type of minister whose spiritual ministry was related to the 'churches' and they used the word 'messenger' to describe him. He it was who represented the local church at the general meetings of the churches in a region, later called 'associations'.[48]

The office of messengers was later to be adopted by the Particular baptists to describe those whom the churches sent to their association meetings but they did not define this office as 'apostolic' nor as an additional 'office in the local church' differing from the recognised 'elders and deacons'.

Inevitably both streams of baptists in England were faced with their relationship with the civil power because of the pressures evoked by Charles I's exercise of what he claimed to be the 'divine right of kings' and the prevalence of parliamentary action to regulate religious matters by legislation, which continued throughout the seventeenth century. When Parliament resisted the arrogant king with force, many baptists lined up with its army and took commissions in it. Indeed they tended to form baptist churches within the framework of their regiments. This was more evident during the Commonwealth period when Cromwell sent his regiments into Ireland to quell revolt and establish peace there. On the other hand, there were those who questioned the propriety of christians taking up arms or having any part in the execution of the king whatever his crimes against the state. Here there are evidences of a lingering 'anabaptist' pacifism and also of their refusal to engage in civil service.[49]

With the removal of the supremacy of the established church which had prevailed in Britain for so long, it was inevitable that a spate of enthusiasts should arise expressing their liberation in irregular and frequently totally unregulated meetings, affirming every kind of conviction and none. Social revolution was inextricably mixed up in these disorderly assemblies. Consequently, the disciplined assemblies of the baptists were often confused with the ephemeral products of the hour. There were doubtless charismatic manifestations among the baptists in some cases; as indeed there had been among the anabaptists of a century earlier. In just the same manner as the biblical and regulated anabaptists had rejected the 'spiritualists' and 'revolutionaries' of their era, so the disciplined fellowships of baptists sought to maintain a distinctive characteristic of biblical order worthy of the gospel. One way in which this showed itself was in the high standard of godly living which they strove to maintain among their memberships. They enforced, for instance, the bible's explicit regulation of the domestic relationships of husband and wife, being prepared to deal with breakdown of orderly marriage in church discipline. In John Denne's church at Fenstanton, a certain Thomas Green and his wife were subject to church censure for constant quarrelling and instructed to put their lazy daughter out to service![50] In another similar marital case when the church at Warboys excluded John Christmas from the fellowship because he did not love his wife Ann as he ought and for speaking hateful and despising words against her... 'Presumably, he afterwards repented and sent for his wife and behaved correctly towards her as he was received back into the church.' Cases also occurred of exclusion from the membership because of marriage to a spouse 'not in the fellowship of the gospel'.[51] Again, the strict enforcement of scriptural regulatives in the seventeenth century by the baptists reflects the same standards as practised by the anabaptists a hundred years earlier.

Cromwell's army was largely officered by baptists.[52] Among these was **Colonel Henry D'Anvers**, who came from a wealthy Staffordshire family and was made Governor of Stafford. He wrote a remarkable treatise on 'Baptism' which is still read today. The former Vicar of Leyton, Eric Lane, was brought to baptist convictions through it and now ministers as a baptist pastor. D'Anvers advocated the doctrine of 'Universal Toleration of Religion', even of Papists, recalling the anabaptists' concern for the similar freedom for Jews and Turks.[53] D'Anvers served in Ireland and after the restoration of the Stuarts became involved in the Monmouth rising, escaping execution by flight to the Netherlands where he died in Utrecht in 1687.[54]

During the Civil War, a quasi-baptist movement arose which majored on the apocalyptic, interpreting the then current history in those terms and anticipating the near return of Christ in kingdom power, in much the same way as had happened a century earlier. They viewed the Stuart monarchy as the prophet Daniel's 'Fourth Kingdom' and its termination as the ushering in of the 'Fifth Kingdom of Christ'. Initially, Cromwell and his Commonwealth seemed to fit this school of thought but as the Protector took more and more autocratic and almost kingly powers, they turned against him as a satanic interruption. As with the extremists in the days of the Münster debacle, such radical ferment threatened the stability of the state and was viewed with increasing concern. Agitation occurred among the baptist churches, and, in at least one of the associations, concerning the joining by baptists to the Fifth Monarchy movement. Kiffin used all his influence against it and succeeded and, as Dr White says, the baptists stopped short of any violent attempt to overthrow the Protectorate even when they held such views.[55]

With the death of Cromwell and the early retirement from public service of his son, the growing agitation for a return to monarchical government, allied to a state church, quickly saw Charles II on the English throne. Despite his promised 'liberty for tender consciences', in little time a harsh suppression of all dissent was being enforced by both king and parliament and the baptists in particular felt the full force of the hostility of the new regime. Initially, action was by lawless mobs in wrecking meetings and baptist chapels, unrestrained by the law in both London and the provinces. Kiffin's chapel was destroyed and some baptists were imprisoned without trial including the Welsh evangelist **Vavasor Powell** and some of the Abingdon association ministers. These churches encouraged one another at this time reporting their 'exceeding cheerfulness and a very lively spirit of faith and prayer is amongst them'.[56] The unfortunate Fifth Monarchist rising of Venner and his men, quickly suppressed, gave the new regime an excuse to begin using legal restraints against dissenters, and particularly baptists, even though he was not a baptist. The Corporation Act 1661 required all civil servants, of all degrees, to take the Oath of Allegiance, to dissociate themselves from war against the king and other disloyal acts. Refusal meant immediate dismissal from office. All new office bearers had to comply with the same requirements and also to 'take the sacrament of the Lord's Supper according to the rites of the Church of England'.[57] **John James**, a Fifth Monarchist pastor of a Seventh-day church in Whitechapel, was executed at Tyburn. **Daniel Axtell**, whose regiment had provided the guard throughout the trial of Charles I and who had been a member of Kiffin's church, was also executed with two other baptists who had been involved in that procedure.[58]

The Act of Uniformity 1662, enforced a total submission to the new order in the State Church and its new Prayer book resulted in the Great Ejectment of its ministers. This barely affected the baptists as most of their men had already resigned under earlier pressures because by conviction they rejected a State Church concept. Dr White names only six baptists among those ejected in 1662 including **Dr John Tombs** of Leominster and **Henry Jessey**, and adds that many of those ejected subsequently became baptists. This latter trend brought many educated and experienced pastors into baptist ranks and provoked the forming of many new baptist churches. For baptists there was one snag left and that the enforcement of the reading of the services of the new prayer book in worship. All gatherings for worship, not conforming to the rule to which he is to conform in public worship, became immediately 'malicious and seditious' assemblies in 'unlawful conventicles under the pretence of religion'. The Abingdon sessional records show many reports of proceedings taken against local people under this regulation; including the widow of the late pastor of its baptist church.[59] Whilst at Aylesbury, twelve baptists were sentenced to death for holding an illegal conventicle. The intervention of Kiffin with the king secured their reprieve.[60] **Benjamin Keach** also suffered many occasions of imprisonment and once his life was saved by an officer of the troop, which had captured the preacher, preventing them trampling him to death.[61] On another occasion, Keach was seized and charged with publishing a seditious 'primer', called the 'Child's Instructor'. Crosbie gives a full account of the court proceedings which reveal the attitude to baptist teaching then current among justices and judges. Keach was imprisoned, fined and pilloried at both Aylesbury and Winslow for it. In the midst of his public suffering, Keach is recorded as saying, 'the cross is the way to the crown'.[62]

In 1664, the first Coventicle Act was passed forbidding more than five persons, apart from the members of the same household, to meet for worship otherwise than according to the rites of the Book of Common Prayer, with severe penalties, including ultimately transportation for seven years.[63] With the passing of a much more severe Conventicle 'Act in 1670, one justice of the peace acting alone could impose penalties on those reasonably supposed to have attended nonconforming meetings, the informer receiving a third of the fine.[64] The king issued an 'indulgence' relieving the pressures on both dissenters and roman catholics but insisting on the licensing of all preachers and the registration of all meeting-places. Within a year, the indulgence was withdrawn but licensing and registration continued and persecution began again, lasting until the king's death.[65] Crosbie highlights the sufferings of the baptists at this time by reference to baptist pastor, **Francis Bampfield**, who was imprisoned in Dorchester gaol for eight years yet was so successful and blest of God whilst in prison that he gathered a church

together within it. When released, he went to London and
quickly gathered a church together, baptising many new
converts and meeting in the hired Pinner's Hall in Broad
Street. He and some members were brought before the
Lord Mayor on 17 February 1682 and they were fined. The
same day they met again for worship in the same place and
were again disturbed roughly during the preaching. This
was repeated the following Sunday and the pastor and
some of his people were sent to Newgate prison. After
several appearances at court, they were sentenced to life
imprisonment. Bampfield, being of a frail constitution,
suffered grievously and ultimately died in Newgate prison,
very much lamented by his fellow prisoners as well as
others.[66] Such were the severe sufferings of many of the
Lord's servants, of whom the baptist historian Crosbie
writes in detail. Among the many, there was none more
famous than **John Bunyan**, though some will doubt his
claim to be 'baptist' in view of his open membership views.
Less still is the evidence to claim as baptist that other
literary giant of the same period, **John Milton**. These two
remarkable men have enriched the whole world with their
writings.

   John Bunyan (1628-88), the immortal dreamer, as the
Bedford tinker has come to be called, commands inclusion
in any study of this kind if for no other reason than his
rugged non-conformity. The classic *'Pilgrim's Progress'* has
made his name known throughout the world of literature,
elevating him into the company of Shakespeare and
Milton. Few baptists have caused such heartsearching
disarray among their own churches as he did through his
advocacy of 'open communion'. Indeed many have been
reluctant to acknowledge him as belonging to their
inheritance.

   Bunyan came from an old norman family, resident in
Bedfordshire from shortly after the conquest. He was born
in Elstow, the son of a poor tinker in 1628. His misspent
youth was followed by army service but whether with
Royalist or Parliamentary forces his biographers disagree.
His first wife, whose name is unknown to us, (nor is there a

record of the marriage,) came from a godly family and brought to John that of which he knew nothing — a warm love and loyalty, a disciplined though simple home life and the enriching benefits of her own puritan upbringing. Her influence made him endeavour to reform his way of life. In 1651, John attended an independent meeting in Bedford, ministered to by **John Gifford**, and was brought to some conviction of sin and despair before coming to assurance of salvation and joining the church. He was soon preaching and this led to his arrest as an unlicensed law-breaker. He spent much of the next sixteen years in prison. He had married a second wife, Elizabeth in 1658 and moved to Bedford. His early publication entitled, '*Grace Abounding to the Chief of Sinners*', was written in prison in 1666. It told of the work of grace in his own heart and gave remarkable insights into his own spiritual pilgrimage. His later work,'Pilgrim's Progress', published in 1678, tells it again in allegory form with such plainness of language and exquisite beauty of expression that it has been for three centuries accounted a masterpiece of English literature. It was his total exposure to the English bible that made this humble countryman's writing so utterly beautiful in its literary style. He wrote a similar allegorical work, '*The Holy War*', and a charming appeal to the sinner entitled, '*Come and Welcome to the Lord Jesus Christ*' but it was the '*Progress*' that has given his name to the world.

Bunyan itinerated throughout Bedfordshire and its neighbouring counties preaching the gospel and founding churches on his own peculiar 'open-membership' lines. It was whilst preaching in London that he was taken ill and died on 31 August 1688, in the home of his friend, John Strudwick the grocer, whose house was knocked down when Holborn Viaduct was built. He was buried in Bunhill Fields and his tomb remains today.[67] John Bunyan held the orthodox baptist view of believers' baptism like all Particular Baptists of his day but he then declared that '*Water baptism (was) no bar to Communion*', as the title of one of his polemical papers is headed. He argued energetically that admission of unbaptised believers into the local church was in order. With the distress of those times in mind and nearly two thousand godly ministers evicted from the

Established church, most of whom adhered to infant baptism, the pull on the heart against a rigid exclusion on principle can be understood, if not shared. Bunyan's immense stature as a popular preacher and writer gave his views great influence and, from that time, baptist churches of open membership order have come into being in England increasingly. This fact places English baptist churches in strange contrast to those in America where to have umbaptised members of baptist churches is more than an absurdity, it is a definite violation of biblical principle.

Now Bunyan was clear in his own mind that his practice of open communion was consistent with scripture and he was at great pains to ensure that others should understand that it was a matter of bibilical conviction with him and not an emotional response to a distressing situation. He sets out his case under two heads;

1. With whom I dare not have communion stating that they are such as are openly profane, that is those who do not profess faith, repentance and a consequential holiness, giving seven reasons for drawing this line.

2. With whom I dare and they are those who are visible saints by calling which quality demands faith, repentance and holiness for this he gives ten reasons.

Under the first head Bunyan is careful to define 'communion' as "fellowship in the things of the kingdom of Christ, commonly called 'church communion', the communion of the saints."

Under his second head he states that there are two ordinances of the church, baptism and the Lord's Supper and that they both are shadowy figures of the death and rising of Jesus Christ. Both are of excellent use to the church in this world but are not fundamentals of christianity nor grounds for communion with saints. He also implies that communicants will be in membership of some church having 'made a faithful relation of their possessing faith and holiness to the church, either personally or through witnesses.' For this he provides copious scriptural proofs. He also requires that in addition to the discovery of their faith and holiness they shall express their willingness to subject themselves to the laws and government of Christ in his church. Surprisingly for a baptist, Bunyan argues from circumcision for such submission. He sees water baptism as a means of strengthening the believer's own faith and standing in Christ but not in any sense does it provide automatic entry to church communion. Persons whose faith and holiness stands in the death and rising of Jesus Christ, though they have not been immersed, have right of access to church communion. He concludes with a '*Short Application*' in which he pleads for strict separation from communion with the profane and exhorts believers to intimate communion with those that are visible saints in holy church fellowship.[68]

John Milton (1608-74), was like many others in the seventeenth century who did not identify themselves with the baptists, yet held and propagated many of their radical beliefs. Toland, Milton's first biographer, [69] says, 'he commenced his religious wanderings from puritanism to calvinism, from calvinism to an esteem for Arminius and, finally, from an accordance with the independents and anabaptists to a dereliction of every denomination of protestants'. Alas! Milton sank into Arianism in his latter days.[70] Yet, for all this, Armitage the American baptist historian lists four baptistic principles held by the poet:

1. The Word of God as the sole rule of faith and here he quotes Milton saying 'that neither traditions, councils nor canons of any visible church, much less edicts of any magistrate or civil session, but the scripture only, can be final judge or rule in matters of religion, and that only in the conscience of every christian to himself'. He also said; I enroll myself among the number of those who acknowledge the Word of God alone as the rule of faith'.

2. Milton defined a gospel church in baptist terms as a 'communion of saints','a brotherhood of those professing faith'. He protested of infants that 'they are not to

be baptised, inasmuch as they are incompetent to receive instruction or to believe, or to enter into a covenant... or even to hear the Word'. No baptist writer of the time so thoroughly refutes the doctrine of infant baptism as Milton.

3. The baptism of believers only by immersion is plainly stated by Milton, who says, 'wherein the bodies of believers, who engage themselves to pureness of life, are immersed in running water, to signify their regeneration by the Holy Spirit, and their union with Christ in his death, burial and resurrection'.

4. Liberty of conscience in all religious matters, Milton propagated persistently as when he says, 'that for belief or practice of religion, no man ought to be punished or molested by any outward force on earth whatsoever'.[71]

Milton's widow was a baptist, a member of the church at Nantwich, Cheshire, and her body rests in the meeting house of that church of which Samuel Creton was pastor and it was he who acted as her executor. But of Milton, his biographer Toland says, 'In the latter part of his life he was not a professed member of any particular sect among christians and frequented none of their assemblies.'[72]

The accession of the roman catholic, James II, to the English throne was followed by numerous plots to unseat him in which some baptists were implicated. Colonel Henry D'Anvers, who has been mentioned above, escaped to Holland, but the two grandsons of William Kiffin were hanged as rebels. **Elizabeth Gaunt**, a London baptist noted for her works of charity, particularly of visiting prisoners in Newgate and whose character was above reproach as her enemies testify, was burnt at Tyburn on 23 October 1685 and was the last person in Britain to suffer death for her faith.[73]

During the seventeenth century, the baptists published many confessions of their faith which are extant and reveal development of their theology and practice throughout the years of persecution during which they grew remarkably and churches were founded throughout the country.

Whilst the 1644 Confession of the Particular Baptists is made over the names of but seven churches in London, [74] much larger companies gathered from time to time thereafter to examine questions of doctrine and order. Such a gathering took place in 1677 when the messengers drafted a new standard expression of their faith and order in much greater detail, specially designed to show that baptists stood in the main biblical line of christianity. It reveals considerable adoption of material from presbyterian and congregational sources, that is, from their Westminster and Savoy Confessions respectively. Such were the difficulties at that time, the Confession was not published. [75] When the accession of William and Mary relieved the pressures on dissenters, Keach and Kiffin extended a nationwide invitation for a gathering in 1689, when the Confession was ratified and became the standard of doctrine and practice of the Particular Baptists for the future. It is commonly called '**The London Confession of Faith 1689**'. [76] The Confession reveals some movement away from the anabaptist influenced 1644 Confession and considerable accommodation to the churchmanship of paedobaptist dissent. For example, it provides for one elder in each congregation, fully stipended and known as the pastor, rather than the former plurality of elders. The local church would approve the appointment by it of other authorised, gifted preachers to assist the pastor, who is normally to be fully stipended by the congregation. Though still stressing the autonomy of the local church, it provides for consultation with others 'for their peace, increase of love and mutual edification'. Additionally, it specifies the use of such interchurch fellowship as a means of resolving 'differences among the members of any church, or points of doctrine or administration wherein either churches in general are concerned, or any one church..'. It affirms that 'It is according to the mind of Christ' that many churches should hold communion together and that it be achieved by the meeting of their 'messengers' who however have no inate authority or 'church power' or any "jurisdiction over the churches themselves." Such meetings of messengers were not entrusted with the exercise of censures over churches or persons, or to impose their determination on the churches or officers. Thus all 'church power' remained in the hands of the individual local churches. The synodical rule of presbyterianism was rejected and independency remained intact.[77]

The Quakers arose in Britain during this century from a 'shattered' baptist church in Mansfield according to Braithwaite, the writer of 'The Beginnings of Quakerism'. He says that in 1648 this society first provided 'George Fox with congenial religious fellowship and, under his leadership, developed into the earliest Quaker congregation'. Whitley says that 'Whole baptist churches changed their views, others were terribly rent, especially in the General wing'. The greatest inroads were made first in the north-west and then in Kent, London, Bristol and Norwich, then spreading over the land and into Ireland and Scotland within three years. He further assesses the impact upon the General Baptists, saying 'that their strength... was drained away' and their principles modified by stress on the immanence of God, the discarding of outward ordinaces and mistrust of a specialised ministry. It was doubtless from this time that the Particular Baptists outstripped the Generals and became the main stream of baptist church life in Britain.[78]

Broadmead, the mixed-membership church in Bristol, was one of those that suffered severely by the secession of a quarter of its membership to the Quakers. Broadmead Church was founded in 1640 as an Independent meeting which later adopted the practice of believers' baptism, though also receiving into its membership paedobaptists and remaining a mixed-membership church. The story of this church is preserved in the 'Broadmead Records' republished 1974.[79] Its predominantly baptist fellowship was no doubt the reason that it was invited to the 1689 Particular Baptist General Meeting when the Confession was published. In the great persecutions of the second Stuart period there were six dissenting congregations in Bristol, which was then Britain's second city. Besides Broadmead, there was a substantial strict communion church named 'Pithay' of which **Andrew Gifford** was the pastor, two Independent churches, a large presbyterian church and a general baptist church of which **Captain Kitchen** was pastor. Besides these, there was a Quaker meeting. All four pastors were in prison at one time in 1675 and the elders of the first four named churches conferred together how best to maintain their meetings and edify their members 'now our pastors are gone'. Edward Tirrill, the benefactor of Broadmead, is reputed to have said that their congregations 'had grown very poor and lean through fines and imprisonments and constant worrying of us every day'.[80] The strict communion church and Broadmead cooperated in providing themselves with their own private burial ground so relieving their dependence upon the Anglican clergy for burial privileges.[81] Edward Tirrill's bequest provided for a stipended ministry at Broadmead which engaged in the instruction of young men for the ministry, subsequently fulfilled in the provision of Bristol Baptist Academy. During their persecutions, the two churches were hard pressed to maintain meetings with their buildings sequestered. There are several intriguing examples of their ingenuity in meetings 'in lanes and highways for several months' and, on at least one occasion, gathering in adjoining houses with a hole in the wall made for the preacher to be heard by the worshippers.[82]

Among those early baptist pioneers in Britain, who lived to see the accession of William and Mary and the realisation of their objective of religious liberty,[83] were the General baptist. **Thomas Grantham** (1634-92) a Lincolnshire farmer who after his baptism at Boston in 1653, became a preacher and founded several churches in the south of that county. Moving to Norwich as pastor, he founded churches in Great Yarmouth and Kings Lynn. The vicar of St Stephens church, Norwich buried Grantham inside his own anglican church and arranged for himself to be buried in the same grave, so high was the esteem for the baptist in that city.[84] The triumvirate of the Particular Baptists were also among that favoured group and so was a remarkable man from the West country, **Thomas Collier**, whose birth and death dates are still unknown.[85] He is first heard of as a lay preacher and evangelist in 1640 whose ministry ranged from Guildford in the east to Poole in the south and well into Devon in the west.[86] He was early recognised as the leader of the baptist churches of the West country and proposed the formation of a Western Association in 1653.[87] The following year there was a discussion about his ordination and he was ordained at Bridgwater in 1655.[88] He published a Confession of Faith in 1656 which was the subject of some concern at a meeting of ministers, including William Kiffin, at Trowbridge in Wiltshire. He also published a Body of Divinity which did not altogether please some of his brethren.[89] He was a critic of the Irish baptist pastors for receiving state pay and wrote more than forty publications, including one to justify the trial of King Charles.[90] Crosby wrote of Collier that he was 'a man of great moderation and usefulness' and printed two letters which Collier wrote to the Taunton baptist church showing the depth of his tenderness and great pastoral concern for the churches of the Western Association.[91] In 1655, the association's churches unanimously appointed him 'the general superintendent and messenger of all the associated churches'. The work of this godly pioneer lives on to this day bearing witness to his life-long devotion to the West Country.[92]

7
The baptist in England after 1689

The 'Glorious Revolution', as the accession of William and Mary in 1689 is called, brought little benefit to the baptists who remained under the restraints of the anti-dissent statutes, being only relieved from them conditionally upon their submission to certain requirements including the taking the Oath of Loyalty before justices at the sessions and the signing of the Articles of the Church of England, with some exceptions. Baptists were permitted the exception of Article 27 on Infant Baptism. However all meeting-houses had to be licenced by bishop, archdeacon or magistrate. The Test and Corporation Acts were not repealed until 1828 and the Conventicle Act in 1813. H. Wheeler Robinson says that 'Baptists were the first in the country to make this demand' for religious liberty and had 'taken their full share of the battle... Their claim was now vindicated; they had the legal right to exist... What would they make of their newly acquired liberty? The answer of the greater part of the eighteenth century is distinctly disappointing, for this was a period of relative stagnation in the history of the baptists'. Having lost their passion for liberty, they also lost their passion for evangelism. 'Even though the 'Great Revival' brought new life to the churches, the baptists were by no means the most responsive to it'.[1]

Hymn-singing gradually established itself as the practice of baptist churches, Keach having begun the practice in 1673 but his church in Southwark did not permit singing every Lord's Day until 1693. In 1692, there was a General Assembly of the Messengers of the London churches to determine a controversy 'about the singing God's praises in the assembly for public worship.'The report advised that none of the churches should buy or distribute any of four books which had fanned the controversy. Though Crosby does not report any decision on the rightness or wrongness of singing, he adds a note that 'thus a stop was put to the troubles that threatened the baptised churches on this controversy; and many of them from that time sung the praises of God in public assemblies.' Keach's book was in use for some time and Joseph Stennett also produced a collection of hymns which two books were later largely replaced in use by that published by John Rippon.[2]

At this same period, as a result of the difficulties of general assemblies at national level due to distance and frequent desire for such fellowship among the churches, emphasis passed to association meetings which largely replaced national gatherings as forums for debate of matters of mutual concern among the churches. The London Association had sporadic meetings and for a time expressed itself in ministers' meetings at the Hanover Coffeehouse. In 1717, the London churches established the **Particular Baptist Fund** for the assistance of needy ministers and the training of young men for the baptist ministry. This Fund still exists and is the oldest baptist fund in existence. It remains the only practical meeting point of Particular Baptists both within and outside the membership of the Baptist Union.[3]

The General Baptists went into a serious decline in the eighteenth century and some of their associations ceased. This trend was to continue until unitarianism destroyed them. The Particular Baptists also suffered a decline in spiritual life, if not in numbers, and antinomianism appeared, that is a view that the moral law is not binding on believers because they are 'under grace' and 'now that faith has come, we are no longer under the supervision of the law.'[4] Many of their ministers became 'hypercalvinists' and adopted a 'supralapsarian' view that God's decree of election preceded his decree to permit the Fall of man. **John Skepp** (c1670-1721), who settled as pastor of the Curriers Hall church in 1710, is said 'to have been so afraid of Arminianism and Pelagianism that he made no attempt to awaken the consciences of the unconverted lest he should despoil God of the sole glory of their conversion'. His successor at that church, **John Brine** (1703-65), followed in his steps, avoiding any reference to repentance and faith, even when preaching on scriptures which of necessity demand it.[5] The rise and development of hypercalvinism is dealt with in detail in a treatise by that title by Peter Toon published in 1967.[6] **Robert Robinson** (1735-90) of Cambridge was one of the few Particular Baptists who lapsed into unitarianism. His theology and writings are forgotten but two of his hymns remains in use, *'Come Thou fount of every blessing'* and *'Mighty God, while angels bless Thee.'*[7]

    Benjamin Beddome (1717-98), pastor at Bourton-on-the-Water, was more typical of the Particular Baptists of that period. He adhered strictly to the historic theology of his church but proved a tender and caring pastor for over fifty years in which his loving concern as a soul-winner and his diligent instruction of young believers, for whose help he produced a catechism, left a sweet savour of his Master long years after his home-call. His hymn, *'Father of mercies, bow Thine ear'* is still sung. In contrast, another son of Bristol who came to minister to the Wild Street church in London, **Andrew Gifford** (1700-84) was ostracised by his brethren because of his open membership views and his voice was almost silenced. However, he gained great fame in court circles and became assistant-librarian at the British Museum.[8] One of Beddome's converts at Bourton was **John Collett Ryland** senior (1723-92), who has been called a 'gruff old calvinist' for silencing William Carey, saying, 'Young man, sit down! You are an enthusiast'.[9]

    It was Baptist laymen that dominated the Georgian period, outstanding men like **John Ward** (1679-1758), director of the East India Company and a member of the Devonshire Square church. When he was appointed Governor of Sumatra, he set such a high standard of personal life as commanded respect of even the Sultan, whose gift of wives Ward refused! Later when Governor of Madras, the same pure life produced a similar extraordin-

ary admiration from society around him. This is a
reminder of the same moral excellence that characterised
the anabaptist fathers. **Thomas Guy** (1645-1724), the
founder of the famous London teaching hospital, was
another such man. We have referred often in this book to
the first baptist church historian, **Thomas Crosby** (c1685-
1752). '*History of English Baptists*' in four volumes was
published 1738-40 and is still a standard work. He was a
shoolmaster and a deacon at Horse-ly-down, Southwark
church of which Benjamin Stinton was then pastor.

Dr John Gill (1697-1771) was the prince of the
hypercalvinistic preachers of this period. He was born in
Kettering, Northamptonshire, and early showed evidence
of very great gifts. His non-conformity excluded him from
a university education but he became skilled in Latin,
Greek and Hebrew. He was converted and baptised at
nineteen years of age and entered the ministry at
twenty-three. He was called to the Southwark church at
Horse-ly-down but failed to secure the necessary majority
to take up the office. However, so great was his following in
the church and congregation, that they met in Thomas
Crosby's schoolhouse from March 1719. Later the Horse-
ly-down congregation left their old chapel and moved
elsewhere. Gill and his church returned to it, using it until
1757 when a new and larger meetinghouse was built in
Carter Lane, Tooley Street, Southwark. Gill remained
pastor until his death in 1771, giving the church fifty-one
years in all. Gill became recognised as the outstanding
scholar on rabbinical learning and was honoured by the
University of Aberdeen with a doctorate of divinity. His
scholarly and exhaustive commentaries on the whole bible
are still in print today. Dr Gill's Complete Body of Divinity
has also been reprinted recently in America. His stern
preaching style shaped the character of preaching among
those Particular Baptists holding restricted communion
who came to be known as 'Strict Baptists' for two centuries
after his death, though not always with the same erudite
distinction! It was his influence which was a major factor in
the retention of a 'High Calvinist theology' of a substantial

part of those churches. It has been rightly claimed that Gill was more accurately a 'High Calvinist' rather than the 'Hypercalvinist' for which he gained a reputation.[11]

It is interesting to note that the early Particular Baptist church in Southwark, which began in 1652, is still maintaining the same doctrinal standards today. In 1668, it called **Benjamin Keach** as its pastor, during whose ministry it moved into new premises in Goat Yard Passage in 1672. Keach's nephew, **Benjamin Stinton**, followed him as pastor in that year. **John Gill** pastored the church from 1719 to 1771. **John Rippon** senior followed Gill being its minister for sixty-three years from 1763 to 1836. During this time the church removed again into new buildings in New Park Street and it was there that **Charles Haddon Spurgeon** became pastor in 1854. He also erected new worship premises for this peripatetic congregation, in Newington Butts, Elephant and Castle and was its pastor until his death in 1892. These prestigious buildings were destroyed by enemy action during the Second World War and have been rebuilt using only the foundations and the former frontage for much smaller premises seating only a third of the original six thousand but providing a full suite of offices, much more useful in the twentieth century. **Dr Peter Masters** is now the pastor. He has initiated a pastor-training scheme, the London School of Theology, and an excellent Tabernacle Bookshop.[12]

The Great Awakening of 1738-42 broke into the decadent christianity in Britain as the Holy Spirit was poured out on the ministries of such great preachers as Whitefield and the Wesleys, Howell Harris and John Cennick. In some sense this presented a further upsurge of protestation of the gospel against the darkness, and even wickedness of the established church, as had occurred in other periods which have been noted. Many baptist principles were recovered and this in spite of the suspicion with which British baptists viewed this revival. The bulk of the dissenting churches reacted no better. **Daniel Taylor**, converted during the revival, became convinced of believers' baptism and requested it of the Particular

Baptists who refused him on account of his arminianism. With others, he started the New Connexion Baptists in 1770 on avowedly arminian bases and a new virile baptist movement came into being, essentially 'General Baptist' but having no links with those churches formerly known by that name, because they had virtually become unitarian.

Daniel Taylor (1738-1816) was born near Halifax and commenced work with his father in the mines when five years old. By 1741 he was a servant in the household of the Countess of Huntingdon who was committed to the ministry of George Whitefield. Taylor began preaching in the neighbourhood of her home at Donnington Park, Leicestershire with much success and converts were gathered together into small groups on 'methodist' lines though they registered their first meeting house as 'independent'. They moved quickly to a baptist church order, substituting 'infant dedication' for 'infant baptism' and insisting on believers' baptism for membership. Taylor became the ordained pastor of a General Baptist church in Wadsworth which arose out of his own ministry, the first baptist church in Yorkshire not of the 'Particular' stream. His friendship with the Lincolnshire General Baptists led to his removal to Lincoln and he preached throughout that area and into Leicestershire. Out of his success a meeting in London was arranged in Whitechapel and a 'New Connexion of Free Grace Baptists' was formed, which title was later reduced to 'New Connexion Baptists' by which they were thereafter known. They declared themselves concerned 'to revive experimental religion or primitive christianity in faith and practice'. They totally dissociated themselves from the unitarianism of the 'General Baptists'.[13]

Whereas baptists profited little, having distanced themselves from the revival, yet the blessing of God which followed it ultimately stimulated a growth in spiritual life and concern for sinners among the Particular Baptist churches. They distinguished between Wesley and Whitefield, recognising the arminianism of the former and the calvinism of the latter. John Gill wrote a defence of predestination and final perseverance in reply to Wesley. As Ivimey records later on, the calvinistic dissenters complained of the 'arminian dialect of Whitefield's language and even of his 'semi-Pelagian addresses'. The one London baptist minister to befriend Whitefield was the ostracised Andrew Gifford who attended the stonelaying of Whitefield's Tabernacle.[14]

Abraham Booth (1734-1806) was pastor of Prescot Street baptist church for thirty years maintaining the historic testimony of that first of London's Particular Baptist churches. Booth was born in Northamptonshire 20 May 1734 a small farming family who were nominal members of the established church. As a child he worked on the farm and had little schooling. He was converted when only ten or eleven through the ministry of some General Baptist preachers who came to his village home in Annesley Woodhouse, Nottinghamshire. He early showed evidences of true piety. He was baptised at Barton during the Midland evangelical revival and almost immediately became the pastor of the New Connexion baptist church at Kirkby Woodhouse at twenty-one years of age. At that time he held general redemption views. He became a weaver and married at twenty-four, opening a school at Sutton-in-Ashfield to help support his growing family.

He had a deep conviction of the sovereignty of God in grace which changed his doctrinal views completely. He resigned his pastorate and started preaching in a room at Sutton-in-Ashfield during which time he wrote the book, now a classic in the English speaking world, 'The Reign of Grace' which has seen at least fourteen editions, being recently republished in America. He was invited to the pastorate of the historic Prescot Street church and on 16 February 1769 was ordained by 'the laying on of hands' as its pastor. From the time he arrived in London he took up a commanding position of leadership and through his long pastorate was responsible for a large number of remarkable projects being initiated. He was prime mover in the forming of the Particular Baptist Fund in 1717 and one of his deacons was a Treasurer of the Fund. His church's giving to it amounted to an average of two hundred pounds a year. He led the formation of the society which later became the Baptist Home Mission and of an Education Society, from which the first efforts to set up a training college for pastors stemmed. Indeed, Stepney College was formed from the effort he began in 1804, though he died before the academy was opened. He was an enthusiast for overseas missionary work and heartily supported Carey, putting him in touch with **John Thomas** who had commenced work in India and was back in London seeking help from Booth. Booth lined up with Fuller on both strict communion and his evangelical calvinism and he remained a close collaborator with Fuller in the Baptist Missionary Society. Booth was behind his deacon Fox who started the Society for Founding Sunday Schools, which later became the Sunday School Union, by merger. Booth was the visionary mind behind much of the forward work of the baptists throughout this period. In his 'Memoirs of Andrew Fuller', Morris said that neither Fuller nor Booth liked being called 'Reverend' and that Booth once said that it was 'a species of profaneness to be so denominated'. The same source gives his readers some fascinating insights into the lives of these, and other remarkable men, who emerged among the baptists at this time.

The first promise of a new evangelical life among the main-stream baptists occurred in the issue of the Circular Letter of the Northamptonshire Association in 1770. Here is a quotation from it: 'Every soul that comes to Christ to be saved from hell and from sin by him, is to be encouraged... The coming soul need not fear that he is not elected, for none but such would be willing to come and submit to Christ'.[15]

Robert Hall senior (1728-91) wrote a book entitled, *'Help for Zion's Travellers'* in 1781, in which he expanded his own sermon preached before the same association in 1779. He summed up his burden in the subtitle, 'an attempt to remove various stumbling-blocks out of the way, relating to doctrinal, experimental and practical religion'. The book became a classic among baptists at home and in America where the same tension between high and low calvinism was also troubling the churches. It was William Carey who commented that, 'I do not remember having read any book with such raptures'.[16] The doctrine of the 'Free Offer of the Gospel', explicit in the 1689 London Confession, which had been suppressed by the rising tide of hypercalvinism, now awoke 'a new era in the history of our denomination', as Ivimey reported. Of Robert Hall he writes that 'It would be difficult to conceive a human mind more completely purged from the leaven of pride and envy... He never made advice a disguise for arrogance... nor even presumed to think himself affronted if his counsels were not followed'. Robert Hall's son, **Robert Hall** junior, (1766-1831) started life as a pupil of Ryland's in Northampton, graduated at Aberdeen University and held pastorates at Cambridge, Leicester and Bristol. He attacked the calvinism of Gill's works, speaking of them as 'a continent of mud'.[17] His influence was great and was used largely to re-open the old controversy among baptists concerning 'open' or 'closed' communion. He was opposed by **Joseph Kinghorn** (1766-1832), a graduate of the Bristol Academy and pastor of the St. Mary's Baptist church in Norwich, who replied to Hall in *'Baptism a Term of Communion at the Lord's Supper*, arguing for the practice of the strict baptists. This is dealt with in chapter fifteen.

Andrew Fuller (1754-1815), another child of the baptist awakening in Northamptonshire, was born the son of a Cambridgeshire farmer and joined the Soham church when sixteen. He had a deep experience shortly afterwards, which Ryland tells in his life of Fuller, which forced him to undertake the care of the church when its pastor left. He was ordained as its minister in 1774 and whilst here wrote an argued case against the hypercalvinist's withholding the invitations of the gospel from the unconverted. Its title was, *'The Gospel worthy of All Acceptation'* and it was published in 1785. This was after he had accepted the call to the Kettering church. Fuller remained a calvinist and repudiated both arminianism and socinianism. This book made an immeasurable impact upon the Particular Baptists, awakened their responsibility to proclaim the gospel to 'all who will hear it,' and paved the way for

'evangelical calvinism' which was to be God's instrument
for the founding of modern world missions. It had other
effects too, principally in hardening the creed of those who
disagreed.[18]

William Carey (1761-1834) was born at Paulersbury in
Northamptonshire, his father being parish clerk and
schoolmaster so that William had a fair basic education. He
was converted in 1779 through the witness of a fellow
apprentice shoemaker named William Manning and was
baptised as a believer in 1783 by John Ryland the Younger.
He had a remarkable gift for languages and soon made
himself proficient in Latin, Greek, Hebrew, German and
French, frequently studying at work at the cobbler's bench.
Moving to Moulton, he joined the church at Olney and was
set apart to preach in 1785. The following year, he became
pastor at Moulton, supporting himself by shoemaking. In
1789, he was called to pastor Harvey Lane baptist church in
Leicester where he preceeded Robert Hall. Whilst here, he
was convicted by the 'Great Commission' and published a
book in 1782 entitled, 'Inquiry into the Obligations of
Christians to use Means for the Conversion of the
Heathen.' At the association meeting of ministers, Carey
proposed that at the next meeting they should discuss their
duty to spread the gospel among pagans. Fuller was
present and expressed himself astounded by the young
man's audacity. Ryland also was there and shocked, sprang
to his feet, crying out 'Young man, sit down! When God
pleases to convert the heathen, he will do it without your
aid or mine!' Nothing daunted, Carey persevered,
preaching his celebrated sermon on Isaiah 54:2,3 at the
Association Meeting 31 May 1792 in which he uttered his
oft-quoted words, 'Expect great things from God and
attempt great things for God'.With little delay the
'Particular Baptist Society for the Propagation of the
Gospel' was formed. This is the society known today as the
'Baptist Missionary Society'.

The East India Company dominated the commercial
affairs of that sub-continent and had had in its employ a
medical doctor, John Thomas who was converted under
Joseph Stennett and baptised by Abraham Booth. Thomas

was called to give up his profession and live in Bengal and evangelise the Indians. He came to London seeking help and Booth introduced him to Carey. The pair left for India in 1793 but were opposed by the East India Company and so set up their base, not in Bengal, but in Serampore instead, where the governor was Danish. In 1799, four further workers were sent out to join them, though two died soon after arrival, so there was then a team of four — Carey, Thomas and Joshua Marshman, an excellent linguist, and William Ward, a master printer. Carey translated the bible into bengali and supervised six complete and twenty-four partial translations of the scriptures as well as publishing several grammars and dictionaries and also, with Marshman, some chinese and sanskrit works. They founded the Serampore College for the training of Indian christians for the ministry among their own people. In Britain, Fuller was Carey's strongest supporter and became secretary of the mission until his death.

Christian missionary enterprise was dynamically reborn and from this humble baptist begininng, stemmed a vast world-wide energetic drive to take the gospel to every creature. The baptist obligation, felt and fulfilled by the anabaptists in the sixteenth century, came alive again and the Master's 'Great Commission' became the over-riding obligation of his disciples everywhere.[19]

John Fawcett (1740-1817) is one of several Yorkshire-men that Morris mentions. He was born in Bradford and was converted under Whitefield's ministry. He became pastor of the Wainsgate church on the edge of the moors going north out of Hebden Bridge and remained there until his death. His love and devotion to his moorland congregation is reflected in the often-told story behind his hymn, *'Blest be the tie that binds our hearts in christian love'*. Having loaded his effects on the wagon in the course of moving elsewhere, his heart could not take it! He moved back to continue a ministry of great commitment and blessing. His tomb stands in the chapel's graveyard to its right.[20]

John Sutcliff (1752-1814) was one of Fawcett's flock having been brought up in the neighbourhood and converted under his ministry. Fawcett sent Sutcliff to Bristol Academy to study for the baptist ministry for which he was convinced the young man was called. So keen was the would-be student that he walked in the depth of winter all the way from Yorkshire to Bristol! Sutcliff's only pastorate was at Olney where he trained men for the ministry and was responsible for recognising Carey's call to preach. Indeed he became one of the main supports for the sending of him out to India. Underwood says that Fuller so esteemed Sutcliff's advice and judgement that he habitually leaned on him.[21]

Samuel Medley (1738-99) was, on the other hand, a Lancashireman whose first pastorate was at Watford before he moved to Liverpool. He stood with Fawcett in the training of ministers and like him also he wrote hymns which are still sung in churches everywhere. The uplifting characteristic of Medley's hymns is found in their climax in the heavenly presence with the Lord. His son was a deacon at the Hackney church and joint-founder of University College, London, which had a strong non-conformist backing.[22]

John Ivimey (1773-1843) was a Hampshire baptist who undertook the London pastorate at the Eagle Street church following Andrew Gifford, bringing it back into the mainstream of Particular Baptist life. Like Booth and Fuller, he was an evangelical calvinist, a strict communionist and a strong supporter of the abolition of slavery, in the cause of which he wrote many pamphlets. He is remembered mostly for his 'History of the Baptists', a standard work to this day and of immense value. He also initiated mission work in Ireland and the Particular Baptist Building Fund.[23]

John Collett Ryland (1723-1792) was a convert of Benjamin Beddome's ministry at Bourton-on-the-Water,

Gloucestershire and was sent by him to the Bristol Academy for training. He pastored the churches at Warwick and Northampton, supporting himself by schools. He is the 'gruff old calvinist' that bid Carey 'sit down!'[24]

John Ryland junior (1753-1825), the son of the above, was a youthful prodigy in the classical languages, having widely read Greek literature and even Genesis in the Hebrew before his twelfth birthday. Like his father, he was a calvinist but in the milder 'Fuller' school with whom he worked closely, as also with Booth and Ivimey. He followed his father in the Northampton pastorate, leaving to undertake Broadmead at Bristol in 1793. Here he became president of the Academy and a close disciple of Jonathan Edwards.[25]

John Rippon (1750-1836) was a Devonian, trained at Bristol, who followed Dr Gill at London's Carter Lane church in 1773 and remained its pastor until his death in 1836, that is sixty-three years in all. During his pastorate the church became one of the wealthiest non-conformist congregations in the country and a generous supporter of missions at home and overseas. His periodical, 'The Annual Register', became an excellent news vehicle among baptist churches. His hymnbook, with its companion tunebook, became widely used. Underwood sees Rippon's 'new global view' as the 'germ' of the later 'Baptist World Alliance'. Probably, Rippon's most significant action was the convening of the initial meeting of Particular Baptist churches which led to the formation of the Particular Baptist Union, the forerunner of the contemporary **Baptist Union of Great Britain and Ireland** (though no Irish churches belong to it.)[26]

In 1798, Rippon's Register listed 445 Particular Baptist churches in England and Wales. These churches enjoyed strong leadership and were awakened spiritually to their evangelistic world task. In 1812, John Rippon and Ivimey, the historian, wrote to all known churches, inviting them to gather to consider the formation of a national union, past efforts towards which had failed. Sixty ministers supported the meeting in the Carter Lane vestry with Rippon in the chair. A document was signed expressing '**A General Union of Particular Baptist Churches**'. Those present and signing represented a little over ten percent of churches in England and Wales. Eleven out of the twenty-one London pastors signed it, reflecting the failure to carry a large party of the Particular Baptist constituency with them.[27] Furthermore, the New Connexion (Arminian) baptist churches were excluded as were the few remaining General Baptist churches which had not slipped into unitarianism. This reflected the clear calvinist doctrine of salvation endorsed by the 'Union' whose constitution expressed its doctrinal content consistently with the historic London Confession 1689.[28] The principal concern of the 'Union' was the unwillingness of four hundred churches to join with them.

Twenty years later, in 1832 an endeavour was made to embrace these churches which had not joined the Union on doctrinal grounds. To achieve this the doctrinal basis was thinned down to a bare minimum. It then read, 'Baptist ministers and churches who agree in the sentiments usually denominated evangelical...'[29] The decline of the Particular Baptists from their original strongly worded doctrinal stance progressed even further in 1873 when the 'Union' expressed concern about the use of the word 'evangelical' in view of the new trends in thought with an emphasis on freedom'. This is not a reflection of the author's prejudice, but a straight quotation from the official *History of the Baptist Union* written by its late general secretary, Ernest Payne (1902-80), a meticulous historian.[30] The removal of the offending word 'evangelical' was an extrovert rejection by erstwhile baptists of their biblical heritage. The 'Union' could no longer claim to stand in the shoes of their fathers of the seventeenth century, nor even of those with whom the nineteenth century had so hopefully begun. This lamentable action had grievous results in loosing suspicion, which bore fruit fourteen years later in the 'Downgrade Controversy'. This 1873 *Declaration of Principle* read, 'In this Union it is fully recognised that every church has liberty to interpret and administer the laws of Christ, and that the immersion of believers is the only christian baptism'.[31]

Charles Haddon Spurgeon (1834-92) was undoubtedly the pre-eminent preacher of the nineteenth century and he stood squarely for the historic standards of the *Second London Baptist Confession* of 1689. This he so highly valued that he re-published it at his own expense in order that it should be freely available and widely read by baptists. He took strong exception to 'the growing departure from the traditional doctrines of Calvinism, particularly those relating to eternal punishment and the substitutionary atonement.' In no way could he stand idly by and watch this progression into liberalism by the Baptist Union. Let us take a closer look at this great preacher who was born in Kelvedon, Essex in 1834, both his father and grandfather being congregational ministers. He was converted when listening to a Methodist lay-preacher in 1850 and baptised at Isleham the next year. He started preaching almost immediately and shortly afterwards became pastor of the Waterbeach baptist church.

Spurgeon was called to London as pastor of the New Park Street church in Southwark in 1854 before his twentieth birthday. This was the historic Particular Baptist pulpit occupied by John Gill, John Rippon and others, but only eighty persons still worshipped there when the youthful pastor was inducted. In very little time all 1500 seats were occupied. This led to the building of the Metropolitan Tabernacle, Elephant and Castle, seating six thousand and even the using of public halls of greater size. His preaching was plain, direct and biblical; some said, 'bordering on irreverence'. But the Holy Spirit's unction rested on it and multitudes were converted. His ministry must be among the most fruitful of modern times. His sermons were published weekly and he wrote many books, the best known of which is his '*Treasury of David*', an extended commentary on the Psalms, designed especially for pastors, hard worked with little time for study.[32]

Volumes have been written on the magnificence of his public preaching which lifted him above his contemporaries in an age when there were outstanding men in baptist pulpits. He was not ashamed of the gospel of Christ, but with apostolic assurance, he was convinced that it was '*God's power to salvation to every believer*' and his whole life's work was a total commitment to preaching it. He himself was mastered by Christ and him crucified, and he was fully dedicated to making Christ real to everyone he could reach with the gospel. He was filled with Holy Spirit, with divine authority resting on his ministry and God gave the appointed harvest that follows 'his word from his mouth'.[33]

Spurgeon had a profound sympathy with the poor and all that were disadvantaged. He ensured that his people did not fail in their brotherly love of their fellows. Spurgeon's Orphanage, his evening schools at the Tabernacle, the Colportage Association and many other agencies gave expression to his practical concern. Often called *'The Prince of Preachers'*, his was certainly the most popular ministry of his day and his death in 1892 left an immense gap in the christian witness of Britain. He founded *'Pastors College'*, not to make pastors but to train those already called to the work. Known as *'Spurgeon's College'* today, it is the only English baptist college remaining with any claim to that rejected adjective 'evangelical'.[34]

Spurgeon was ever ready to contend for the truth and was early embroiled in the fighting off of the inroads of the 'new learning' which were enervating gospel preaching among Victorian baptists. The Particular Baptists, to whose historic confessional position he ever avowed his allegiance, were departing progressively from their biblical roots. First, they had embraced 'arminianism' and then the 'modernist heresies' of the new learning and that was more than he could stand. He withdrew from the Baptist Union in 1887, a union which he saw as lacking any credal convictions. To reject the word **'evangelical'** and to have no credal base was incomprehensible to him. Furthermore, the welcoming of the arminian baptists into fellowship was a total destruction of the Union's foundation. Fundamental concern for a biblical definition of faith and order had ceased to be a matter of concern. Spurgeon said of the Particular Baptists of his day, that they 'are going down hill fast'. Spurgeon's withdrawal from the Baptist Union was the climax of fifteen years controversy in which he had striven hard to re-establish the Baptist union churches in the historic doctrinal position without success. Only a few ministers and churches were prepared to take the same separatist stand, as Dr Payne says, 'The strength of the churches remained behind the Union and the fact that so few followed Spurgeon in leaving it, showed that the majority had come to regard a national union as essential to their well-being and the existing Union adequately safeguarded the concern all felt for the essentials of the faith.'[35] Dr Payne does not define what his last phrase meant, nor is it clear that the Union churches, viewed generally, were certain what was truth vital to baptist church witness at that time. Indeed, the Union was openly striving to embrace all who called themselves 'baptist' within its fellowship. In 1893, it welcomed the New Connexion (arminian) baptists and the remainder of the former General Baptist churches without demanding a confession of faith from them. To be fair, in 1904 the constitution was modified again and some doctrinal content restored and this has since been further strengthened in order to affirm the Deity of Christ.[36]

The struggle of Spurgeon to restore a biblical basis to the Baptist Union came to be called the '**Downgrade Controversy**'. Many saw it as a personal conflict between Spurgeon and another leading baptist of his day, **Dr John Clifford** (1836-1923).[37] Dr Clifford was certainly an outstanding preacher with a considerable following. His mother was an extraordinary, faithful christian woman and has often been likened to Susannah Wesley, and rightly so, because she trained up her son in practical godliness. When John left home to enter college, his mother counselled him, '*Find out the teaching of Jesus; make yourself sure of that; then stick to it, come what may!*' It was advice which he was to pass on to many others and it became his own watchword for life, according to Robert E Cooper's essay on Clifford.[38]

Clifford's family were Derbyshire people and he was educated in denominational schools and went to work in a lace factory at ten years old. He was converted at fourteen and of this experience he wrote later, 'it seemed as though a light shot from the very face of Jesus Christ into my heart...' He was baptised seven months later and began work on a course of self-education, including church history, French and Latin. Even in those days, he gathered a group around him to teach each other how to preach. He had a strong

sensitivity lest he should preach the Word of God
unworthily. At eighteen, he was admitted to the lay
preachers plan of the New Connexion baptists of Nottinghamshire and a year later entered their Midland College at
Leicester. In his second year he became student pastor at
Market Harborough and was asked by that church to
become their pastor on completion of his course, which he
felt unable to do. In 1852, he moved to London to pastor
the New Connexion church in Praed Street, Paddington,
continuing his studies at London University, securing three
degrees over the following eight years. His views were
often labelled 'liberal' and even heretical, but he quickly
became a leading voice for all arminian baptists and very
influential on the Baptist Union Council.

As we look back it will seem surprising to us that the
strongly calvinist Spurgeon and the arminian liberal
Clifford were close friends. Indeed, during the Downgrade
Controversy, Spurgeon wrote to Clifford assuring him that
he had no quarrel against him, because Clifford was openly
a 'General' baptist and had always been so. Spurgeon said
his quarrel was with those claiming to be 'Particular
Baptists' but who were leaning towards modernism. He was
a passionate preacher, who attracted young men particularly to his rich and very powerful ministry as a forthright
non-conformist, social reformer. Politically he was a liberal,
a champion of temperance and a prime mover in the
formation of the Baptist World Alliance, but he was not
ecumenically minded, saying, 'a belief in any priesthood,
other than that of all believers, made union impossible'.
Clifford's biographer mentioned above adds '... he passed
that combined sense of social concern and personal faith to
a vast company whose lives are, in consequence, committed
to the work of Christ in all its aspects'.[39]

Undoubtedly, Clifford was an outstanding man and
remarkably held Spurgeon's respect despite their strong
differences. Of course, as Spurgeon openly said, Clifford
could not be accused of moving away from the historic
doctrines of the Particular Baptists to which he had never
given his assent. Clifford was at all times an arminian
baptist in upbringing, training and life's ministry. Of the
sharp contentions in Baptist Union circles during this

period, Dr Payne says, 'Within living memory there have been secessions over 'Fullerism' and 'Open Communion', but on the main theological issues raised by Spurgeon,... no schism took place.'[40] The value of the last remark may not be accepted too easily in the light of the furore that has recently followed the publication of a book entitled, '*C. H. Spurgeon and the Modern Church*', written by a baptist minister who stands doctrinally in the tradition of Spurgeon.[41]

Though Spurgeon, because of his open communion practice, did not close ranks with the independent, or strict baptist churches, who still held to the old 1689 confession, his stand affected those churches considerably in their rejection of antinominan tendencies and the recovery of an evangelical calvinism which has borne fruit in the twentieth century. His works follow him. The Baptist Union, however, did not immediately enjoy such benefits but progressed in its downgrade direction, away from its historical roots in both doctrine and practice. Increasingly it lost baptist distinctiveness and became a 'free church' concerned to take its place in the fraternity of christendom. Shortly after Spurgeon's death, a new secretary took office whose broad ecumenism was to dominate the union churches' witness in England for the next several decades.

John Howard Shakespeare (1857-1928) was undoubtedly the architect of the modern Baptist Union which today holds together 1863 churches in England and Wales, with a church membership of 152,385. Dr J. C. Carlile described Shakespeare as 'an ecclesiastical statesman' and his work as the achievement of some measure of cohesian among baptist churches of strong independent convictions and growing divergence in doctrine and practice. Many see the edifice that he built as a most remarkable contribution to christian witness in Britain whilst others see it as a product of pragmatism in which organisational oneness has overruled the cherished liberty, simplicity and scriptural government of the historic baptist movement.

Shakespeare was the son of a Yorkshire baptist pastor and was influenced as a youth by the cultured but modernist ministry of James Thew, of whom Ernest Payne says, his *'advanced theological opinions gravely disturbed Spurgeon.'*[42] He was trained at Regent's Park College and became pastor of the St. Mary's Baptist church in Norwich for fifteen years. This he left to become the General Secretary of the Baptist Union in 1898 which office he held for twenty-six years. Dr Carlile said that the coming of Shakespeare saved the Union from being shattered by the Downgrade Controversy.[43] Undoubtedly, those that stood with Spurgeon in his efforts to maintain a pure, evangelical commitment to biblical truth and practice would have questioned this as 'salvation'!

Shakespeare was totally ecumenical in outlook, being committed to a unified Free Church and even one church only in England. He was willing to accept some form of re-ordination from anglican bishops in order to achieve the recognition of baptist ministers in an united church, adhering to the theory of 'apostolic succession.' His baptist forebears would have shuddered at such unholy compromise. He took part in conversations between the free churches and those bishops who were seeking unification of all churches in Britain. Shakespeare revealed his commitment to this union in his book, *'The Churches at the Crossroads'* published in 1918.[44] So sweeping was the spirit of compromise which he engendered, that when the Archbishop of York addressed the Council of the Baptist Union in April 1921 on this subject, Shakespeare afterwards wrote to him, *'Your address was so persuasive ... that if someone had risen and moved that we accept episcopal ordination, it could have been carried. I think that perhaps this is an exaggeration bbut something very near it would have been reached.'*[45] Shakespeare's organisational genius had dominated the first twenty years of this century but suspicion in the churches was aroused at this point and Shakespeare began to lose their confidence. Re-ordination remains rejected as a general policy by the Council.[46]

His vigorous leadership led to great initiatives for church extension in urban areas, the setting up of new funds for special purposes, improved support for the ministry and the erection of a prestigious new headquarters on the site of the old Eagle Street chapel in central London. He transformed the Baptist Union from being a 'servant of the churches' into the managerial directorate of a national body. Various baptist funds and societies were progressively brought under central control. Dr Payne sums up this period succinctly in these words, '*A new century, a new leader, a new paper, new departments and new responsibilities.*'[47] Indeed, looking back we may observe that a '*new thing*' had come into being. By 1915, baptist Britain was divided into ten dioceses and a '*bishop*' appointed to each '*see*' though discreetly called a '*superintendent*'. It is true that there are many financially independent churches which disregard the superintendents at the present time. Yet their subscribing membership of the Union makes them willing parties in the politics and actions of it. The colleges resisted central control though yielding some influence and the Baptist Missionary Society refused to be absorbed. Early in this period the Union's 'Objects' were modified giving authority to its Council, as the official voice of the churches, to speak on their behalf '*upon such public questions as the Council may from time to time determine*'. The significance of this is seen in the various ecumenical conversations and declarations that followed. In what might seem a 'transvestite miracle', ruggedly independent baptist local churches were transformed into the hierarchical dress and appearance of the episcopal churches of christendom. Dr Payne observes of the Baptist Union, that '*It had ceased to be a voluntary society*'.[48]

In structuring the Union with great skill, the premises on which he worked gave rise to the problems of the years after the First World War. His elimination of those criteria, which we have repeatedly noted as baptist distinctives and the foundation of all true christian evangelical witness, inevitably provoked a situation in which many baptist ministers and some churches left the union. Indeed, Dr Payne acknowledges as much when he says of Shakespeare that '*he underestimated the difficulties, theological and practical, in the way of fulfilling his dreams which had come to master him.*' This historian adds '*The baptist denomination, which he had led so brilliantly, was preplexed and grew distrustful of what he was at.*'[49] Yet he goes on, within twenty years of his death both a 'British Council of Churches' and ' 'World Council of

Churches' had come into being'.[50] The former began in 1942 with the Archbishop of Canterbury as president and baptists recognised and accepted as sister churches those whose heresies they had historically condemned! The World body followed, being proposed in 1941 but not actually brought to birth until 1948 after the end of World War Two. Dr Payne says, in his official *'History'*, that *'the Baptist Union had accepted the invitation to join in 1939'*. The implications of the Union's participation in these ecumenical councils provoked unease among the churches and a vigorous opposition developed including some secessions from the Union.[51]

Similarly in 1971, the Rev. Michael Taylor, Principal of Manchester Baptist College, in his sermon as the appointed preacher at the Annual Assembly of the Baptist Union expressed himself in language impugning the deity of Jesus Christ, and the Council took no action to rebuke or dissociate the churches from the implied heresy. There were renewed protests from member churches and their ministers and some further secessions. Considerable unease has continued to date and many independent baptist churches have come into being as a result. The churches have tended to stand aloof from the 'official voice' and many have retained only a tenuous link. The Union has endeavoured to recover an 'evangelical' appearance and there are evidences of a spiritual renewal and respect for their historic heritage among many of its affiliated churches. The shrinking number of churches in the Baptist Union is still double those which retain their independence in Britain. It has to be acknowledged that the mantle of the historic baptist movement of the past centuries here is more faithfully carried by those who retain their independency in church order and still adhere to the faith once delivered to the saints. This is a sad fact but the evidence submitted above shows that the Baptist Union, as presently constituted and acting in the name of baptist churches, is no longer reflecting the biblical standards of our heritage nor fulfilling the historic ministry entrusted to them. Lest this should be taken as an unreasoned judgement, the decline of the main body of baptists in Britain from the beginning of the seventeenth century until the present time is now set out.

Now by the expression 'main body of the baptists in Britain' is meant those baptist churches springing from the Spilsbury church and its influential ministry in the 1630s. The churches which sprang from the church founded twenty years earlier by Helwys which held to Universal Atonement and were known as 'General Baptists' progressively slipped into unitarianism and only a small number remained as baptists being either merged into the arminian body of 'New Connexion Baptists' or into the Baptist Union at the end of the nineteenth century.[52] It was the 'Particular Baptists.' with their 'calvinistic' doctrine of salvation who became the mainstream of English baptist churches. Indeed, this became largely true throughout the expansion of baptist churches worldwide. The *First London Baptist Confession of Faith* issued by the seven London churches in 1644 represents the doctrinal stance of that 'mainstream' and the decline thereafter can be referred back to that position with advantage.

Baptist decline in Britain can be set out in the following fifteen steps:

1. In 1643 onwards, the admission of unbaptised believers to the Lord's Supper and, subsequently, into membership of the churches. Lumpkin comments, 'The Lord's Supper is not restricted to those scripturally baptised as in the *London Confession 1644*'.[53]

2. In 1677/89, the drafters of the *Second London Confession* were motivated by a strong desire to be seen to be as true churches, as were the presbyterians and congregationalists. Hence they worded their confession as closely to that of the Westminster and Savoy confessions. Lumpkin comments '*It was important that dissenters form a united front... by a show of doctrinal agreement among themselves*'.[54]

3. In the eighteenth century the decline of the Particular Baptists into antinomianism and hyper-calvinism and General Baptists into Arianism.[55]

4. In 1832, the Baptist Union eliminated the 1689 London Confession as the standard and substituted the vague words, *'baptist ministers and churches who agree in the sentiments usually denominated evangelical'*.[56]

5. In the 1850s, the dropping of any reference to the distinctive doctrine of Particular Redemption and the disuse of the adjective *'Particular'* in the titles of Union and Mission.

6. Thereafter, the penetration of the *'New Learning'* into baptist pulpits and churches.[57]

7. In 1873. the dropping of the word *'evangelical'* in view of the new trends towards intellectual freedom![58]

8. In the 1880s, the refusal of the Union to affirm baptist doctrinal orthodoxy despite the plea of Spurgeon.[59]

9. In 1887, the failure of evangelical baptists to withdraw with Spurgeon and to assert anew the rule of scripture among their churches.[60]

10. In 1893, the merger of all baptists into the Union regardless of doctrinal convictions and practices, without any credal commitment being demanded.[61]

11. 1900 onwards, the transformation of the Union from a fellowship of free, independent churches into an entirely new hierarchical society.[62]

12. In 1915, the imposition of Area Superintendents as a first step towards accommodation to episcopacy with an eye to ultimate union.[63]

13. In 1921, the near acceptance of re-ordination of baptist ministers by anglican bishops so acknowledging the exclusive validity of the theory of apostolic succession.[64]

14. The acceptance of heretical churches as equal partners in Christ in order to achieve the formation of (1) The Free Church Federal Council, (2) The British Council of Churches and (3) The World Council of Churches.[65]

15. 1971, the refusal of the Baptist Union Council to discipline or rebuke their Annual Assembly preacher, Michael Taylor, who publically impugned the deity of Jesus Christ.[66]

The failure of the Baptist Union churches throughout this long period of doctrinal decline is highlighted by a study of their failure to protest effectively against the successive actions of their leaders as one negation of truth gave place to the next. There have always been a few clamouring voices for action but as we have noted time and again in the course of their history, they were few and ineffective. There has prevailed a 'stay-in-it-to-win-it' philosophy which is characteristically non-baptist. In chronicling the spiritual decline of the Baptist Union, there is no comfort to be found in doing an unpleasant task from the knowledge that there are many evangelical churches still found in it who have not bowed the knee to Baal. The unwelcome reality is that Baal has been set up in high places and the leadership has progressively sold its biblical heritage for a mess of ecumenical pottage. The question must be asked, 'Is there not still an adequate body of churches to raise their protest and recover their birthright?' This book makes its appeal to those who still cherish their baptist heritage and desire to honour the Word of God as supreme in all matters of faith and practice, to awake out of sleep while it is still day. The historical mission of baptists has been to stand against the inroads of apostasy at every step of its invasion of the pure and simple testimony of the churches of Christ. That failure forfeits the right to the descriptive 'baptist' and from a strict biblical standpoint, 'christian' also, for the scriptures lay down a standard of total separation from everything not conforming to the truth as it is in Christ Jesus our Lord.

8
The Strict Baptist churches

The early years of the nineteenth century saw a renewal of the controversy among the Particular Baptist churches. The former differences over the restriction of the communion of the Lord's Supper to baptised believers, in which Bunyan had participated strenuously, continued to be a bone of contention with both the Rylands and Robinson of Cambridge on the one side debating in public with Abraham Booth, the strict communionist, on the other, When Booth died, **Joseph Kinghorn** of Norwich took up the stand for the historic baptised communion principle.

Furthermore, the questions raised by **Andrew Fuller** on the 'Free Offer of the Gospel' had not been settled and occasioned a further tendency towards division among the churches. The divide was parallel to that on the communion issue. Fuller was a strict communionist, as was Ivimey the historian and most of the Welsh baptists but there was already a growing body of churches following Bunyan and practising first an Open Table and then Open Membership. Now Fuller brought a further divide as the churches responded by a rejection or acceptance of his moderated and evangelical calvinism.[1] The result was there arose churches which were 'strict' and against Fuller, 'open' and against him, and some 'strict' who were for his view and open communionists who opposed him. The 'strict anti-Fullerism' churches tended toward hypercalvinism and came to be called 'Gadsbyites' after the name of one of their leaders, William Gadsby, a Manchester minister.[2] These churches expressed their 'anti-Fullerism' explicitly, stating that 'saving faith was not a natural duty but the sovereign gift of God'. They also declared that 'the invitations of the gospel were not for the unregenerate'.[3] However, by no means all adopted this extreme reaction to Fuller. Many of these conservative churches retained a healthy concern for the unsaved masses and freely preached the gospel to all people, setting forth the invitations of the gospel as extended to 'all creatures' as Christ in the Great Commission clearly commanded. However, the Particular Baptist churches of Britain were fragmented in the early years of this nineteenth century. Yet, in the providence of God, their weaknesses were to be turned to strength during the industrial revolution in England. The growth of new towns everywhere, as the working population of the country exploded, led to the widespread planting of non-conformist churches in which baptists enjoyed a substantial share.

Growth of Particular Baptist churches also took place in rural communities such as East Anglia. In 1769, six churches in Norfolk and Suffolk came together to form an association, namely, Claxton, Shelfanger, Worstead and Yarmouth, in Norfolk, and Wattisham and Woolverstone in Suffolk.[4] Their Declaration of Faith was explicitly 'Particular Baptist' but liberty was given to the churches in the matter of open or strict communion.[5] Similar strains that we have noted in other parts of the country came to bear on this association in the 1820's. **Cornelius Elvin** (1797-1873), pastor at Bury St. Edmunds, led the broader section and he was an ardent open-communionist.[6] **George Wright** (1789-1863), who led the other churches, had been an arminian before his conversion to a calvinistic scheme of salvation. He took his calvinism seriously, being a strident advocate of Particular Redemption and also of strict communion.[7] The outcome was a breakdown of fellowship and the separation of the churches into two groups. **The Suffolk and Norfolk New (Strict) Association** was formed in 1829 and held its first gathering in the following May at Beccles. This association declared itself 'Particular Baptist', holding 'strict communion' and was opposed to Fuller's duty-faith concept. This latter article stood for one hundred and twenty years when it was rescinded as an expression of obsolete hypercalvinism no longer adhered to by the churches. Ultimately, the greater part of the Suffolk churches joined the 'new' association.[8] This 'New' association soon expressed its title as the 'Suffolk and Norfolk Association of Strict Baptist Churches' and became the first to be called 'Strict Baptist'. The remainder formed the Suffolk Baptist Union in 1846, embracing Aldeburgh, Bury St. Edmunds, Botesdale, Barton Mills, Diss and Eye.[9] A year later, the only open-membership church in the county was received into the Union exhibiting the breadth of its faith and order. The Norfolk churches formed a Norfolk Baptist Union and the 'Old' association ceased to exist.

Similar moves in the London area led to a meeting in the Eagle Street baptist church in 1841 to form an association of churches standing clear of the diminishing doctrinal commitment of the 'Baptist Union'. They formed the 'Strict Communion Society' of churches of whom Underwood records, 'They did not feel drawn to the followers of Gadsby but felt some affinity with the Strict Baptists of Suffolk'.[10] Though this society failed to hold the support of the London churches, it claimed strong support among those in the north where it survived as the 'Baptist Evangelical Society' engaging in missionary enterprises on their behalf. They sent missionaries to Germany and Denmark in support of the work of Johann Oncken of Hamburg.[11] The northern churches held tenaciously to their faith and order long after the commitment of those elsewhere had weakened. They trained their ministers by placing them alongside experienced pastors for three years. Later they founded the **Manchester Baptist College** on a constitution which was explicitly committed to both *Particular Redemption and Strict Communion*. As the influence of this group faded the college fell into the hands of the Baptist Union area of influence. Today, after having been amalgamated with Rawdon College, of which Underwood the historian was Principal, and renamed the 'Northern College', it has become little more than a hostel for students of Manchester University.

In 1846, the London churches seceded and formed a London Strict Baptist Association whose full title was

'Association of Strict Baptist Ministers in and about London' but it lasted only six years during which time it met monthly. **William Norton**, the editor of the '**Baptist Tract Society**' was a prime mover in this. In 1849, another grouping of Strict Baptists emerged called, 'The New Association of Particular Baptists in London' and this joined the older group in 1851 and changed its name to the 'Association of Baptists holding Particular Redemption and Practising Strict Communion'. It seems to have met with little success, possibly on account of the length of its unmanageable name![13]

It was not until 1871, that the London Strict Baptist churches succeeded in forming a stable association with twenty-two founder churches. It was named, '**The Metropolitan Association of Strict Baptist Churches**'. Its centenary was marked with special gatherings and a commemorative handbook stated that sixty-one churches with about two thousand members were in fellowship.[14] The term 'Strict Baptist' came to be a convenient common denominator for those churches which, alone of all groupings in the British Isles, still held to the historic confessions of the seventeenth century. Underwood stated in his '*History of the English Baptists*' that the London Confession 1689 'is not now endorsed by British Baptists except by some who have remained Strict and Particular'.[15] He wrote that in 1945, since which time there has been a revival of calvinism generally among evangelicals in this country and there have emerged many new churches calling themselves by various names and none, some using the name 'Reformed', 'Evangelical' or 'Grace' baptist churches. The secession from 'Union' churches has continued and the independents have greatly increased their numbers. The seventeenth century baptist confessions have been re-discovered and a growing appreciation of baptist heritage exists.

As the twentieth century draws near to its last decade, and doctrine and church order are discounted in the frantic obsession to achieve a universality among professing christians, there is a parallel but counter strengthening of biblical authority. Consequently, there is new 'unity' developing among baptists, both the old and the new, in a return to biblical normality in church life. An instance of this is the emergence of 'Grace Baptist Assembly' which expresses the fellowship of baptised churches holding the doctrines of grace. Unlike the 'Baptist Union' and other established bodies, it claims no authority over churches whatsoever but strenuously affirms the historic creeds in unqualified biblical terms and strives to further such fellowship by all permissible means. An interesting example of this trend is found in the re-naming of the 'Strict Baptist Mission,' which had lasted 120 years, as 'Grace Baptist Mission' and so providing a common instrument of mission for all those churches adhering to the historic Particular Baptist confessions.

There was a **'Northern Union of Strict Baptist Churches'** for some years but this has been replaced by an informal fellowship of churches which loosely expresses its common commitment through the **Grace Baptist Assembly** which has been mentioned above. In 1927, there was a coming together of like-minded churches in the '**Cambridgeshire and East Midlands Union of Strict Baptist Churches'**. Those also find national fellowship in that same assembly.[16]

Grace Baptist Assembly was not the first expression of fellowship among these churches. A '**National Federation'** existed for twenty-two years from the end of the Second World War. Its failure has been attributed to the non-participation of the 'Gospel Standard' (that is, those Strict Baptist churches which tend towards hypercalvinism and are strongly anti-Fuller; they are so-called by the name of their periodical), and other churches fearful that it might develop into an authoritarian organisation such as the Baptist Union. This failure was followed by a totally unstructured assembly of pastors and deacons which met a real need and led to regular gatherings for prayer for revival in which there was some degree of success. It was out of this '*prayer fellowship*' that the present '**Grace Baptist Assembly'** was born. It brings together the pastors, elders and deacons of like-minded churches and provides a national forum for worship, prayer and discussion of doctrinal, practical and social concerns. It exercises no control over the churches and only actually exists when it is

in session! Any conclusions reached in the assemblies
become applicable to the local churches only if and when
they themselves formally adopt them. The historic independence of the churches is not infringed but their
baptistic interdependence is recognised and expressed.

The churches linked in that assembly publish a monthly
magazine called 'Grace' and have an active publishing
house known as *'Grace Publications Trust'*. Those other Strict
Baptist churches known as '**Gospel Standard**' churches, to
which reference has been made, also publish some
excellent literature. Despite the immense amount of
christian literature published in Britain today, but a very
small proportion of it remains true to the historic baptist
heritage. This is not the case in the United States where
baptists continue to provide a constant flow of publications.

As is frequently the case, the story of any group of
interests is best illustrated in the lives of its leaders. For this
reason, some outline sketches of some of the personalities
among the Strict Baptists follows at this point in this book.

John Stevens (1776-1847), minister of the baptist church in
Meards Court, Soho, was an influential activist in the controversies which led the emergence of the Strict Baptists as a
definable grouping of churches in England. He took a harder
line than Booth but was not so isolationist as Gadsby. Stevens'
principal controversy was against Fuller and the 'Free Offer'
and he condemned the notion that 'saving faith was a legal
duty', i.e. that it was the universal duty of every man to believe
the gospel whether or not the Holy Spirit made faith possible.
Stevens also claimed a following of ministers and churches
throughout the land similar to those that followed Gadsby.
They claimed that they were standing for the original 'Particular Baptist' position and practising church communion
restricted to believers immersed on a profession of their own
faith. They came to call themselves the **Strict and Particular
Baptists**, a title that came to be shortened to **Strict Baptist**. In
practice, both these groups, the followers of both Stevens and
Gadsby, are generally referred to by that name.

Stevens was born of humble parentage in Ardwinkle,
Northamptonshire 8 June 1776 but seems to have been

brought up largely by his maternal grandmother who provided him with as good an education as was available in the neighbourhood. The rector of the parish church at that time was Dr Haweis, a man beloved of both George Whitefield and Lady Huntingdon, and he was noted for the fervour, simplicity and spirituality of his ministry. It was under this anglican rector's ministry that John Stevens was brought to a need of Christ as Saviour whilst only fifteen years of age. His coming to a mature faith in his Saviour took place under the ministry of **Richard Burnham**, pastor of the baptist church in Grafton Street, Soho, after he came to London to live. He it was who baptised Stevens and ultimately set him apart for the ministry. When Stevens returned to his home village to preach, the old rector would steal unnoticed into the meeting to listen to him, well pleased with the gospel he preached but not with his non-conformity! He commenced a church in St Neots, Huntingdon, in 1799 and remained pastor for five years. For six years he pastored the church at Boston before accepting the call in 1811 of the Grafton Street baptist church, Soho where he had been blessed in his youth. The growing congregations made necessary a move to York Street, St James' two years later. Then a new chapel was built in Meards Court, Wardour Street, known as Salem Chapel, where he laboured on until his death 6 October 1847.

Stevens had published his first book in 1803, amplified it in 1814 and revised and republished it in 1829. It was a refutation of the 'moderate calvinism' of Fuller, a rejection of all offers of the gospel and of the notion that saving faith was a natural duty of all men. So ardent was he that he created a school of followers who began to insert in their credal statements and in the trust deeds of their churches a new article which was to endure for a hundred years. Another significant publication was 'Doctrinal Antinominaism Refuted' in which he sought to establish the 'Place that the Law of God had as a Rule of Obedience for the Saints', as the subtitle stated.

This he issued to rectify the tendency among the **'Gadsbyites'** to fall away into antinomianism which in the previous century had stultified the growth of the churches

and stifled an effective envangelical testimony. The third
subject that occupied his pen, and often his pulpit, was the
subject of the 'Saviour's Pre-existence' in which he argued
for the eternal plurality of Deity as well as for Deity's
essential oneness.

Stevens was an earnest missionary, itinerating constantly,
preaching the gospel, encouraging believers to gather in
local fellowships and helping them to build places of
worship. He was also convinced that the work of the
Particular Baptist Missionary Society and kindred institutions were means that the Lord blessed with real success.
His biographer says that he had a deep sense of the divine
commission to 'Go into all the world and preach the gospel
to every creature, baptising...' and that it was 'a cause that
bears so evidently the stamp of divine authority'.[17]

It was not suprising that such a ministry should bring to
birth an able scholar who would produce the first detailed
confessional statement for the now separated strict
communion baptists. **William Jeyes Styles** (1842-1914) of
the Meards Court church was a protegé of Spurgeon and a
student of his Pastor's College. He published in 1887 'A
Manual of Faith and Practice' which he said was designed
for young and enquiring christians and in which he set out
to systematise Strict Baptist standards of faith and order. In
1902, he issued a 'Guide to Church Fellowship' which
recited the 'Articles of the Faith and Order of a Primitive or
Strict and Particular Baptist church'. It was based on the
'Declaration of Faith and Practice' of John Gill 1720. These
books met a need at the time but had been lost sight of
within fifty years.[18] It is an interesting and instructive study
to compare these works of Styles with those published in
1966 and 1971 by his successors of a century later. Here no
mention is made of the duty faith problem, Christ is
absolutely the Eternal Son of the Father and the gospel is to
be presented to all men as worthy of acceptation. The 'high
calvinism' remains but all tendencies towards hypercalvinism and antinomianism are totally absent. The Strict
Baptist at the end of the twentieth century stands in the
historic heritage of the Particular Baptist Confessions of
the seventeenth century and is an earnest propagator of
the gospel in all the world.[19]

William Gadsby (1773-1844) was born at Attleborough, near Nuneaton, in 1773, the son of a roadmender. He had little education, being apprenticed at 13 years of age to a ribbon-weaver. He was a lively, sporting type, a ring-leader of his fellows. When only 17, he was convicted of sin by the sight of three burglars being hanged at Coventry. Telling of his conversion, he said, 'God's peculiar love was shed abroad in my heart by his blessed Spirit... and... I was led to believe in God's free mercy and pardon and could... say "He loved me and gave himself for me"'. He worshipped in the Independent chapel at Bedworth but later was baptised and joined Cow Lane baptist church, Coventry. After marriage, he began preaching in a barn at Hinckley and in a chapel built for him at Desford where he was ordained and became the pastor. In 1805, he was called as the pastor of Back Lane Chapel, Manchester, which he took out of the Yorkshire and Lancashire association immediately.

Underwood speaks of him as a 'pulpit genius' with a remarkable voice which could fill the old Free Trade Hall as few of his contemporaries could do.[20] One of these was Robert Halley, later Principal of New College, London, who said of Gadsby, 'He was a preacher made especially for the working classes and the common people heard him gladly. He could speak the dialect of the place... knew his business well and succeeded where many men greater than he utterly failed. A man of plain sense, he sought to be nothing more than a plain preacher of Christ's plain gospel, 'Christ crucified for sinners.' He had not a particle of affectation... He spoke English well. Scripture he knew by heart and quoted with verbal accuracy. His thoughts were natural, closely connected, logically arranged and lucidly expressed... no man spoke with more seriousness or gravity... He was called an 'antinomian' but no man in Manchester lived a more moral life or presented a more beautiful example of christian discipline and self-control.'
[21] In an unpublished thesis, the late **Kenneth Dykes**, Principal of Manchester Baptist College, said that Gadsby was a fervent evangelist, founding twenty-nine chapels in Lancashire as a result of his itinerant preaching in the towns and villages. **John Warburton** (1776-1857), later pastor at Trowbridge, and **John Kershaw** (1792-1870),

pastor at Rochdale for over fifty years, were converts of Gadsby's ministry. His strong convictions against Fuller's 'Free Offer' and 'Duty-Faith', with his high calvinism, made him a natural leader of those who shared his views. His magazine, 'The Gospel Standard', ensured him a wide audience and its followers were often called 'Gadsbyites', though later by the name of the magazine (founded 1834). Gadsby travelled more than 60,000 miles in his preaching tours and preached between 10,000 and 12,000 sermons and became known as 'The Apostle of the North'. When he died he stood in the forefront of God's spiritual army contending for the great truths of the gospel of grace. It is now 140 years since Gadsby died and still his magazine continues to be published and his collection of hymns is used.[22] His works follow him.

William Tiptaft (1803-64) and **Joseph Charles Philpot** (1802-69) were clergymen of the Church of England who seceded in the mid-Victorian period because of the drift of the establishment into a doctrinally mixed church. They joined with the 'Gadsbyites' and the latter became the editor of the 'Gospel Standard' and greatly influenced its circulation. Indeed Philpot's ministry stamped a characteristic on the preaching among those churches for a century afterwards. He emphasised the need to find in the believer's own experience the ground of assurance of salvation rather than by objective faith in Christ of Calvary. This was a reaction to the 'easy-believism' of the revivalist preaching which had become prevalent in his days among evangelicals generally. Unfortunately this emphasis bred introverted religious concern and produced believers who lacked assurance. There remains today the need to demand an 'inner experience' of the Holy Spirit's work accomplishing and accompanying salvation, the need to see the ground of assurance as external to man, lying in the finished work of Christ at Calvary and his acceptance as the sufficient sacrifice at the Throne above once for all. The 'Gospel Standard' movement grew strongly at first but from the turn of the century there has been a steady decline. Slightly more than half of their chapels closed during the past eighty years and others have moved into the evangelical mainstream of Strict Baptist churches.[23]

Joseph Charles Philpot (1802-69) was the son of a Kentish rector and was himself educated at Oxford and was elected a Fellow at Worcester College in 1827. He left anglican orders after meeting another seceder, **William Tiptaft** (1803-64), his close associate, had built a chapel in Abingdon for a dissenting group which he pastored. Philpot was baptised by Warburton at Allington and served the Strict Baptists for the rest of his life, pastoring churches at Allington, Oakham and Stamford. For more than twenty years he was editor of the Gospel Standard, keeping in place Gadsby's volatile son, John, who 'combined ability to speak the language of Zion with considerable business acumen!' John, who printed his father's magazine, inherited it and was in a position of considerable influence but lacked his parent's grace and tender spirit. Philpot sparked off a troublesome controversy when he preached a sermon on the 'Eternal generation of the Son' in 1860. The editor of a competing magazine, the 'Earthen Vessel', unwisely printed an article from a contributor attacking Mr Philpot's exposé. The outcome was very un-Christ like and the controversy left its marks on Strict Baptist churches for a long time. It was not that Philpot's view was unorthodox, nor that the other editor differed from him, as **Charles Banks** ultimately revealed, but that an implication grew that Strict Baptist ministers, not of the 'Standard' following, were unsound on the Eternal Sonship of Jesus Christ, whereas this was not the case. Philpot's published sermons have enjoyed a wide circulation and still are read as the best of the experimental school which he fostered. A fuller treatment of his life and ministry, and that of Tiptaft, is to be found in 'The Seceders', the volumes of which are still in print.[24]

Stanley Delves (1897-1978) is another who became a much loved pastor and sought after preacher among the Strict Baptists in recent times. He was born at Rushlake

Green in Sussex, the youngest son of the village blacksmith, his father being a deacon in the local baptist chapel. He was a lively, adventurous lad and a quick developer when he entered business life in Tunbridge Wells where he was brought to faith under the ministry of **J. G. Evans**, the pastor of the baptist church at the 'Pantiles'. After military service which took him to Russia, he commenced preaching in the village chapels of Kent and Sussex, preaching his first sermon in the Forest Fold chapel, Crowborough, of which he became pastor three years later, in 1923, and remained so until death, completing an outstanding and wonderfully fruitful ministry of fifty-five years. The church grew and became one of the most thriving Strict Baptist churches in Britain and their pastor's ministry must be acknowledged as the most remarkable for spiritual power and fruitfulness in the present century. Stanley Delves favoured no party or section among the churches which he served so well for so long but came to be loved and esteemed by all. This was expressed by the representative nature of the vast gathering at his jubilee service in his lifetime and at his funeral.[25]

George Bird was a contemporary of Stanley Delves and one who also exercised an outstanding ministry among the Strict Baptists. He was born, schooled, converted and baptised in East London, his father being a deacon at West Ham Tabernacle. He was among the first students admitted to the **Strict Baptist Bible Institute**, under **James Willoughby**, and his first pastorate was in Cambridgeshire. He later became the pastor of Bethesda Baptist church in Ipswich and sustained a fine ministry there with congregations in excess of a thousand. His voice was frequently heard on radio and TV on the national networks and his gentle, winsome presentation of the gospel was greatly used through his long years of usefulness.

It is true that the first half of the twentieth century was a period of decline for Strict Baptists, but it can now be said that the second half has seen a reversal of this trend. The evangelical churches have been the subject of the revival influence of the 'neo-reformed' movement and they have regained spiritual vigour, rediscovered their doctrinal heritage and given themselves to aggressive church founding and missionary enterprise at home and abroad. Several churches, in the new towns of this era, bear witness to the new outlook. Many of the 'Gospel Standard' churches have benefitted from the same stirring of the Spirit, though their growth has not been in terms of new churches, but in new ministries such as their publications department and their chain of residential Bethesda Homes for the elderly.

Speaking of the 'neo-reformed revival' of the second half of this century, the name of a principal leader in it cannot fail to get a mention here despite his not being a 'baptist.' **Martin Lloyd Jones** said in 1974, 'the Strict Baptists were one of the few 'denominations' (his word!) which held to the historic christian faith and remained unaffected by the inroads of twentieth century modernism'. Writing in the Baptist Times, the organ of the Baptist Union, **Lester Gaunt** said in 1929, 'the Strict Baptists are the salt of the earth and causes of truth, greatly beloved and devoutly served... The great doctrines of Divine Sovereignty, Predestination and Election to Eternal Life, are the very marrow of their teaching. Their members travel many miles to obtain sound doctrine.'[26] Both Underwood and Whitley, baptist historians of this century, say that Strict Baptists alone have remained true to the London Confession of Faith 1689'. Another such author bears a similar testimony in speaking of the Strict Baptists in Suffolk. He says, 'I cannot speak too highly of them... they are blessedly loyal to the fundamentals of our faith'.[28] Let Underwood continue, 'they have repudiated arminianism and become ardent evangelists' despite having 'retained high calvinist doctrine.'[29] Strict Baptists have maintained missionary work overseas for 150 years and active home mission ministry too. They have promoted three libraries for public use including the world-wide 'Evangelical Library' which was the child of a deacon of the Beddington chapel.

It is interesting to note that in the decline of church attendance in the ending of the twentieth century in

Britain, the evangelical baptists, together with the evangelical house group churches, alone show growth. This was
stated by Peter Brearley in the BBC's radio programme
'Sunday' on 2 December 1984. He said that one in fifteen
British christians attended house churches. This reflects
the rejection of the traditional churches by this generation.

Baptist Union churches have shown a decline of
one-third in the number of their churches between 1921
and 1971 and more than half in their membership. This
decline came earlier with the Strict Baptist churches and
seemed to stop from 1950 on and growth to begin again.
This appears true also among the growing number of
independent evangelical baptist churches outside both
groups, and outside of all ecumenical involvements. It may
be that these churches, will increasingly become the
effective voice of the gospel in this land as they recover the
simplicity, spontaneity and separated purity which marked
the primitive baptists and which were the hallmarks of
apostolic christianity.[30]

9
The baptist in Wales, Scotland and Ireland

The ancient Welsh Celtic churches have been noted in an earlier chapter as also their decline under Roman pressures. The Lollard preachers from England carried the 'new faith' into Wales and made converts, of whom **'Holy Rhys'** is famous (1390). But the first evidence of a baptist church appears to be that formed in Olchon in the Gower in 1633 at which **Howell Vaughan** preached. The Welsh historian, Thomas of Leominster, states however that the church at Ilstone near Swansea founded in 1649 is more certain. During the Commonwealth, Cromwell sent his preachers into Wales and there were two Oxford graduates with baptist convictions among them. **Jenkin Jones**, who had been a captain in Cromwell's army and had raised a troop of one hundred and twenty horse at his own expense, often appeared with a sword in one hand and a bible in the other. He was appointed parish minister in his home town but was ejected at the Restoration, his estates forfeited and he himself was imprisoned. There is no record of his death. The churches founded by Jenkin were Particular baptist and strict communion. **John Miles**, who was sent to Wales by the Glasshouse church, Broad Street, London, gathered several churches on an open communion basis. The church at Ilstone was one that he founded but these churches later became strict communionist or paedobaptist, according to Armitage.[2] He also relates how **John Tombs**, who has been referred to previously, disputed publically in St Mary Parish Church, Abergavenny, on 5 September 1653 concerning 'Believers' Baptism' and names this the first such public debate in

Wales. **Vavasor Powell** (1617-71) was one of the most fiery of Welsh itinerant preachers during the Commonwealth period and after. Whilst himself of independent convictions, he taught the baptism of believers only and that by immersion. He himself was baptised during the course of his ministry in 1656 but the churches he founded were not included in the Welsh association because of their entirely open membership and Table. He suffered grievously because of his convictions, first at Cromwell's hands because of his Fifth Monarchy views and then by the Stuarts for his subborn dissent. He wrote his 'Confession of Faith' in prison, calling it 'The Bird in the Cage, Chirping!' He died in the London Fleet prison.[3]

A chain of baptist churches sprang up in the wake of Cromwell's army moving to suppress the Royalist groups in North Wales. Many of these adopted the Fifth Monarchy views of Powell and later the American Campbellite modification of Sandemanianism. **David Lloyd George**, the British Prime Minister of the First World War was a member of such a church at Criccieth.[4]

In a similar way, the campaign led by **Colonels Rede** and **Deane** occasioned the formation of a string of baptist churches throughout South Wales.[5] During the Commonwealth period ninety baptists accepted appointments to the Establishment. Twenty-six were ejected from Welsh pulpits at the Great Ejectment 1662.[6] The Welsh baptists continued to prosper despite the oppression of dissenters by the Stuarts. By 1672 there were two hundred and ten baptist ministers licensed to preach in Wales and two hundred houses licensed for worship.[7] When the General Assembly of Particular Baptists in London 1689 met, there were several Welshmen present and two signed the Declaration.[8]

Baptists were not to the forefront during the eighteenth century revival but in the following century growth was phenomenal. **Christmas Evans** (1766-1838) was converted and joined a presbyterian church. A narrow escape from death caused him serious thought and he was baptised and joined the church at Aberdaur. From that church he was sent to pastor five small baptist churches in the Lleyn peninsular. Due to an accident, he lost an eye and was often known as the 'one-eyed preacher!' His ministry was with great power and the churches in Anglesey and North Wales grew astonishingly. The last revival in which he was involved was that of 1828-30 when more than six thousand believers were added to the churches. When he died in 1838, the churches had got rid of much of the weakness that 'Sandemanianism' had caused and Whitley says, 'he left the churches of North Wales well-grounded and hopeful'.[9] Indeed, twenty years later there was another revival with very substantial growth and ten years afterwards again remarkable blessing was showered on these churches.

The Welsh churches were diligent in training their men for their ministry. The first training centre that they provided was at Pontypool, being commenced in 1732. It pre-dates Bristol's College quite substantially. The Trosant Academy was next and dates from about the same period. In both projects **Morgan Griffiths** of Hengoed was prominent. Abergavenny College was founded in 1807 but was transferred to Pontypool. Haverford West and Llangollen Colleges were founded in 1839 and 1862 respectively.[10]

Scotland

The Pictic church, founded by Ninian and his successor, Kentigern, has been represented as being somewhat like the early Celtic church in Wales, evangelical and baptistic up to the time of its suppression by Rome. Columba's mission from Ireland in the sixth century, which was based on Iona, produced churches conforming to Roman rites. Sadly there is little hard history to help formulate a detailed picture of these early Scottish churches.[11] There does seem to be evidence that they baptised by immersion and believers only. The long gap between the fifth and sixth centuries and the establishment of baptist churches by the Parliamentary army of occupation during the Commonwealth period in 1646, is a reflection of Roman catholic domination only just broken by the Reformation under John Knox. Cromwell's army had many baptist officers who led baptist worship for their men but left no indigenous churches behind when the army was withdrawn in 1660.[12]

John Glas founded a sect in 1725 to restore the simplicity of New Testament church life and his son-in-law, **Robert Sandeman**, developed it into a movement, even starting a church in London. This led to them being called 'Sandemanians' after him. **Archibald M'Lean** left the Church of Scotland and joined them but at that time they were still paedobaptists. M'Lean went to London and was baptised with two fellow members by John Gill who sent them back to Glasgow to commence baptist work there. This they did and their churches were called 'Scotch Baptists'. They ordered themselves differently from the English churches which led to that distinction. The 'Scotch Baptists' had a plurality of unpaid elders, despised an educated ministry and appointed no full time pastors. They practised communion like Gill but unlike him they held that 'Justifying faith was a natural intellectural matter'. They required an intellectual consent to their beliefs as a basis for membership. Much of this they had carried over from John Glas. They had twenty-two churches in 1822 but none of them survives though Underwood says that a few became Strict and Particular Baptists.'[13]

Andrew Fuller, the English baptist, argued in vain with the Scotch baptists in an endeavour to bring them to conform to a biblical understanding of faith. In the end he persuaded **Christopher Anderson** (1782-1852), a convert of the Haldanes to whom reference is shortly to be made, to commence 'English Baptist' services in Edinburgh which he did, forming a church there. Anderson was a graduate of Edinburgh University and trained for the ministry under Sutcliff in England, intending to go as a missionary to India but his health had ruled him out. His ministry in the Scottish capital was very fruitful and he founded a training institute and also commenced baptist mission work in Ireland. Anderson's churches were calvinistic in doctrine and, inevitably, a non-calvinistic church sprang up and established its own college for arminian baptists.[14]

Sir William Sinclair founded a baptist church at his castle Keiss in Caithness which has some claim to have been the first indigenous baptist church in Scotland but it ceased after his death.[15] The foundationary work done by the brothers Haldane has lasted.

Robert Haldane (1764-1842) and **James Haldane** (1768-1851) were wealthy aristocrats and were converted in 1794, both in the same year but quite independently. James resigned his commission in the army and became minister of a new independent church in Edinburgh for which his brother funded a new chapel. Robert sold the family estates and devoted the whole proceeds to the furtherance of the gospel. In 1808, the two brothers were convinced of believers' baptism and were immersed and from this time their work was specifically baptist. Their energetic ministries spread baptist teaching throughout the country and many baptist churches were founded, all on calvanistic and open communion lines. Robert's greatest work was in Switzerland where he wrote, lectured and published mainly in Geneva where he stamped his mark. The 1816 visit resulted in a rich harvest of very able scholars such as Merle d'Aubigné, Theodore Monod and César Malan. Their impact on the French evangelical scene was immeasurably great.

Ultimately, the several streams of Scottish baptist life were brought together in a Baptist Union of Scotland whose doctrinal statement reflected nothing of the historic calvinism concerning the atonement, typical of the Haldanes, and it provided for open communion. The historic strength of 'calvinism' among the Scottish Presbyterians doubtless occasioned this reaction as it also did in the Netherlands.[17]

With the reviving of a concern for the reformed faith in the mid-twentieth century there has come into being a small number of baptist churches adhering to the Particular Redemption doctrine of atonement as stated in the London Confession 1677/89. These, like their sister churches in England, remain outside the union and tend to find their fellowship with the Grace Baptist Assembly, a relatively new informal grouping of baptists which takes the 1677/89 standard of doctrine. There are about two hundred baptist churches in Scotland today.

Ireland

Early christianity in Ireland conformed to Roman pattern and its missionaries planted catholicism everywhere. Danish and English conquests suppressed the Irish and trampled on their religion. The Stuart king, James I filled Ulster, the northern province, with Scottish colonists who transplanted their presbyterian faith into Ireland. Following the terrible massacre of protestants by the catholics in 1641, Cromwell sent to Ireland an army which contained many baptists who planted their churches wherever they set garrisons. According to Thurlow, in 1655 there were twelve governors of towns and cities who were baptists. The withdrawal of the army led to the shrinking of the number of churches remaining. Probably the first indigenous baptist church was founded by **Thomas Patience** who had been assistant to Kiffin in London. He formed a baptist church in Dublin in 1652, with others in Waterford, Clonmel, Kilkenny, Cork, Limerick, Wexford, Carrickfergus and Kerry. These churches made little headway and the baptist cause in Ireland remained weak until the conversion of Carson to baptist views.[18]

Alexander Carson (1776-1844) may well have been the most eminent of the Irish baptists. He was a Greek scholar and was offered the professorial chair in Greek at Glasgow University provided he conformed to the 'standards' of the Church of Scotland. Though a Scot, he settled in Ireland at Tobermore as a Presbyterian pastor in 1798 but soon became convinced of the scriptural character of the baptist doctrine of the church and seceded, vacating his living, and took to preaching to crowds in the open air or in barns. His scholarship is reflected in his writings of which his classic work on *'Baptism – Its Mode and Subjects'* has remained a standard work, being recently republished in the United

States. He helped Haldane with his Commentary on the Romans, providing the linguistic expertise. Carson was a voluminous writer, a profound logician and a very fruitful preacher. He has been called, 'The Jonathan Edwards of Ireland.'[19]

Christopher Anderson has been met in Scotland as the founder of a baptist work in Edinburgh. He commenced evangelical work in Ireland in 1813, forming the 'Achill Mission' and the 'Society for Propagating the Gospel in Ireland', This extended the baptist witness considerably.[20] Towards the end of the nineteenth century, the evangelical revival in Ireland greatly enriched the baptist churches and stirred them up to missionary ministry overseas. These churches formed the Irish Baptist Mission and established a field of work in Peru which is still prospering. But more of their outreach was channelled through undenominational societies which was a typical pattern in Ireland.[21] They formed themselves into an Irish Baptist Union with eighty-six churches having four thousand four hundred members. In recent years it has separated from the British Baptist Union on account of the latter's accommodation of liberal doctrine and ideas and because the Irish are determined not to compromise their baptist churchmanship by membership of the World Council of Churches. Neither are they in membership with the Baptist World Alliance for much the same reasons.

During the troubles attending the North-South tensions of post World War Two years, the Irish Baptists have been seen as christians without sectarian bias. When there were incidents nearby, the residents of Irish Baptist College made their premises available to help catholics and sought to bring aid at all times without regard to a sectarian political discrimination. This action underlines the baptist rejection of political ties between church and state and highlights the historical reality that baptists are not protestants any more than they are catholics! The Irish baptists are found in both north and south Ireland and their Union spans the secular frontier, effectively ministering to both communities.

10
The baptist in Europe

France

In tracing baptistic witness in Mediterranean Europe, the emergence of the 'Puritans' or 'Cathari' during the Middle Ages has already been noted. They were particularly strong in the south of France and were frequently called 'Albigenses' after the name of one of their principal centres in France, Albi which stands on the river Tarn, 76kms north-east of Toulouse.[1] By the middle of the eleventh century, Albigenses were very active, testifying vehemently against the corruptness of the catholic church and the godlessness of its priesthood. There was no clear concensus of teaching among them and many were in error on the person of Christ, denying the reality of his flesh.[2] Others among them were mystics but many were plain gospel preachers convinced of the authority of the Word of God and striving to apply its practical teachings on godly living to the churches and their ministers. They were responsible for making several translations of the scriptures into the vernacular tongue and conducted their public ministry in the common language. War was waged on them and many were put to death in the twelfth century. There is no evidence that they objected to infant baptism and only in the basic ethos of their protestations can they be said to be baptistic.[3]

Two outstanding preachers of that period were Pierre (or Peter) de Bruys and Henri of Lausanne.[4] Some biographic detail of these two remarkable men is to be found in chapter three together with some information on their ministries. The Albigenses in southern France suffered persecution at the hands of the catholics but their persistence for so long as an effective witness against the corruption of Rome, displays the widespread unease throughout the country at that time. In 1167, a conference of their teachers was called at St. Felix-de-Caraman, near Toulouse, in which greetings were brought from like-minded churches as far afield as Bulgaria and Romania. This has led to suggestions that they were themselves of Bogomil origin. This contact with Balkan christians was repeated in 1201 but its benefits quickly came to an end as ferocious efforts were made by the catholic authorities to wipe out the whole movement and take away any freedom of thought and religion. A military crusade, led by the Englishman Simon-de-Montfort, crushed all resistance and the independent states of the region were all brought under the rule of the King of France and conformity enforced. Believers were scattered far and wide and darkness fell on the land once again. Previous reference has been made to Peter of Lyons, who also belongs to this period, but he and his followers were driven from the city and found refuge in Bohemia where, after many years of fruitful service, he died[5]

It is interesting to note that the Council of Tours, called by Pope Alexander III in 1163, forbade any intercourse with the Waldenses because they 'taught a damnable heresy long since sprung up in the district of Toulouse'. Waldensian believers had moved into France from the Piedmont valleys and became identified with French baptistic protest already there.[6]

Strassburg and Cologne remained centres of dissent long after the Albigenses had been forgotten though there is some evidence that they had penetrated the other large cities in the north and east of France. This may account for the strong 'puritan' testimony residing in those two cities of great influence, which, we must recall, were essentially part of the sphere of influence of France. The free-city of Strassburg was to become the scene of the remarkable ministry of Johann Tauler, of Martin Bucer the magisterial reformer and some anabaptists like Johannes Denck.[7]

The colonisation of Provence, by the Waldensian

christians, had turned it into a prospering country. There
they built up their communities and established missionary
work beyond their own area. Francis I, persuaded by
catholics at his court, set out to destroy these dissenters and
did so with such great violence that it troubled him on his
deathbed. His son, Henri II persecuted the growing
reformed churches with even greater ferocity, beginning in
1550 by burning French Protestants, known as Huguenots,
at the coronation of his queen, Catherine of Medici.
Primed by his mistress, Diane of Poitiers, to whom the king
donated all the sequestered protestant estates, the king
shed blood throughout his kingdom.[8] Almost all the
Huguenot movement was 'reformed' in the Genevan
pattern and not baptist; but the severity with which
protestantism was exterminated was the cause of the
suppression of any typically baptist witness in France in this
period. Its story is told in detail in Wylie's documented
'History of Protestantism.' Religious wars between the
catholic throne and the protestant princes saw the triumph
of the former. In this the fact that French protestantism
was not baptist is plainly seen. No true baptist would take
up arms in the defence of his religion. Genevan reform,
with its roots in the Constantinian marriage of Church and
State, would resort heartily to the sword to win liberty for
religion. Catherine Medici was mistress of France by now
and her determination to make France catholic provoked
her policy of extermination of all dissent, which climaxed
in the ultimate massacre of St Bartholomew in October
1572 and the harshest suppression of all religious dissent
thereafter. Twenty years later, the Edict of Nantes gave a
brief respite to the dissenters but this was revoked in 1685
and eight hundred Huguenot meeting-houses were destroyed. Throughout this period almost all baptist witness
was buried beneath the sufferings of protestants in
general.[9]

Going back some years to the publication by Erasmus of
his Greek New Testament in 1516, Professor Le Fevre at
once begun teaching his students at the Sorbonne
University in Paris from the bible. Totally independent of
Luther, he asserted that 'It is God alone who, by his grace
through faith, justifies to eternal life.[10] He it was who led

Guillaume Farel to Christ and influenced many of the aristocracy of France towards a simple gospel. Le Fevre published the Psalms and the New Testament in French and the Word of God became the great theme of conversation in high circles laying the foundation for the strength of the later Huguenot movement to which reference has been made.

Farel preached the gospel everywhere and Jacques Briçonnet, Bishop of Meaux was converted, making his town an evangelical centre from which christian literature was distributed throughout the land.[11]

In 1533, bible readers gathered together for study and worship in the kingdom of Navarre in south-west France. They were encouraged and helped by the saintly **Queen Margaret**. They met in the castle lower hall for breaking of bread and sharing of the cup, with the queen taking a humble believer's place.[12] It was at this time that the student Jean Calvin was forced to leave Paris and move to Poitiers where he met some of these Navarrean believers. Servetus, the Spanish anabaptist later to be put to death as a heretic with the approval of Calvin, had his roots in the same area, attending the university of Toulouse and his story has been told in chapter five.[13] There is a need to notice here the evident anabaptist character of these believers in Navarre.

The dominance of a 'Genevan' protestantism in France submerged all free church dissent from the Revocation of the Edict of Nantes until the nineteenth century, when once again reformed, or non-catholic churches, began to include dissenting assemblies. A farmer in 1810, hunting through the attic of his farmhouse one day, found a French bible and began to read it. This awakened spiritual life in him which he shared with his neighbours in the little Flanders village of Nomain. A little place of worship was built for this new christian group. It is said that some English christian soldiers, from the battlefield of Waterloo (1815), were quartered on the village and joined in the worship in this chapel. In 1819, **Henri Pyt**, a recent convert of Robert Haldane's ministry in Geneva, came to Nomain and began to teach baptist principles with the result that France's first baptist church of the modern era was formed.[14]

Later **Casimer Rostan**, a native of Marseilles and an ardent and able baptist missionary, settled in Paris in 1832 and began to preach and baptise converts. **Isaac Willmarth** followed him and linked up the church in Paris with the Flanders churches, which had sprung from Pyt's work. Some American missionaries came to strengthen this baptist work in France but the outstanding pioneer of this period was a Frenchman, **Jean-Baptiste Crétan** whose fruitful labours continued over fifty years. During this period baptist meetings were often raided by the police and many baptists lost their livelihoods and had to emigrate to the States because of the persecution. But the baptist pioneers persevered and God blessed their labours.[15]

French baptist work divided itself on a north and south axis. That in the north was known as 'La Fédération des Eglises Baptistes du Nord de la France' and included Belgium within its province. **Pastor Philémon Vincent** and his family were the outstanding leaders of this. Those churches in the south formed 'L'Association des Eglises Baptistes Franco-Suisse' which had a centre in Paris and three main areas of work, the South Cevennes, the Montbéliard district and the French-speaking Bernese Jura. They engaged in country-wide evangelism led by **M. Sainton** and in large evangelistic campaigns led by **Dr Ruben Saillens**.[16] The latter left a fine legacy of hymns and a hymnbook still used to this day, *'Sur les Ailes de la Foi'*, which has seen eight successive editions.[17] Later Dr Saillens left the baptists and formed an undenominational pastoral training college at Nogent [18]

The ethnic ties between the Bretons of North-west France and the Welsh were not long in producing a new work by a Welsh baptist in Brittany. **John Jenkins** commenced his evangelical mission in 1843 and several baptist churches sprang up in that part of France, many continuing to this day. At one time, there was a school at Morlaix and thirteen preaching centres. This work was supported by British churches but today it is part of the work of the French 'Fédération'.[19]

Canadian baptists gave support to baptist work in the Alsace and Swiss Jura with the result that the work of some few indigenous churches was extended and a sizeable group of churches exists there today. Some of their pastors have been trained in the Canadian Toronto Baptist Seminary. This bond remains effective today as the Canadian Seminary is bi-lingual, teaching in English and French. The result is that these French pastors are fluent in English and this has provided good ground for the building of ties between them and the British evangelical baptists.

Early French baptist work, as has been noted, depended greatly upon the support of the American Missionary Society of Boston.[20] This latter developed into an American Mission Board and came to reflect the changing theology of some of its member churches. Suspicions of 'modernist' heresy raised large questions among the French baptists who had stood firmly for a conservative evangelical position. In 1920, **M. Arthur Blocher**, pastor of the Paris church, meeting in the American owned church buildings in *Rue de Lille*, seceded on doctrinal grounds and later vacated the said chapel and built another in northern Paris called the 'Tabernacle' which remains independent to this day.[21] The next year the French churches of the two groupings met to unite to form a national union and to face the questions of doctrinal infidelity. The outcome was that their president, **Dr R. Dubarry**, **M. Georges Guyot** and four other pastors withdrew from the others and, meeting in the hall of the nearby St. Lazare railway station, formed a new thoroughly evangelical fellowship to be known as 'L' Association Evangélique d'Eglises Baptistes de Langue Français' with an initial six churches in membership.[22] Over the years this grouping has grown and now embraces 15 churches in France, 8 in Switzerland, and one each in Belgium, Madagascar and Martinique. It also has a significant number of other centres of work with groups of members which will in due time be formed into local independent baptist churches.[23]

The remaining churches in the old 'North' and 'South' groups united to form a 'Fédération des Eglises Evangélique Baptistes de France'. This body is in membership with the European Baptist Federation and the World Baptist Alliance but not with the World Council of Churches.[24]

The American baptists have continued to support baptist

work in France, including some of the independent baptist
missionary groups not aligned with either the American
Baptist Convention or the Southern Convention, such as
'Baptist Mid-Missions'. This organisation has a base near
Bordeaux and has founded a number of baptist churches
in the country.[25] Other baptist influences have been strong,
including the Darbyists (Christian Brethren), Pentecostal
and other churches. It is claimed that there are about two
hundred baptist churches of all types in France today, but
this must be counted meagre in view of the sixty million
population and the honoured history of baptist witness in
France from early times. What an urgent need there is for
baptists to strive to spread their biblical message throughout this illustrious nation. The American missionary,
Adoniram Judson, once said that 'an evangelised France...
would furnish stimulation to all the intelligent classes of
Europe'.[26]

Germany

The story of the anabaptists of the sixteenth and
seventeenth centuries has been told. The location of so
much of their witness, progress and missionary spread, as
well as their subsequent falling away, took place in those
lands which in due time were welded into a united
Germany. Sadly, since World War Two it has been rent
apart into two separately governed entities. Over the years,
the eastern and western frontiers have undergone constant
change. In anabaptist times, Strassburg was a german city
and the centre of much lively witness. Alsace and Lorraine
are now in France. In the east, much of what we call Poland
has been Germany and much once part of Poland is in
USSR.

The rise of the baptists in Germany in modern times is
very largely the story of a remarkable man, **Johann G.
Oncken** of Hamburg, which must now be told in a brief
biographical review. Not Germany only, but the Netherlands, Hungary (and Romania) Poland, the Baltic States of
Latvia, Lithuania and Estonia (now part of the USSR) the
Scandinavian countries of Denmark, Norway, Sweden and

Finland have all been fields in which baptist pioneer endeavour, church-planting ministry and subsequent growth stems from his ministry. Today, after the Catholics, Lutheran and Reformed churches, the baptists form the largest christian grouping in Europe.

Johann Gerhard Oncken (1800-84) was one of a small group of seven persons who were baptised on 23 April 1834 in the river Elbe at Hamburg, at night because of strong opposition. Few at the time would have viewed the occasion as significant but from it stemmed the rebirth of baptist testimony in Germany and its neighbouring lands. Oncken was born to a Lutheran family on 26 January 1800 at Varel, on the Saxony coast north-west of Bremen.[27] Though confirmed in the Lutheran church at thirteen, he remained ignorant of the gospel until a Scottish merchant was attracted to him and took him back to Scotland to live in his home and work in his service for the next nine years. There he was taught the scriptures and greatly influenced by that godly presbyterian household. His conversion took place in London at a Methodist chapel through a sermon on Romans 8:1.[28] The Continental Society sent him back to Hamburg in 1823 as a missionary to his own people.[29] His first sermon was preached in a private house to eighteen people and **C. F. Lange**, who was to become his close colleague, was converted.[30] Oncken turned to street preaching and drew great crowds by his powerful ministry. This aroused great opposition from both Lutheran and Catholic clergy who incited the police to suppress 'the English religion'..[31] To qualify as a Hamburg citizen and so avoid expulsion, Oncken commenced a booksellers business which remains today the official publishing unit of the German baptists, 'The Oncken Press'. On the birth of his first child, he became convinced that there was no biblical ground for infant baptism but that believers only should be baptised and that by immersion. It was at this juncture that the now famous 'Baptism in the Elbe' took place.[32] The next day, 24 April 1834, the first modern German baptist church was founded in Hamburg and within two years it grew to sixty-eight members.[33]

It was at this point that the American Baptist Missionary Society of Boston commenced supporting his work. The city authorities were incensed by this disturbing preacher's success and he was imprisoned twice and all baptist services forbidden. However, the more they tried to stamp out this 'new sect', the more Oncken's witness prospered. Eventually, the influence of British and American merchants, on which Hamburg's prosperity so largely depended, eased the persecution and ultimately religious freedom was gained. In 1836, **Julius Köbner** was converted and baptised, and the following year **Gottfried Wilhelm Lehman** also.[33] These three men formed a mighty triumvirate, preaching the gospel throughout north-eastern and central Europe with extraordinary success. They were called affectionately, 'Kleeblatt' (=Cloverleaf).[34] Lehmann became the pastor of the first baptist church in Berlin. Köbner and Oncken founded the first baptist church in Denmark in 1838 and the first in Sweden ten years later. Work in the Netherlands commenced in 1847 with the first modern baptist church founded that same year. The American Society gave considerable financial support for widespread missionary work throughout Europe and baptist churches sprang up everywhere. Oncken, as reviewed later, had a large hand in the birth of today's immense baptist community in Russia. The German churches were founded on clear 'Particular Baptist' lines reflecting the historic 1689 Confession, but as the pressures eased and religious freedom was gained, so there began a decline in the spiritual vitality and biblical discipline giving place to arminian doctrine and also later, to liberalism. Yet this remarkable story of God's grace in reviving biblical baptist witness in modern times, almost throughout Europe, is told largely in the life and work of one remarkable man, Johann Oncken, who has been called, 'The Father of the Continental Baptists'.[35] He died on 2 January 1884 at Zürich.[36]

Gottfried Wilhelm Lehmann (1799-1882) was born in Hamburg on 23 October 1799. As a small boy, he was sent to an uncle in Friessland and grew up among earnest

christians, some of whom were Mennonites. He was led to
Christ in his youth and early felt a great urge to proclaim
the gospel. He went to Berlin as a student at the Academy,
studying foreign languages and engaged in christian
propaganda there. Oncken baptised him with five others
on 13 May 1837 and the next day the first baptist church of
Berlin was formed. Lehmann was appointed pastor and
served in that office until his death in 1882.[37] Throughout
his ministry, he shared with Oncken and others in the
missionary outreach of the German baptist churches, of
which there were 162 in 1886. Today there are 593
churches with 89,000 churchmembers in the two Unions of
Evangelical Free Churches of East and West Germany
according to the World Baptist Alliance Yearbook for
1985. Whether all these churches are truly baptist is not
clear. In addition there are numerous 'baptist' type free
churches, generally keenly evangelical, having resisted the
general trend towards modernism, which cannot be
numbered precisely because of their independency.

Denmark

Julius Köbner, (1806-84) to whom reference has already
been made, was born the son of a Jewish rabbi, on 11 June
1806 at Odense in Denmark. He was a gifted young man
and in pursuit of his ambitions, he moved to Hamburg. On
the first occasion of hearing Oncken preach he was
convicted of sin and, coming to faith in Jesus Christ, was
baptised on 17 May 1836. Hearing of groups of believers
which had separated from the Danish State (Lutheran)
Church, he returned to his homeland in 1839. He found
such a group in Copenhagen which had also seen the error
of infant baptism. Oncken joined Köbner in ministry there
and soon eleven believers were baptised and Denmark's
first baptist church was formed. Subsequent visits led to
more conversions and their baptisms with many baptist
churches being formed in other cities. Bitter persecution
followed and several pastors were imprisoned. **Pastor
Monster** of Copenhagen suffered imprisonment five
times, but religious freedom came in 1849. It was Köbner

who compiled the first baptist Danish hymnbook and he served the Copenhagen church for a further ten years. Today there are 44 baptist churches with 3737 members in Denmark without adding in the several free churches not associated with union.[38]

Sweden

The seventeenth century saw the settlement of both pietist and Moravian Brethren communities in Sweden but they became loosely linked with the State Lutheran Church after a time and lost their distinctive baptist characteristic. During the eighteenth century, there were secessions from the State church of many concerned christians but little evidence of baptist witness until 1847 when **F. O. Nilson** returned home from Hamburg where he had been converted and baptised under the ministry of Oncken. He began preaching in the little village of Veddige, near Gothenburg, forming a church there. He was sentenced to banishment for his persistent dissent and went to America whilst the little church he left behind was severely persecuted but survived, In 1854, a different beginning of baptist work in Sweden was made at Stockholm by two furriers, who also had been baptised by Oncken at Hamburg. Together with seven others they were formed into the first baptist church in Stockholm. Itinerant preaching led to baptist churches springing up all over the land and by 1866 there were nearly two hundred churches with almost seven thousand members.[39] Today the 380 churches have almost 21,000 members.

Norway

In 1857, **Fredrik L. Rymker**, a Danish baptist, settled in Porsgrund, near Skien, and began to preach the gospel. A church was formed 22 April 1860 at Tolnaes, near Skien, comprising seven members. Swedish pioneers also evangelised their neighbouring country in the following year. A Norwegian expatriate baptist from Boston, USA, was sent to do similar work in his native land, with the support of English Baptists, and his ministry was most fruitful. The 'Ebenezer' baptist chapel in Bergen is a lasting testimony to his work which continues to the present time. Baptists suffered harshly under the Lutheran dominated local governments but persecution seemed to strengthen their resolve to persevere with the gospel without compromise. Dr Rushbrooke says that at one time 'many Lutherans believed and preached that believers' baptism is an unpardonable sin and that baptists are eternally damned since they wilfully reject the saving grace of infant baptism'.[40]

Finland

The first baptist church in Finland was formed in 1856 on Foglo in the Aland Islands and the first on the mainland at Jacobstad in 1869. There are two streams of baptist churches in the country, arising out of the language divide. There are the Swedish speaking churches and the Finnish language churches. Baptists have not been persecuted in Finland but the impact of an agressive 'pentecostalism' movement has greatly impaired the clear baptist testimony to biblical faith and practice.[41]

Switzerland

'The Baptists appeared first in Switzerland about 1523...' states the Schaff-Herzog Encyclopedia under 'History of Baptists in Europe'.[42] Enough has been written already for the reader to trace baptist church history back to the earliest centuries of this christian era and also for him to understand the false conclusion which the quotation draws. Certainly, a remarkable revival of the baptist witness broke out in Switzerland around the year cited, which was to give a virtual new birth to the movement. Sadly, within a century of that new beginning, baptist churches were dying out again and magisterial reform became the only effective alternative to revived catholicism. The home of those 'Swiss

Brethren', which laid the foundation of the modern baptist movement, has not retained a strong baptist testimony. One half of the cantons which form the Confederation are roman catholic and the remainder protestant after the style of Zwingli's moderate churchmanship. In the German-speaking cantons there are some baptist churches which appear to have sprung from Johann Oncken's evangelism and his itinerant preachers. They are affiliated to the European Baptist Federation and the Baptist World Alliance. With considerable support from both the American Conventions, American Baptist Convention and the Southern Baptist Convention, they maintain a seminary at Rüschlikon, near to Zürich, which trains men for the baptist ministry in all European countries. It has done good work in supporting pastors in the churches of the Eastern bloc.[43]

In the French-speaking cantons of Western Switzerland, the baptist churches are keenly evangelical, totally independent and wholly committed to a conservative theology. They find fellowship in an Association of French Speaking Evangelical Baptist churches which spans frontiers to include France and Belgium. They also individually express wider fellowship in the Association Baptiste Evangélique, known in Britain as the Fellowship of Evangelical Baptist Churches in Europe, or just FEBE. These French language churches also maintain a missionary presence in Madagascar and Martinique.[44]

It would be a serious omission to pass over the remarkable impact of the Scottish baptist preacher **Robert Haldane** during his residence in Geneva. Burdened with a sense of the need for the gospel on the mainland of Europe, Robert and his wife arrived in Geneva in 1816. They commenced teaching a group of twenty to thirty students which met in their home, giving expositions of the Epistle to the Romans by interpretation. Such careful exposition was entirely new to his hearers who were attracted by Haldane's knowledge of the scriptures and his utter belief in them as the Word of God. These bible readings proved to be of abiding worth in the lives of many gifted men who were to exercise distinguished ministries themselves. Among them were **César Malan**, whose hymns are still sung in evangelical churches, **Merle D'Aubigné**, whose *History of the Reformation* is still an acknowledged classic, **Adolphe Monod**. **Félix Neff** and others who carried what they had learned throughout the French-speaking world. These students suffered for their commitment to the truth at the hands of Calvin's successors, the Swiss Reformed Church. However, the Word of God prevailed and little independent groups of believers arose from this witness, although many became identified with the 'Christian Brethren' or Darbyist assemblies rather than the evangelical baptists.[45]

However there are some Swiss baptist churches holding to the evangelical calvinism of Robert Haldane and his emphasis on a pure church maintained by total submission to the scriptures. Close by Calvin's cathedral in Geneva, and near to the meeting-place of Haldane's group in La Pélisserie, such a baptist church meets under the pastoral care of **Guy Appéré**, who has had books published in both French and English. Yuille says that Haldane's ministry in Geneva changed the face of continental protestantism.[46]

In 1847, Johann Oncken, the German baptist pioneer, extended his evangelistic tour of Bavaria into Switzerland and formed a church at Hochwart of a few believers whom he had baptised. The baptist church in Zürich was formed two years later and in 1856 **I. I. Hofer**, from the Hamburg Seminary became resident missionary and over fifty persons were baptised and added to the church. Two further missionaries were sent from Hamburg in 1859 to commence work in north-eastern Switzerland and churches were gathered in Bischofzell in Thurgau and at Herisau in Appenzell, both in the vicinity of St. Gallen where the remarkable anabaptist ministry had once prospered. Baptists were persecuted, their infants compulsorily christened, their meetings broken up and fines with loss of property inflicted on them. It was not unitl 1874 that the constitution of the Swiss Federation was revised to grant religious liberty. In German-speaking Switzerland there are today 23 baptist churches and two Italian in the Swiss Baptist Union, European Baptist Federation and Baptist World Alliance. There are nine French speaking churches in the Association Evangélique des Eglises

Baptistes de Langue Française, the Association Baptiste Evangélique et Européan' and outside all world bodies.[47] The European Baptist Federation has a Theological Seminary at Rüschlikon near Zürich for the training of pastors from all European countries, particularly those behind the Iron Curtain.

Paul Besson was a remarkable Swiss baptist who after some years of evangelism in France, went to South America to preach the gospel and founded baptist churches at the invitation of some French-speaking imigrants already established in Argentina. His greatly successful life's work is detailed later in the next chapter.[48]

Italy

The presence of christians in Italy, before Paul reached Rome as a prisoner, is evident from his own writings and the story of their persecution under successive emperors is very well documented. In claiming kinship for baptists with those early Roman believers, Dr J. H. Rushbrooke says of baptists,[49] 'They point with quiet assurance to the dark pools in the catacombs and to the beautiful baptistries which adorn the country from the Alps to Etna--sermons in stones that tell of primitive belief and practice'.

In earlier chapters the witness of faithful christians through the Dark Ages and into Middle and Modern times has been traced. The Bogils and others in Northern Italy and then the Waldenses whose churches, much modified, continue in the present day, have been noted. Savonarola of Florence lit the reforming torch in the fourteenth century and Servetus and **Juan de Valdés** and others during the Reformation period carried on the testimony.[50] The Counter Reformation almost stamped out the baptistic churches of that time.

Contemporary baptist work seems to have begun with the work of a Wiltshire baptist, **James Wall**, who started work in 1863 at Bologna, and **Edward Clark** in Spezia. They lived by faith and often in very low circumstances until a committee was formed in 1868 to help them. In 1870, Wall removed to Rome and carried on until 1901, when he died. His widow, and afterwards, their daughter carried on a caring ministry for the poor of the city. Others joined them in Naples, Turin and Genoa in what was then called the 'English Mission'. In 1891, the Baptist Missionary Society took responsibility for the work, excepting that at Spezia which continued as a separate ministry.[51]

American Southern Baptists began work in Rome in 1872 sending **George Boardman Taylor** in 1873 who laboured until his death in 1907. A theological school was opened in 1901. Growth was considerable and in 1918 it was possible for it to become self-governing. Social work and extensive christian publishing has marked the development of baptist work in Italy. Italian baptists' literature work led by **Lodovico Paschetto** for many years, has been particularly successful. The British Mission was amalgamated with the work started by the Americans in 1923.[52]   The evangelical baptist churches of France have supported independent baptist home mission work in the northern industrialised cities. This has led to the founding of six new churches in that area. There are a number of other independent baptist churches and outreach ministries in other parts of the country, largely the result of individualist endeavours of converted ex-priests who have left the roman catholic church. A few others have come into being from the secession of keen evangelicals from the Italian Baptist union because of its rationalist tendencies.

Austria

The anabaptists were prominent in Austria during the sixteenth and seventeenth centuries but the catholic 'Counter Reformation' blotted out all dissent both baptist and protestant, leaving one reformed church to survive in Hallstätt in Upper Austria. It was not until **Marschall** and **Hornung**, Austrians who had been working in Hamburg and converted and baptised by Oncken, came to Vienna in 1846 that baptist witness revived in this country. Visits from Oncken encouraged the formation of a little church in the capital, meeting in the house of an ex-catholic, **Karl**

Rauch who with nine others was imprisoned for a while. In 1862 an Englishman, **E. Millard** returned to Vienna and heartened the few remaining baptists there and the church was reformed on 20 December 1869. The first pastor, **A. Meeris**, was appointed 1879 and served four years before emigrating to America and he was followed by **Julius Peter** who later took a prominent part in baptist work in Yugoslavia. Baptists were constantly suppressed by the Austrian authorities and even as late as 1917, a hall and its funds was seized and its work terminated because it was 'Suspected of working for the cause of the repeatedly forbidden baptist church'.[53] The baptists have persevered despite the opposition and the severe sufferings of the nation throughout the rest of this century. Today, Austria is free and prosperous again and the baptists have about thirty centres of work of which twelve are constituted churches of the Austrian Baptist Union and the remainder represent the witness of independent missionary endeavours of the evangelical baptist churches of Switzerland, France and England.[54]

Russia

The penetration of Eastern Europe by the anabaptists of the reformation period has been noted.[55] The baptistic Polish Minor church was virtually eliminated in the Roman Catholic Counter Reformation. The many pockets of Mennonite churches along the Baltic coast suffered a similar fate though some moved further east into Russia, as also did at least one Hutterite community surviving the efforts-at suppression of all 'protestant' witness.[56] Those that survived became very successful farmers and were highly esteemed by landlords everywhere. Catherine the Great of Russia became empress on the assassination of her husband, Peter III in 1762. She was an agnostic but a shrewd woman without principles, and cruel. With a view to raising the economic worth of her vast unoccupied lands, she extended a welcome to Mennonite farmers from Prussia and the Baltic States to settle in free grants of lands and a first colony was set up on the river Dneiper island of

Khortitsa and subsequently many others were founded
between 1788 and 1796 to her great advantage. The
Mennonite colonists were permitted to retain their German
culture and language and to practise their religion
provided that they undertook not to proselytise their
neighbours. They proved themselves industrious and
became very prosperous but their spiritual life declined.
Their history is told in some detail in Smith's *'History of the
Mennonites'*. There were times when pressure was brought
by the State to restrain or limit their prosperity and this has
been interpreted as religious persecution.[57] Some 18,000
emigrated to the United States in the 1880s but 100,000
remained in Russia up to the time of the Bolshevik
revolution in 1917. After World War I they suffered
considerable privations, especially during the 1922 famine
and large scale emigration began again, mainly to Canada
and Paraguay.[58]

During the opening years of the nineteenth century,
endeavours were made to promote the Gospel in Russia by
British christians, the Bible Society and the London
Missionary Society being prominent in this. The German
Baptist Mission, based in Britain, which had sponsored
many of the missionary tours of **Johann Oncken** of
Hamburg, encouraged him with finance for work in Russia
and Poland. The German evangelist reached the Mennonite colonies and began baptist witness amongst them using
the German language. He also visited the Government
Minister in St. Petersburg (now Leningrad) and told him
that 'God has called us to preach the great truth of
believers' baptism among Europe's millions... If the
Imperial Government tries forcibly to suppress the baptists
in Poland and Russia, they will discover that it is a very
difficult thing to try and destroy a genuine religious
movement'.[59] The first baptism recorded of a pure Russian
convert on the profession of his faith was in 1867 and the
Russian baptists of today claim the commencement of their
work from that date. That same year a wealthy merchant,
Nikita Voronin (1840-1905) was baptised and threw
himself and his substantial resources behind aggressive
baptist evangelism. In 1871, he baptised **Vasili Pavloff**
(1854-1924) who become a leader amongst them and the

same year **V. I. Ivanoff** (1846-1919) joined the new movement and so provided a trio of powerful preachers as leaders of the baptists in Russia, which led to widespread establishment of baptist churches throughout the Union.

A British peer, **Lord Radstock**, himself a member of the 'Plymouth Brethren' movement, gained access to the drawing rooms of St. Petersburg, preaching the gospel, and was instrumental in some leading aristocrats being converted. Among them was **Colonel V. A. Pashkoff** who became a passionate missionary among the Molokans and Stundists. The former were dissenters from Russian Orthodoxy and the latter keen Bible christians who met in groups and were of a pronounced baptist type. Pashkoff tried to secure the union of these 'baptistic' evangelical christians but failed to unite them completely. His efforts laid a strong foundation for the later achievement of union in 1944 which ensured that there was a spiritual bond among these churches stronger than the USSR Government's legal imposition of an organisational union.[60]

During that period, **I. S. Prokhanoff** (1869-1935) was born, converted in 1877 and sent to Britain for training in Bristol Baptist College. He became prominent in this century as a baptist leader. Persecution and imprisonment or banishment to Siberia became the lot of the early baptists. In 1905, an edict for religious toleration was made but off and on suppression remained official policy. However, baptist churches grew in strength right up to the Bolshevik revolution, publishing their own periodicals and literature, attending baptist conferences outside their own land and founding a bible school in St. Petersburg. The revolutionaries first gave liberty to the baptists, attracted to their 'democractic' form of government which stood in contrast to the traditional Russian Orthodox church with its hierarchical government. When Stalin came to power in 1929, the constitution was altered so that christians could no longer engage freely in 'religious propaganda'. The new code allowed only 'freedom of worship'. In 1930, deportation to Siberia was re-imposed as a corrective for all those engaged in 'religious propaganda'. In 1944, Stalin forced all evangelicals to unite in an **'All-Union Council of Evangelical Christians-Baptists'** organisation with the requirement that all 'evangelical churches whether baptist, brethren, pentecostal or seventh-day or not' should conpulsorily register with it.[61] About 75% churches were refused registration in an endeavour to reduce drastically the number of christian churches still gathering through-out the Union. When Stalin died in 1953, some relief came temporarily to the baptists but in 1962/3, Kruschev launched a new offensive against all religion, bragging that he would exhibit the last christian on television in 1965. During that period about 10,000 churches were closed. One result of all this pressure was the formation of a national fellowship of unregistered churches which en-joyed some effective leadership and spiritual prosperity.[62] This is called the **Council of Evangelical Baptist Chur-ches**. Today it is said that these churches greatly outnumber the registered churches and one estimate gives them as having three million members. A reliable source says there are at least 2,000 unregistered churches in Russia today.[62a]

The AUCECB introduced some 'New Statutes' for church government under pressure from the government and these diminished the autonomy of the local churches and gave more power to the central office. These regulations also prohibited 'unhealthy missionary man-isfestations... aimed at stopping evangelism. Baptisms of young people between the ages of 18 and 30 years of age were ordered to be kept at a minimum. Children were forbidden to attend worship services with or without their parents and the baptism of those under 18 years was forbidden.' Unregistered churches lost their meeting houses in many cases and started gathering for worship in their homes. This was followed by police visits, searches for bibles and hymn books and other christian literature which when found was confiscated. The formation of their own national committee, even though illegal, strengthened their hands greatly. Pastors **F. Prokofev, Gennardi Kriuchkov** and **Georgi Vins** formed an action group commonly called the 'Initiative Group' and wives of imprisoned leaders formed their own **Council of Prison-ers' Relatives (CPR)**. Though it was forbidden for churches or individuals to give financial aid to other church-members, yet as soon as fines and loss of jobs brought hardship, they all gave assistance to one another with typical christian generosity.[63]

Technically, there is religious freedom in USSR, but christians cannot conduct evangelisation of any form and Sunday schools, youth clubs, camps or other similar activities, are forbidden. The registered churches are permitted only a token amount of printing of literature and it is forbidden to listen to foreign radio broadcasting.

Article 227 of the penal code has a clause which makes it illegal for minors to participate in religious activities 'which are harmful to the health of the citizens and encroach on the personal rights of the individual'. This is used effectually to bar attendance at any kind of christian activity. In 1966, a decree banned all Sunday school and informal religious education given by parents to their children. It authorised the removal of children from parental care if they refused to allow their children to attend the State's indoctrination meetings and youth clubs. In effect the practice of religion is stripped down to the bare attendance by adults at services and almost everything else is made illegal. Inevitably christian pastors and workers, and indeed private christians too, break the laws of their land because they cannot but preach the gospel and seek to lead their fellow men to Christ, both young and old. At any one time it is estimated that there are 150 unregistered pastors in labour camps or prison. Christians are not born again to be silent! The christian's faith cannot be bottled up within himself. It is for the world! Every new government raises hopes of greater freedom but the christian does not trust in princes but in his almighty Master. All christians everywhere, who enjoy relative freedom to practice their religion, ought to sustain their brothers and sisters in Russia by prayer and every practical means.[64]

Georgi Vins (b. 1924) is the son of a well educated baptist family, his father being a missionary in Siberia when Georgi was born. His father was sent to a prison camp for three years shortly after the birth and died two years later during the Stalinist purge of christians in 1929. His mother strove to give her boy a good education and nurtured in him the convictions of his father. In time Georgi proved

himself an able proponent of the christian faith, a good
expositor of the scriptures and a caring pastor for his
people in a baptist church in Kiev. He joined Prokofev and
others in forming the independent fellowship of unregistered churches in 1960 (Initsiativnoki). He was sentenced
to three years of 'special regime' in 1966. Though a
qualified engineer, he was compelled to work as a labourer
and every endeavour to dispose of him was enforced. He
was again sent to prison in 1976 for five years to be
followed by five years in exile. Worldwide protests and the
personal appeal of **President J. Carter**, himself a baptist,
led to Vins and his family being allowed to emigrate to the
United States in 1979 but he had to give an undertaking
not to return to his homeland.

Visitors from the west should attend worship in these
baptist churches where they will experience a warm and
gracious welcome and be inspired by the spiritual vitality of
the large congregations. The central church in Moscow is
easy to find, has services at 10, 2 and 6 every Sunday and
midweek meetings on Tuesdays and Thursdays at 8pm.
The congregations on Sunday overfill the church building
and number 2,500 with about 500 standing. Seats are
reserved for overseas visitors in the gallery. The church in
Leningrad worships in a former Russian Orthodox church
with its traditional onion top tower.[65] It too is well filled
despite having been extended to seat more in 1894. It is
reached by Metro to Udelnaya and bus number 38 from
across the road to Poklonnaja Gora. The bus stops outside
the church which stands at No. 29A Bolschaja Osjornaja
and its services are at 10 and 4 also with midweek meetings.
You will also be welcomed to churches in Minsk, Lwow,
Alma-Ata, Taschkent, Tallinn, Narva, Parnu Tartu, Riga
and Vilnius. The latter place has historic interests in that it
was an anabaptist centre during the 16th and 17th
centuries.

The Balkans

The witness of the 'Bogomils', who embraced a puritan
form of christianity in the ninth century, has been noted in

chapter three.[66] The spread of Paulician believers into the
northern Balkans led to their receiving that local name.
They were effective witnesses to the simplicity of a biblical
faith and church order. They maintained a strong
evangelistic conviction which was to spread their influence
throughout southern Europe. They were devout christians, with a distinctively peaceful nature evidencing a close
communion with God. Indeed it was their piety and
practical godliness which marked them out from the
catholics who found the Bogomils' puritanism a rebuke to
their own indifferent, and often blatant, worldly standards.
For instance, **Basil**, a physican, is remembered as being an
outstanding witness to the gospel. He rebuked the laziness
of those whose made religion an excuse to avoid the
responsibility to support oneself and to contribute to the
community welfare. A tireless preacher and able teacher,
he laboured for forty years (1070-1111) in the Balkans in
the region we know as Bulgaria today. These Bogomil
communities, their slavic name meaning '**Friends of God**',
sent their messengers to similar groups of believers in the
south of France in the thirteenth century and may well
have had much to do with the strength of the Albigenses
there. They were still to be found in the Balkans in the
sixteenth century, according to Broadbent. Many baptists,
fleeing from persecution by both catholic and protestant
countries to the west, found refuge among them at that
time. Hutterite communities from Austria and Hungary,
also sent their messengers among them, but little remained
after the oppression of the Catholic Counter Reformation
in the following century.[67]

It was not until Oncken sent his missionaries into the
Balkans in the nineteenth century that a baptist witness
again appeared.[68] **Kargel** a german evangelist, baptised
eight converts and formed a church at Kasanik in 1880.
The same year another church was formed in Rustchuk
and a Hamburg trained minister became its pastor,
developing a chain of village churches, and so began the
modern baptist movement in Bulgaria. The Bible Society
sent a german colporteur into the country to help
strengthen it and he did some excellent pioneer work.
Another German named **Klundt** founded several chur-

ches, including that at Golinski, which was almost entirely composed of converted gipsies. Another church was founded in the mountains at Barkowitza by **Peter Igloff** and **Spas Raitscheff** gathered a church at Mertwirtza before going into Sofia, the capital city, to establish a church there.[69] American baptists sent a missionary into the south, starting a work there and their generosity played a large part in the expansion of baptist witness in Bulgaria up to the outbreak of World War Two, since which time the country has been dominated by the Soviets and the churches have had a severe testing time. The Moscow-dominated government has severely repressed christian witness but today there are still about twenty-five baptist churches in Bulgaria which continue to meet but lack the spiritual vitality of their Romanian neighbours.

Baptist churches in **Romania** have a similar history, being commenced by a national, converted under Oncken's ministry and baptised by him eleven years earlier. He returned to preach to his countrymen in 1856, commencing work as a colporteur in Bucharest. Here he was joined by several German baptists and a small church was commenced. An English lady, **Miss Elizabeth Clarke** from Canterbury, joined them. Oncken sent them a pastor in 1863, **August Liebig**, who also ministered in baptist churches founded by Russians in the Danube delta. Several gifted men gave themselves to pastoring these churches, including **Daniel Schwegler** (1878-1905), **Johann Hammerschmidt** (1906-1910) and an American, **B. Schlipt** (1911-12) and others since. The boundaries of Romania were extended in 1919 and brought in a large number of baptist churches from the annexed Hungarian territory. Today the baptists are strong and active in Romania, numbering in excess of a thousand churches and comprising the ninth largest group in the world. Soviet-style government severely oppresses them but persecution has brought spiritual prosperity. The size of the congregations and the number of churches has been growing to the great embarrassement of the marxist politicians and special measures are being enforced to restrain baptist growth. Restrictions on proselytising and religious propaganda have always been characteristic of soviet administrations.

The considerable harrassment of pastors, and provocations in restraint of buildings permitted to be used, have caused many to suffer penal consequences, Some pastors have opted for emigration after periods in prison. Probably **Pastor Wormbrandt** is the best known of these. His writings have been translated into many languages and read all over the world.[70]

In **Yugoslavia**, there is greater freedom of worship though some typical soviet style restraints exist. Substantial baptist congregations are to be found in the major cities with a total of about sixty churches in the whole country. There is some fellowship with western churches and some limited evangelism is possible though anti-proselytism laws exist.[71]

Greece has only a very few churches though there has been a revival of evangelical witness of a baptist character in recent years. Neighbouring Albania claims to have stamped out all religion throughout the nation reports the existence of small underground groups of believers still maintaining their christian faith in spite of the most severe regime in the Balkans is reported.

11
The baptist in the New World

The United States of America

The settlement of colonists on the eastern seaboard of North America began in earnest in 1607 when British emigrants formed a colony, naming it Virginia, for their late queen Elizabeth I, and the Church of England was made the established form of religion until 1776. Initially, it was tolerant of other christians but later enforced conformity. In the thirty-two years from 1768 to 1790, two hundred baptist churches were founded in Virginia.[1] Episcopy was not popular in any of the new colonies. The New England states were settled by the Pilgrim Fathers and other migrations from 1620 onwards and again an established state religion was imposed, in this case that of the Independents comprising oppressed puritan congregationalists and anglicans. The Independent state-church enforced their paedobaptist calvinism in just the same way as Virginia had imposed the Church of England, both groups persecuting all dissenters, which mostly meant baptists.[2]

Boston was the chief point of entry for these early settlers, and the state of Massachusetts secured its charter from Charles I in 1628 and its established congregational church remained entrenched until 1834. It was the last state to grant liberty of conscience. Harvard and Yale colleges were founded in 1638 and 1701 respectively. The first baptist church in this state was formed in 1665 at Boston but it suffered oppression for a full century. Connecticut, chartered as a state in 1638, also established

Congregationalism with a toleration for presbyterians, with whom it had few differences. Maryland received its charter in 1632 as a privately owned colony for catholic émigrés and established the Roman Catholic church but gave toleration to other christian faiths until 1692, when the Church of England took over control. The Carolinas were founded as Church of England establishment colonies without tolerance. Georgia, founded rather later, gave toleration to all christians except Roman Catholics. New York began life as a Dutch colony called New Amsterdam and they made their national church the establishment with no toleration of other faiths until 1652 when they allowed a Scottish Presbyterian church. The colony was captured by the English in 1664 and again the intolerant anglican church was imposed on the newly named New York. It remained intolerant of any other denominations and persecuted them. The English Quaker, William Penn, set up Pennsylvania in 1681 and gave tolerance to all.[3]

There were few, if any, baptists among the Pilgrim Fathers and early baptist colonists appear to have worshipped among the congregationalists. **Roger Williams** was one of these and he actually served as an assistant minister at Boston for a time. However, he was ultimately banished from New England and started a new colony in 1636 at Rhode Island, calling it Providence. He formed his fellow baptist colonists into a fellowship of which another Englishman, **John Clarke** was a member. The first church formation in a formal sense at Providence took place in 1639. However, John Clarke was sent from Providence to found a baptist church on the island, at Newport, which he did possibly six months before Williams formed his Providence congregation into a church. American baptist historians generally quote the Roger Williams church as the first baptist church founded in their country but it may well be that Clarke found the first at Newport. According to Lumpkin, the Providence church had no confessional basis.[4] Unlike the other North American colonies of that period, Rhode Island gave full religious freedom to all citizens. A congregation of Jews was able to worship freely in Rhode Island from 1658 and it was probably the only place in the world where such liberty was granted to them.[5]

Roger Williams and John Clarke secured the colony's charter from Charles II in 1663 by personal appeal. Williams, often referred to as the 'Apostle of Religious Freedom' for his work in that field, was not a successful pastor leaving his church after only six months and being replaced by **Chad Brown**. Besides these two churches, five other baptist churches were founded in this colony in its first fifty years.[6]

Religious intolerance in the colonies was frequently bitter. Massachusetts passed an Act in 1644 to banish all baptists from the state. Four quakers were hanged in Boston between 1656-60[7]. Rhode Island baptists also suffered when travelling into the New England States, as for example, when Dr John Clarke, with Pastor Obadiah Holmes and Deacon Crandall, visited a member of their church living near Boston. The puritan magistrates seized them and committed them to prison. There was no prison in Lynn, so the alehouse was used! All were fined heavily but Holmes refused to pay and so strong were his principles concerning the unscriptural involvement of magistrates in religious matters that he suffered a public whipping of incredible severity... thirty fierce strokes with a three corded whip. Sadly it was an action supported by the Congregational clergy. The full story can be found in most American baptist histories.[8]

Roger Williams (1599-1689), the founder of the Rhode Island community, was born in Wales, educated in Pembroke College, Cambridge and ordained into the Church of England ministry. Being opposed to the high-churchmanship of Archbishop Laud and because of the oppression of all evangelicals in Britain, he left Bristol for Boston, arriving early in 1630. He ministered in a congregational church until 1635 when he was banished for preaching 'baptist heresy'! He settled in Rhode Island in 1635, founding the baptist church there three years later. After leaving his pastorate, he became a member of the 'seekers', a mystical group akin to the Quakers. He spent his years in the cause of fighting for religious freedom for all men throughout the American States.[9]

Dr John Clarke (1609-76) was born at Westhorpe, Suffolk on 8 October 1609. His father's name was Thomas Clarke and his mother's maiden name was Rose Kerridge. He was one of eight children of whom six were to emigrate to America and settle in New England. John was given a good education in both law and medicine in London and appears to have studied also at the University of Leiden in the Netherlands. He had a 'high repute for scholarship and ability in languages including Latin, Greek and Hebrew and in theology'. He had attended the baptist church pastored by John Spilsbury in London for a time, emigrating to Boston in New England in 1637 being twenty-eight years old. He left Boston with about three hundred colonists to join Williams in Rhode Island, having been persecuted as 'baptists' by the ruling congregational magistrates. They formed a new colony on the Island of Aquidneck in the Narragansett Island in 1638, purchasing it from the Indians. The group had bound themselves as a 'Bodie Politick' in a solemn convenant submitting their 'persons, lives and estates unto our Lord Jesus Christ, the King of kings and Lord of lords, and to all those perfect and most absolute laws of his given in his holy Word of truth, to be guided and judged thereby'. Here Clarke formed the first baptist church in America, moving to Newport at the other end of the Island where a more commodious settlement was possible. Though Williams had a worshipping congregation at Providence before this, it had no creed and was not properly formed as a baptist church. Clarke went to England and ultimately secured from Charles II a colonial charter in 1663 which guaranteed 'full liberty in religious concernments', governing Rhode Island until 1843. Clarke was America's first baptist pastor and the founder of an expanding movement which was to become the largest non-roman catholic group of churches in the United States. He died on 20 April 1676. With Roger Williams, Clarke had worked continuously for religious freedom and has been called the 'first great exponent of Soul Liberty' a phrase which remains associated with his honoured name.[10]

Dr Henry Dunster was the first president of Harvard

and was greatly admired for his successful leadership in establishing this important educational centre. However, admiration stood for nothing when he became a baptist. He was immediately dismissed. He was probably the greatest living authority on oriental languages in his day and gave Harvard twenty years brilliant service. The shock of dismissal occasioned his premature death five weeks later.[11]

The formation of Associations, that typical characteristic of baptist life in the Old Country, began in America in simple meetings called for fellowship and worship. Increasing persecution of the baptists, however, provoked the need for collective assistance to resist such oppression where the religious establishment was unrelenting. The cluster of five churches around Philadelphia formed the first association, called the Philadelphia Association in 1707. By 1743, there were nine such churches and they formally adopted the London Confession of Faith 1689 with small adjustments. It was printed by that remarkable American, Benjamin Franklin! **Elias Keach**, the son of Benjamin Keach, the prominent London pastor, who had shared in the drawing up of that original, came to America as an unbeliever but was given opportunities to preach on the strength of his father's reputation! However, he was converted, baptised and became the pastor of the Pennepack church in the Philadelphia Association. It was Elias who handled the revision and the addition of the two articles (i) No 21 in favour of hymn singing and (ii) No 31 requiring the laying on of hands at baptisms and ordinations. These two additions were those advocated by his father. The appendix on Strict Communion was not included, as indeed it was not in Britain. But the new Article No. 31 did refer to baptism as a prior qualification to admittance to the Lord's Table, doubtless because all American baptist churches practised Strict Communion. This revision of the London Confession became the standard baptist confession in the States and is known as **The Philadelphia Confession of 1743**. The formation of this association led to more effective mission work and the founding of more churches so that 'in 1770 it had so increased as to contain thirty-four churches exclusive of

those which had been detached to form another association'. Association fostered educational and philanthropic
enterprises and strengthened the impact of baptist churches on their communities. The Charleston S. C. Association was next formed in 1751, the Kehukee N. C. in 1765
and the Warren Association in Rhode Island in 1767. As
early as 1729, the General or Arminian baptist churches
formed an association in Rhode Island but the Warren
Association did not grow out of it, the latter being
calvinistic in doctrine.[12]

As in most States, during the colonial period, Virginia
suffered a severely enforced conformity to the Church of
England practice. No one was allowed to teach or preach
publically or privately who was not a communicant
member of this church. Furthermore, no planter could sell
his harvest until he had paid the church tax for the support
of the anglican minister. Such laws remained in force until
1775, except during the Cromwellian Commonwealth
period. In particular, opposers of infant baptism were
picked out for severe treatment. They were taxed,
whipped, hunted with dogs, beaten, poisoned and held
under water until nearly dead. Quakers, as well as baptists,
suffered in this way.[13]

Robert Nordin was sent to minister in Virginia in 1714
and the first baptist church was organised there. Later the
Philadelphia Association churches sent **Shubael Stearns**
and **Daniel Marshall** and the number of baptist churches
in Virginia grew speedily. These two men of God exercised
a most fruitful ministry and their calvinism became the
creed of most of the State's churches. The churches united
to form an association called **The United Baptist Churches
of Christ in Virginia**. The normal description of a church
at that time was 'a baptised church of Christ' and there was
never a doubt that the church members were all baptised.
This must be contrasted with the development of open
membership in Britain referred to elsewhere. Such
prosperity attended these churches that their number had
grown to 227 by 1793 and made up one third of all baptist

churches in the whole of America.[14] As these various groups worked together there arose a tendency to modify the calvinistic element in their confession. This arose chiefly through the impact of General Baptist churches which were affected by the revivals and so began working together with the Particular Baptists in mission. Lumpkin traces the decline in the calvinistic content of doctrine among these churches, commencing with the 1801 Confession of the Union of Kentucky Baptist churches, then the Ten Articles of 1816 and the well known New Hampshire Confession of 1833, which became the standard of the so-called Landmark churches. The progression can be followed on through the Free-Will Baptist confession of 1911, the Southern Baptist Convention of 1925 and the Regular Baptist Association (Northern Secession) of 1933.[15]

The impact of the revivals on the baptist churches during the ministries of **Jonathan Edwards** (1703-58) and the seven visits of **George Whitefield** (1714-70) strengthened the calvinistic nature of the Particular Baptists' doctrine but more importantly, moved some of those in the General Baptist sector towards a moderated calvinism. There were hard-line calvinistic baptist churches formed during this period, such as those which ultimately formed the Primitive Baptist Association, declaring against all revivalist ministries and evangelism at home and abroad. These were akin to the hypercalvinists in England at the same time. By and large, the product was to merge baptists into a moderated calvinism which became reflected in the subsequent confessions as related above from Lumpkin and which has been characteristic of almost all American baptist churches since. It might be well to stop at this point to pay tribute to some of those men whom God used during the period just reviewed.[16]

Isaac Backus (1724-1806) was born into a congregational family at Norwich, Conn., in 1724. He was converted during the Great Awakening in New England in 1841 and, after much hesitancy, joined the local congregational church which took the 'Half-way Covenant' position. That is, it was a mixed membership church, not demanding evidence of regeneracy but allowing those who had ceased to attend regularly at worship and Lord's Supper to retain 'covenantal status', which permitted their children to be baptised as if they were born to believers. Backus condemns the laxity of discipline and lowness of spiritual life in this church. Under the influence of the revival, truly spiritual members began to leave such churches and join, or form, new fellowships demanding a regenerate membership. Backus with fifteen other members withdrew and founded such a 'Separatist' church, as they came to be called. Two years later he formed a similar church in Middlesborough, Mass., before becoming convicted of the New Testament doctrine of baptism for believers only. He was baptised by Elder Periera of Rhode Island and the first baptist church in Middlesborough was commenced. Bitter persecution by the Congregational State Church led to widespread pressure for religious freedom and Backus quickly became a leader in the campaign. In one six month period he travelled three thousand miles and preached one hundred and twenty-five sermons. He lived to see the whole country freed from colonial rule and most States give religious freedom to their citizens... that is... all except Massachusetts, which had been the first to impose religious conformity and was the last to repeal it in 1834. Virginia, once an intolerant anglican stronghold, removed all disabilities as early as 1786.[17] Backus tells how his mother refused to pay church taxes and was violently seized late one cold, wet night and haled to prison where she languished for thirteen nights. At the time, she was ill and her life was risked by such heartless action. It appears that the tax officer deliberately chose that time, believing that she would yield rather than risk her life. Backus has preserved for us the letter she wrote to her children as she triumphed by faith over adversity. Listen to her brave words, 'O the condescension of heaven! Though I was bound when cast into this furnace yet I was loosed and found Jesus in the midst with me!' Backus published forty-four books including a three volume 'History of the Baptists' and he earned the admiration of his successors for his precise accuracy.[18] Throughout the nineteenth century, the American baptist scene produced many outstanding preachers, pastors and evangelists. It was a century of immense growth. One such minister was...

Richard Fuller (1804-76) had graduated from Harvard law school and established a profitable legal practice by the time of his conversion in 1831. Speaking of his overwhelming experience of Christ as his Saviour at that time, he said, 'My soul ran over the love and joy and praise; for days I could neither eat nor sleep'. He gave up his profession and became the pastor of a small church which under his leadership grew to 2,600 members of which twelve out of every thirteen were black. His ministry stressed the authority of scripture and the importance of a close walk with Christ. When he preached it was as though he had come from the presence of God, says Armitage. His personal discipline and effective example came from a solemn sense of his being altogether his Master's man.[19]

John Leland (1754-1841) was born at Grafton, Mass., and was baptised at Bellingham in 1774, two years before the Revolutionary War. He joined and became the pastor of the Mount Poney baptist church in Culpepper county. He spent fifteen years evangelising Virginia, baptising seven hundred persons on a confession of faith. He was a calvinist but would not be bound by the inhibitions of Gill. The correct way of addressing sinners exercised his tender spirit constantly but he says that at one time when he was preaching, his 'soul got into the trade winds' and he forgot Fuller and Gill and all the controversies and five hearers were saved. There was nothing sensational about his preaching but a tender unction which led sinners to the atoning Lamb. He fought the last battles for religious liberty and saw Isaac Backus life's work through to completion. Baptists rose as a man during the war and suffered consequently from the British who destroyed their meeting houses and harried their flocks wherever they triumphed. The baptists came out of that trial with religious freedom as well as liberty for the colonies. Those desiring to follow the baptists through that campaign will find much interesting reading in Armitage's '*History of the*

Baptists' or the '*History of the Baptists in Virginia*' by Robert
Baylor Semple.

Adoniram Judson (1788-1850) and his wife, **Ann
Heseltine**, were sent to India in 1812 as America's first
overseas missionaries. En route, they were converted to the
truth of believers' baptism and were immersed on arrival in
India. They resigned immediately from the paedobaptist
society that had sent them out and their colleague, **Luther
Rice**, returned to the States to seek support from baptist
churches. The British colonial government opposed the
setting up of the mission in Bengal and the Judsons sailed
for Rangoon in Burma where they arrived in July 1813.
American baptists sent out four further missionaries to
strengthen the work during the next few years. They
studied the language and then began preaching the gospel
in a hall in 1819. That year the first converts were baptised,
declaring themselves Christ's even though to change
religion was a capital offence in Burma. Judson appealed to
the Emperor in person but was rejected. The work
progressed until war with Britain broke out and the
Judsons were arrested. Expecting the city to be shelled,
Judson and a colleague were prepared for beheading in a
public place with the executioner being instructed to let his
axe fall the moment the first shots were fired into the city.
In fact the executioner was so scared when that happened
that he ran away. The missionaries were returned to
prison. Progress in Burma was very slow but, when the land
to the north was ceded to Britain, openings occurred to
preach the gospel there. The Karen people responded to
the gospel in considerable numbers and some thousands
were saved. Judson translated the Bible into Burmese and
into five other languages as well. He died convalescing at
sea in April 1854.[21]

American baptists responded to the awakened awareness
of the need of the pagan world for gospel preaching and
they sent their missionaries everywhere in increasing
numbers. Earnest missionary zeal has marked baptist
outreach right up to the present time. In Britain, we have
benefitted by the flow of consecrated men coming here

since World War II ended. God graciously overruled the posting of American servicemen here during the war years in order to stir up many christians among them to serve the Lord in pagan Britain. From the time of Judson until now, there has been a growing stream of dedicated American baptist missionaries going into all the world.

Looking back a little, the formation of the **Philadelphia Association** in 1707 started a sequence of such associations being formed as the number of baptist churches increased and the whole country was ultimately evangelised from coast to coast. In the south in 1845, the **Southern Baptist Convention** was formed. Though this body has not been altogether faithful to its biblical foundations, it has become the largest body of baptists in the world. This grouping has been the strongest of all baptist bodies working for world evangelisation and has funded by far the greatest number of missionary projects in the world. The northern states produced the Northern Convention which later was renamed the **American Baptist Convention** but this grouping has drifted into liberalism and has lost momentum as a spiritutal force. It has been overtaken by the Southern Convention which now is eight times larger. There have been many secessions on doctrinal grounds and because of various contoversies. It is said that there are about forty different kinds of baptists in the States today. The principle independent baptist groups, which have adhered to the historic faith are the **Northern (Negro) Baptist Association**, **The Regular Baptist Convention** and the **Bible Baptist Fellowship**. Each possesses its own organisation and all maintain extensive missionary work at home and overseas.[22]

The old '**Landmark**' baptists gathered their churches into a new 'American Baptist Association' and in 1950 numbered two hundred thousand members. Their confession ceased to contain any distinct doctrine of the atonement, that is, neither General or Particular Redemption, but stated that the crucifixion and suffering of Jesus Christ was vicarious and substitutionary. The same characteristic is found in the seceders of 1950 who formed the 'North American Baptist Association.' The 'Goodchild' or 'Conservative Baptist Association Confession' of 1947 says that 'Christ made atonement for the sins of the whole word.' Similarly, the articles of the 'Bible Baptist Union of America' are universalist. The '1963 Statement' of the 'Southern Baptist Convention' gives a fuller atonement article in which redemption is related to the believer and so avoids either a 'general' or 'particular' position, but it does recognise 'election' specifically and takes note of the 'sovereignty of God' in other aspects of salvation. It cannot be called 'calvinistic' and probably expressed the elimination of a 'limited atonement' from mainline American baptist articles of faith.

Landmarkism arose among the Southern Convention baptist churches as a conviction that the only true New Testament churches were baptist churches, all others being mere human societies. Similarly, its advocates asserted that only baptist ministers were validly ordained gospel ministers. They ruled that their ministers should not preach in any other pulpits, nor ought the ministers of other denominations to preach in baptist pulpits. The popular slogans of the movement were 'Non-affiliation in pulpit ministry, and 'non-pulpit affiliation.' They rejected the validity of baptisms, even by immersion, by ministers other than baptists. They went so far as to claim a direct succession in the ordination of baptist ministers back to John Baptist. They counted valid the actions of the local church only, refusing increasingly to co-operate with conventional decisions. There are those in the late twentieth century who still adhere to these views and they are generally found in the non-conventional of the south.[23]

The **Dutch Mennonites** first emigrated to America in 1643, arriving at New York. They have become in the main paedobaptist churches and have spread throughout North America with pockets in Canada, including the 'Amish' sect in Ontario. They have also set up colonies in Paraguay in South America. They retain some of their 'anabaptist' characteristics, especially their pacifism. They have been industrious workers wherever they have settled, as indeed they were in Europe. They have been very successful in mental health ministries and in agriculture. A full account is to be found in Smith's Mennonite History.[24]

The ties between British baptists and those of North

American have remained close despite the War of Independence. Indeed all but two of the Particular Baptist ministers in Britain at the time sent their fraternal encouragement to the 'rebels'. British baptists sent books for their ministers in 1717 as well as later. The baptist churches of Rhode Island were visited by the non-baptist Whitefield during his evangelistic campaigns and great growth followed. The strengthened churches founded Rhode Island College, now known as Brown University. In the constitution of 1764, provision was made for one third of the fellows and the Trustees to be other than baptists. The membership of these churches doubled in the ten years to 1774.[26]

Speaking of the growth in numerical strength among the baptist churches of North America, it is astonishing to note the remarkable progress, in view of their starting as the oppressed minority in twelve out of the first thirteen States. There were thirteen baptist churches in the Colonies in 1688, of which seven were in Rhode Island but by 1740 there were thirty-seven churches with three thousand members. In 1790 the total membership had grown to 6,500. Twenty-five new churches were founded during the first half of the eighteenth century and in the second half the increase was 825 new churches. In 1886, there were 28,953 baptist churches and today the published figure for baptist church members is approaching 50 million, outnumbering all other churches except the Roman Catholics.[27]

During the Civil War of 1861-65, baptists fought on both sides and both claimed that 'God was with them' expressing their convictions in their battle hymns. For the North Julia Ward wrote: '*God's truth is marching on!*' While for the South the Confederates sang, '*Lay Thou their legions low, Roll back the ruthless foe; Let the proud spoiler know, God is on our side.*' The surrender of the South to the North brought little reconciliation but most negroes became baptists as they enjoyed their freedom. No doubt they recognised that 'freedom' was a principle for which all baptists had struggled from the very foundation of the nation. The folk traditions of the 'south', together with negro influence, contributed largely to the emergence of the distinctly

'American sacred song' and its typical emphasis on congregational singing.[28]

The American baptist churches have provided a great incentive for church evangelism the world over. They have also given to the world a series of remarkable evangelists such as **Billy Graham**, who reflects in his ecumenical missionary endeavours the breadth of doctrinal development among them. He shares his platform with church leaders which no baptist would have done in earlier centuries. He preaches the gospel in fulfilment of the 'Great Commission' but it is shorn of its precept to baptise converts. Yet, despite these departures from the historic baptist position, he preaches 'The Bible says...' retaining, as the great bulk of American baptists have, the conviction that the Word of God is the christian's sole authority.

Canada

Baptist witness in Canada began in the Maritime Provinces of Nova Scotia and New Brunswick, the former being the first province to come under British rule in 1713. An unknown Dutchman was the first to bring a baptist testimony to Canada when he came and preached in 1752 at Lunenburg, to a colony of French and German settlers. In 1758, the provincial government declared the Church of England to be established but it allowed freedom of worship to other christians, Roman Catholics excepted. Colonists from New England emigrated to Nova Scotia in 1760 and set up their baptist church at Sackville in 1763 but they returned to New England in 1771 and this church ceased. **Nathan Mason** was its pastor and leader.[29] **Henry Alline** (1736-84), a 'New Light' preacher, campaigned as an evangelist, after the style of Whitefield, and was greatly used to promote a spiritual revival and in the founding of many new churches. He was born in Newport, Rhode Island and came to Nova Scotia in 1760. He had been converted at twenty-seven years and was a congregationalist. He seldom baptised but was willing that his members should be immersed if they so desired. The churches he formed were really congregational though some have considered them 'open-membership baptist churches'. After some years, Armitage says, 'numbers of them appeared to have seen the need for greater conformity to gospel faith and practice and at first resolved themselves into baptist churches practising open communion.'[30] These 'Alline' churches were by far the strongest of the baptist churches. The Horton church, founded in 1778 with Rev. N. Pearson as minister, was one of these. Alline died 36 years old in 1784. The first association was formed at Granville in 1800 with six member churches, all except Halifax having open communion. The association took responsibility for the appointment and ordination of ministers until 1827 when this was handed back to the churches. During the last half of the eighteenth century and the first half of the nineteenth there were some notable preachers such as **Theodore and Harris Harding**, **Edward Manning**, **Joseph Crandall**, **Thomas H. Chipman** and **James Manning**, whose fruitful labours built up and strengthened the churches. **Edward Manning** may well have been the most gifted of them all. He also was a convert under the Alline ministry. He used to itinerate, preaching the gospel, often in the depth of winter, travelling in snow shoes from place to place. His first pastorate was at Cornwallis in 1795; then when he moved to the strict communion church at Annapolis remaining there until his death. Armitage says that Manning 'was imbued with deep piety and a fervency of spirit.' He championed the cause of religious freedom and met the Church of England's intolerance and persecution with the 'firmness of a man born to rule his own spirit'. Another convert of Alline, **Theodore Harding**, was pastor at Horton for sixty years from 1796-1855.[31]

Another notable worker in Canada was **Dr. John Mockett Cramp DD** (1796-1872), who was an Englishman, born at Broadstairs, in Thanet, and baptised in 1812. He was trained for the ministry at the Stepney Institute, London and assisted his father as pastor of the Broadstairs church for fourteen years before moving to Hastings in 1840 as pastor there. In 1844, he crossed the Atlantic to take charge of the Montreal College, being supported by the Canadian Baptist Missionary Society. He moved to

Arcadia College in 1857 and laboured incessantly there until his death. He wrote many books but his *'History of the Baptists'* is the best known.[32]

The Canadian baptists formed the 'Society for the Maintenance of Foreign Missions' in 1838 and sent missionaries to Burma to aid the work started by Judson. Later they also sent men to India. **Dr. Tupper** was the Secretary of this work for many years and gave himself without stint to further the cause. At his Jubilee service, he said that he had travelled 146,000 miles, preached 6,750 sermons and taken part in 3,430 other meetings. He had married 238 couples, conducted 542 funerals and baptised 522 converts. This remarkable man had only ten weeks schooling as a boy yet became proficient in Hebrew, Greek, Latin, French, German, Italian, Syriac and a few other tongues! God greatly honoured the devotion of this Canadian baptist minister.[33]

Home Mission work led to the extension of baptist witness across the whole breadth of the Dominion of Canada from the Atlantic to the Pacific. Baptist churches were based on the London Confession 1677/89 and therefore Calvinistic in salvation doctrine. Free-Will baptists immigrated from the United States and established churches akin to the English General Baptists and received support from the New Connexion baptist churches in Britain. These two streams of baptists merged in 1906.[34] Evangelism among the Micmac Indians of the Maritime Provinces and Quebec was begun by **Dr. Silas Tertius Rand** in 1829 and he worked among them for forty years, giving them the scriptures in their own tongue.[35] The first baptist church in Ontario was founded in 1776 at Beamsville, near the Niagara Falls and had an American origin. The first in Quebec was commenced at Caldwall Manor in 1794 and was followed by churches at Hallimand (1798) and Phillipsville (1803). A church of 'Scottish Baptists' was founded at Eaton with **John Gilmore** of Aberdeen as pastor. This church developed a strong 'Brethren' characteristic. Churches in the provincial capitals, Toronto and Montreal, were founded in 1828 and 1830 respectively. There was also a group of strongly calvinistic baptist churches, almost all of Scottish origin, derived from the ministry of the Haldanes.[36]

Having noted the forming of a baptist church in Toronto, mention must be made of a remarkable baptist layman whose beneficence enabled much forward work to be done. **William McMaster** was born in Tyrone, Ireland, in 1811, received a good English private school education and arrived in Canada in 1833 and soon became a prosperous merchant. His commercial success led to a life in public service, including Parliament, and he was greatly honoured by the young nation. McMaster financed the Baptist Home Mission Society and the college which was to become the McMaster University.[37] In 1851, there was some reorganisation of the Canadian baptist churches and the Regular Baptist Missionary Society was formed and Regular baptist churches separated, identifying themselves with the historic baptist standard with its calvinistic doctrine of salvation and with fundamental church-manship.

With the colonisation of the vast hinterland, a great variety of ethnic groups set up nationalistic communities and in some cases established their own churches. A Swiss church came into being at Grand Ligne, Quebec and early became baptist. It reached out with the gospel among other Swiss groups, establishing churches. Similarly, German and Dutch churches were formed and, as mentioned earlier, Mennonites also arrived and set up their communi-ties bringing with them their particular brand of 'Amish' anabaptist practices.

The President of McMaster University and minister of Bond Street baptist church, Toronto, **Dr, J. H. Castle** built the beautiful Jarvis Street church.[38] This church later withdrew its support for the McMaster University when liberal influences were admitted there. The Jarvis Street church built its own Theological Seminary during the pastorate of **Dr. T. T. Shields** (1890-1955). This remains a biblically orientated training college for the baptist ministry and has prepared men of many nationalities whose ministries have spread round the globe. There has been some fragmentation of the Baptist Churches in Canada. **Regular Baptist Churches** represent the most conservative in doctrine and practice and the **Fellowship Baptist**

Churches are generally keen evangelicals though not so distinctive in doctrine nor as separatist. The churches of the **Canadian Baptist Union** comprise the bulk of the others with considerable variety in their characteristics and tendency towards liberal theology. These latter are affiliated to the Baptist World Alliance and the World Council of Churches, whilst the others are not.

The Caribbean and Central American Republics

Jamaica was discovered by Christopher Columbus in 1494 and it was ruled by Spain until 1655, when the British captured it. The Spanish enforced the catholic faith, whilst the British brought the Church of England as an establishment. An American negro preacher, **George Lisle**, together with **Moses Baker**, began evangelising the island in 1783 and founded churches. The Baptist Missionary Society sent missionaries there in 1814 and very considerable spiritual growth developed among the negro population. Baptists became the largest religious body, outstripping both the residual catholics and the anglicans. They suffered as a consequence when the negro population struggled to secure a reasonable degree of freedom and standard of living in the two insurrections of 1831 and 1865. Baptist missionaries were arrested and imprisoned as collaborators with the rebels. The baptist church memberships trebled between those two dates to above thirty thousand. **William Knibb** (1803-1845), a B.M.S. missionary sent out to Jamaica from the Kettering church at twenty-one years of age, did the most to secure the final abolition of slavery in British dominions, according to Underwood.[39] The planters opposed the missionaries vehemently, flogging their converts and burning their homes and chapels. Knibb toured Britain pleading for 'abolition' and succeeded in securing the liberty of his negro brothers by Act of Parliament. The day fixed was 1st August 1838 and back in his land of adoption among the enslaved people he loved, Knibb led the rejoicing as their freedom became a fact. Underwood relates how a coffin was made containing 'the whips, branding irons and other badges of slavery and screwed down' and buried. At the midnight hour as the day of freedom dawned, he cried, 'The hour is at hand; the monster slavery is dying! The monster is dead! let us bury him! The negro is free!'[40] Today, the baptists dominate the country though they have divided up into many groupings, particularly as pentecostal influence has spread among them.

American baptists have been responsible for the spread of the evangelical message in the other islands, founding baptist churches in **Cuba**, **Haiti**, the **Bahamas** and elsewhere. Throughout the Caribbean islands today there are over thirteen hundred baptist churches, very many with large memberships. However, in some islands the catholic faith still dominates; in others, such as in **Puerto Rico**, the baptist churches remain weak because of the financial dependence upon their American mother churches.[41]

Mexico was colonised by the Spanish and annexed by them in 1519. It regained its independence in 1821 and is today a republic, its capital city being the fastest growing metropolitan city with the world's largest population. The Spaniards imposed the catholic faith which still dominates the religious scene even though its power was greatly limited by the independence wars because it stood against the republican movement. The last century has seen the most amazing growth of protestant churches, mostly of a baptist type though predominantly pentecostal in character. The National Council of Christian Churches formed in 1921 to unite the protestant churches excluded the baptists, who typically remained apart. Today there are about twenty-five million evangelical christians in Mexico.[42]

Similarly, the mainland republics south of Mexico have been areas of catholic prevalence for the same reasons. Non-catholic missionaries began working in these lands during the nineteenth century and American baptist and pentecostal influence has steadily grown since the beginning of the present century. In general there is religious freedom today because of the British and American

influence. It is said that there are about three hundred and
fifty baptist churches with a membership of about thirty
thousand believers spread through the **Central American
Republics**. Most of the missionary work has been done by
undenominational societies, resulting in the emergence of
evangelical churches of considerable variety in character.
Such a situation has made possible the ravaging of their
witness by cults and sects, heterodox in nature, and which
are present in strength throughout the area.[43]

South America

The countries of South America were discovered, colonised and exploited by Spain and Portugal and the Roman
Catholic faith was imposed in all cases. The catholic faith
has retained a large measure of loyalty of the population
though it has accommodated itself to the primitive animism
of the American Indian peoples. More recently it has
adopted the charismatic features of the indigenous
pentecostalism which has been the outstanding development on the religious scene in South America in this
century.

    Brazil, which is a Portuguese speaking nation, has the
largest baptist community with about three thousand five
hundred churches and nearly half-a-million church members. The movements for national liberation of the last
century not only gave the people their national identity but
also a love for individual freedom which spilled over into
religious philosophies. This has produced the characteristic distinctiveness of South American churches which have
a strong indigenous nature. Self-governing churches of
baptist type appealed to their liberated souls. Baptist
churches were formed when numbers of Southern Baptists
from the United States emigrated to Brazil following their
loss of the Civil War.

    Chile received its first missionaries from Southern
Baptist churches in the United States in 1917 and the
emergence of similar churches there is of a more recent
date. Baptists churches number now about 166 churches
with 14,000 members. There is a similar number in **Bolivia**

though the total membership is lower. Waldensian émigrés came to **Uraguay** during the 1850s and Mennonites entered **Paraguay** during the same period and have formed their own communities there. Recently there has been talk of the amalgamation of the latter with the liberal Methodists which indicates the extent of their departure from their anabaptist heritage.[44]

Argentina was evangelised by Swiss baptists who had emigrated from their homeland in the mid-1850s. They sent for a baptist minister and **Paul Besson** answered their call. His influence not only extended to the formation of baptist churches in that country but was instrumental in the removal of many of the catholic-imposed restrictions on non-catholic christians, including the right of christian burial. His story must now be told as one of the outstanding missionary stories from the South American continent. There are four hundred baptist churches in Argentina with twenty-five thousand members.

Paul Besson (1848-1932) was a remarkable Swiss who was used extensively for the founding of baptist churches in Argentina. The Swiss Anabaptists of the sixteenth century were very active evangelists and set an example for all baptists to follow. Besson achieved just such a work in South America. He was born in 1848 at Nods in Canton Bern, his father being a French-speaking minister of the Swiss Reformed Church and his mother from Waldensian stock. He entered theological college at Neuchatel in order to follow in his father's steps. He trained under Professor F. Godet and others before going on to Leipzig and Basel universities and was ordained pastor at Liniers, Neuchatel in 1871. Almost at once, he was involved in Godet's controversy, arguing for the separation of Church and State, and he resigned his living as the price of obeying his conscience. Already baptist principles were stirring in his heart and he began itinerant preaching of the gospel including that 'baptism was for believers only' and was himself immersed as a believer whilst ministering in Lyons in France. Whilst here he was twice imprisoned for his evangelistic activities. As a convinced baptist, he would not 'ask permission of civil authorities to preach the gospel', being convinced that the State had no rights in spiritual matters, which were between the believer and his Lord.

After working six years in France for the American Baptist Mission Board, he followed some members of his church to Argentina to preach the gospel where there was great need. He arrived in Buenos Aires in 1881 completely penniless and immediately began preaching the gospel among the colonies of Swiss and French settlers as an itinerant. He became rapidly known as an agitator for religious freedom. Liberty to practise religion according as each man's conscience demanded was guaranteed by the constitution of the republic but in practice such liberty was not permitted, due to the stranglehold of the Roman Catholic church on the police. Marriage and burial was limited to that church and all dissenters from it either had to conform or lose out. In 1853, he founded the first baptist church in Buenos Aires and remained its pastor for forty years. He was a scholarly preacher but also exceedingly fervent, possessing a powerful voice and commanding the attention of his hearers. He translated the New Testament from Greek into South American Spanish. One of his successful battles with the State was the provision of public cemetries for the burial of non-catholics. When his fruitful ministry came to an end in 1932, his mortal remains were laid to rest in just such a cemetery in Buenos Aires. His ministry of over fifty years in Argentina was immensely important in laying a strong evangelical basis for the development of baptist churches and for his tremendously useful struggle to secure freedom for all evangelical witness in that country.[45]

12
The baptist in Africa

The Donatists, with their distinctly baptist type testimony, thrived in the Northern civilised areas of Africa during and after the fourth century though their witness was almost extinguished by persecution engendered by Rome. The rise of Islam in the seventh century and its rapid spread throughout **North Africa** diminished christian witness in the Arab countries. Throughout these seven states today there is little indigenous christian testimony. In **Egypt** and the **Sudan**, undenominational missions have established churches of independent evangelical character, though some are baptistic. There is one baptist church in **Libya** and three in **Algeria**, eight in Egypt but none in **Tunisia**. South of the Sahara there are forty-one separate nations with six off-shore island countries. British and American missionaries have worked in **Nigeria** since the early nineteenth century. At present there are about 900 baptist churches with about 150,000 baptised members in Nigeria. Nearby **Liberia** was evangelised by American negro baptists from 1852 and today there are 25,000 baptist believers there. British baptists worked in the **Camerouns** where today there are 16,000 church members.[1] **Alfred Saker** from the Strict Baptist church at Borough Green went to the Camerouns in 1844 and a survey of his life and work will serve to highlight the typical missionary's labours in founding christian churches in West Africa.

Alfred Saker (c1815-80) was born at Borough Green, the youngest son of the village millwright and engineer. He was frail of body but possessed a brilliant mind which was early evident to his parents who did their best to give him as good an education as limited local resources could provide. He was sent to Sevenoaks to stay for sixteen months and was converted one Sunday when, hearing a hymn from the baptist chapel, he entered and heard God's Word preached. *'All have sinned and come short of the glory of God.'* The visiting preacher went on to lead sinners to Christ for salvation. Alfred had come to know Christ as his Saviour whilst fifteen years old and began to serve him as his Master, as he was to do with such amazing commitment for fifty years to come. Returning home, he began attending the Borough Green Baptist chapel where Mr Bolton was pastor and he commenced to teach a Sunday school class almost at once. Later he became the Superintendent but was not baptised until 1834. He moved to Devonport Dockyard for work and attended Morice Square baptist church there. He married Helen Jessup in 1840, the stalwart christian woman who would share his pioneering lifework in Africa.

The Baptist Missionary Society sent Mr and Mrs Sturgeon to Fernando Po, the Spanish island colony in the Bight of Biafra, to commence mission work there and there came an urgent call for help which was told at mission meetings in Devonport chapel. The Sakers offered to go to Africa and were accepted, arriving on 16 February 1844 with three other couples, travelling via Jamaica, where one couple stayed. They settled at Fernando Po in Clarence, joining the workers already established there. Saker commenced evangelising on the mainland of the Camerouns (=prawns are plentiful!) 10 March 1845 taking with him a converted African ex-slave, Thomas Horton Johnson who was to be his close colleague for years afterwards. They set up a station called 'Bethel' among the Duallas and set out to learn the language. He taught at first in the broken English that the traders had brought to the people. But Saker quickly mastered the local language and reduced it to writing. The first native convert was baptised 5 November 1849 and a little church formed that day was the first in the Camerouns. The first six missionaries that joined Saker died from the disease ridden climate. The colony was called, 'The White Man's Grave'. In four years the church grew to twenty-four and in eight years there were over one hundred converts. Saker's health suffered and one child was lost and Mrs Saker had to return to England. Yet he laboured on against the opposition of the pagan chiefs and their witch doctors and God gave his servant the increase in a spiritual harvest.

When the Spanish ordered all non-catholics to leave Fernando Po, Saker bodily moved all christians to a new settlement on the mainland at Victoria which he himself built on unoccupied land. He equipped it with steam sawmill, printshop, brick-kiln and rules for community life. In time, it was to become an established British administrative centre. For the first time christians had a 'quiet Sunday' in which to worship. Saker translated the whole Bible into Dualla and actually printed it in his own works. His daughter supervised the setting and proof reading and natives did the printing. Utterly worn out, Alfred Saker died 13 March 1880. Baptist work is maintained by British and French baptists.[2]

Southern Africa

The first baptist church in **South Africa** was founded in 1820 at Grahamstown by the baptists among four thousand picked immigrants who were settled there. Whiteley says that the tree where the carpenter conducted the first service is still shown to visitors. The next baptist work occurred when disbanded German soldiers were settled in Kaffaria after the end of the Crimean War.[3] **Hugo Gutsche**, one of Oncken's Hamburg students joined them as pastor and many other Germans emigrated to build up the work. This German baptist church commenced work among the native population in 1888 with **Carl Pape** as missionary and within four years there was a native evangelist at work with him. The earlier work was financed from Britain by the Baptist Missionary Society and in 1894, when a group of Australians volunteered for service in South Africa, since which time the co-operation between the two countries has continued. A South African mission enterprise arose to reach the workers in the gold fields. This was sponsored from Britain and extended its ministries considerably. American baptists provided a Telugu speaking missionary to work among the immigrant workers from India which has led to the establishment of churches in Natal. Some ministry has been maintained among Tamil speaking Indians also. Baptists in South Africa have opposed apartheid in contemporary times and it is obvious that their own very existence has been from many races from the first. There are about a quarter million baptists in the Republic today, seventy per cent of which are non-whites.[4]

Malawi, formerly called **Nyasaland**, became one of the earliest missionary fields of the Australian baptist churches when they sent workers there in 1890s, whilst **Zimbabwe (Rhodesia)** was first missioned from South Africa in 1905. The British Baptist Missionary Society sent workers into **Angola**, then a Portuguese colony, in 1878. They established a Mission base in San Salvador and evangelised the northern parts of the country. American baptists commenced their ministry there in 1880, based themselves at Bihe and majored on the southern half of the country.[5]

Zaire, former Belgian **Congo**, received its first baptist missionary in 1877 when two missionaries from the Camerouns were transferred to work there. The Germans had invaded the British Camerouns and expelled their nationals. Those two pioneers in the Congo were **George Grenfell** (1849-1906) and **Thomas J. Comber** (1852-1887). The former did some remarkable exploration work and remained an authority on the northern Congo for years to come. The latter died ten years after arriving there. These pioneers were joined by others shortly afterwards and Congo became a prominent mission field for baptist work.[6]

H. Holman Bentley (1855-1906) worked tirelessly at linguistic work, reducing the native language to writing, compiling a dictionary and shaping a grammar. He also completed the translation of the New Testament. The Congo exacted a heavy price for its missionaries because of its many health hazards.[7] In more recent times, missionaries suffered massacres during the Lamumba rebellion of 1964-65. The present regime has 'nationalised' christian churches and made the separate work of baptist churches difficult though not impossible. Some who escaped death, have returned to continue to work there, including **Margaret Hayes** whose story she tells in her book.[8] Belgian baptists are relatively few in number but they have not forgotten their former colony. Pastor **Bron-Jens Berge**, formerly of Brussels, has paid frequent visits to the baptists in the Kivu province to encourage their pastors and to hold bible training courses.

The Southern Baptists sent two negro baptist missionaries to **Liberia** in 1821 and today the baptists form the largest christian communion in this country, its president being a church member. These early American baptist missionaries were **Lott Carey** and **Colin Teague** and they laid a fine foundation even though the former lost his American Missions Board support over a policy disagreement. Lott Carey wanted to persevere when others would have retrenched. Lott Carey's own name became attached for a long time to the indigenous baptist movement in Liberia.[9]

Nigeria was first missioned by non-baptists in the early years of its colonisation by Britain. The name of Mary Slessor will always be recalled. The first baptists were Americans from neighbouring Liberia, Southern Baptist missionaries in 1849. **Thomas Bower** was the pioneer but he died after but one year's labour in Nigeria.[10]

Madagascar, the large island off Africa's east coast, has not been neglected by baptists. There was a phenominal growth of christianity in the nineteenth century but it was the catholics who gave the Malagassies their first bible in their own tongue. Today, there is a small baptist presence in Madagascar and French baptist workers from both the Federation and Association churches support it.[11]

13
The baptist in Asia and Australasia

India

India was reached by christian evangelists in the first or second century of the christian era, traditionally by the **Apostle Thomas**. Today there is a christian community which claims continuity from the beginning, known as 'Mar Thoma", with a quarter million membership.[1] Roman catholic missionaries have also witnessed through the centuries but modern missionary work is usually said to have begun in India with the arrival of **William Carey** in 1798. But this is not strictly correct, for this honour rests with Danish Lutherans and the German missionary they sent to the Malabar Coast of southern India in 1706. **Bartholomew Ziegenbalg** (1683-1719) laboured for thirty-six years and achieved a solid foundation for those that followed after.[2] He and his colleague, **Henry Plutscho**[3] established a church, schools and a print shop. They issued a substantial amount of literature in Tamil, thirty-two works in all, including a New Testament. Additionally, they issued fourteen books in Portuguese, the 'lingua franca' of southern India, the Portuguese having been the first to colonise it. **Christian Schwartz** (1726-98),[4] also sent out by the Danish Mission worked in India from 1750 until his death in 1798. William Carey was certainly the first baptist missionary and his work laid the foundation for the modern missionary movement's methodology. The base set up at Serampore, with its schools, press and Indian Bible Society, became the centre of a worldwide outreach. Forty versions of the scriptures in Asian tongues were produced and an effective source of back-up

213

for Asian ministries provided.[5] American, Canadian and Australian baptists followed in his wake and baptist missionary commitment to the Sub-continent was prodigious from that beginning. Today there are 6,500 baptist churches in India with 800,000 members, still but a small fraction of the vast population of the country. The Baptist Missionary Society, which commenced with Carey, Fuller and Booth, continues to be a major instrument in gospel outreach in India. The Strict Baptists also made India their major field of operation. Their society, which is a church-based entity, formerly known by their name, is now called 'Grace Baptist Mission' and began work in India in 1861 and has continuously sustained a gospel mission among the Tamil speaking peoples of South India and also in Malaysia.[6]

Sri Lanka has today about five thousand baptists, mostly among the Tamil-speaking citizens. Work in this island, formerly known as Ceylon, was begun by Dutch reformed church missionaries in mid-eighteenth century. The internal tension between the ruling tribe of Singhalese and the Tamils has restrained all missionary extension work.[7]

Pakistan and **Bangladesh** have mainly Muslim populations and christian evangelism has been difficult, especially in the former which claims to be an Islamic state. There is only a small baptist presence in Pakistan but a somewhat larger group of baptists in Bangladesh, which are found particularly in the north of the country. They number about fifty thousand.[8]

Independent Baptists gave support to the Baptist Missionary Society in its work in India from its inception. In fact, the Baptist Union had not been formed and all British Particular Baptists, whether strict communionist or not, joined hands in sending Carey and others into the sub-continent. In the Tamil-speaking country of the south-east, an Indian christian named **John Christian Arulappen** (1810-67) who had received a missionary school education, commenced a gospel ministry which was formed into a church of baptised believers in 1840 in Sivagasi in the Rhamnad District. Though much persecuted, this little baptist church prospered and Arulappi was able to leave it in charge of a local preacher and travel further afield, forming other baptist centres. Certain Strict Baptist churches in Britain supported his labours as also did some christian brethren assemblies. This work dispersed when Arulappen died, some properties being passed by his family to the anglican 'Church Missionary Society' and some became associated with the christian brethren movement. However, the ground work of the Strict Baptist Mission's work in South India can be attributed to this indigenous evangelism of Arulappen.[9]

The independent work in India of the **'Strict Baptist Mission'** was born in the vestry of the central London baptist church in Keppel Street near Covent Garden in 1861 and in the following year it was shaped into a nationwide mission. An Anglo-Indian, **Henry Fenwick** was appointed the first missionary and he commenced his work at Tulleygaum, a populous village between Bombay and Poona. Just prior to this, a British soldier, **Mr A Wilson**, had formed a baptised church in Chintadripet in Madras and an Anglo-Indian brother, **Mr H. F. Doll**, a civil servant, was sent out by this church to preach in various places. Mr Doll became the supervisor of the Mission's work on the field and through his leadership a baptised Brahmin convert, **Coopoosawmy Row** began a church in Poonamalee and other workers were entrusted with extending the ministry. None of these early workers was a 'Missionary sent from England' but all the work was being done by residents working in their own areas though supported from the United Kingdom financially. The work expanded into the Tinnevelli district and into Ceylon as well as expanding throughout the Madras area.[10]

Samuel Hutchinson and **Ernest Alfred Booth** were the first missionaries to be sent out from the British churches to join the indigenous work in South India and they sailed in February 1895 since which time a succession of workers from the home churches have joined hands to strengthen the work. With the advent of **David Morling** (1879-1942) the mission field was extended into Salem District and several churches were founded there. With the end of the Second Great War, the mission took action to strengthen the indigenous leadership of the churches but it was not until 1969 that the Mission's work and all its property trusts were transferred to Indian leaders and the whole ministry was indianised. From that time there has been a constant reduction in expatriate staff and it is foreseen that in a few years there will be no foreigners engaged directly in the Indian missionary ministry.[11]

The Strict Baptist Mission opened and maintained several schools, some at higher elementary level, but mostly at simple elementary grades in villages. The number of schools in 1956 was forty-two with 4,220 scholars. Hostels were opened for children and young people and extensive medical work was maintained in which **Dr Ruth M Harris** principally figured together with numerous trained nurses who formed a Ladies Zenana Auxiliary of the mission. The world-authority on leprosy treatment, **Dr Paul Brand**, was the child of SBM missionaries and the great burden of his useful life was born in the midst of missionary life in India.[12]

The Mission has gained the support of many independent baptists, particularly of those that maintain the old confessional commitment to the doctrines of grace. To reflect this broad backing and to mark the successful transition of its policies into a fully church-based movement whereby it is not in any sense a 'missionary society' but a specialist aid to the evangelistic outreach of local churches which maintain complete independence, the name of the growing international work has been renamed '**Grace Baptist Mission**'. Today it services missionaries working around the world, on behalf of numerous independent baptist churches, but its first hundred years work was entirely in India and Ceylon (Sri Lanka).

David Morling (1879-1942) was born in Ipswich on 12 November 1879, his father being the pastor of Zoar baptist church in that town. He was called to go as a missionary worker to India whilst his father was a pastor at High Wycombe of which his wife was also a member. He left for India in 1903, commencing his work in the Madras area but soon the up-country need claimed him as a pioneer missionary in the Salem District where he founded a church in Sendamangalam. He assisted Missionary Brand in further pioneer work on the Kolli Hills and later he founded the church in Namakkal town and others in villages along the Cauvery River. In 1929, he took charge of the Tinnevelli field and commenced the Tamil Baptist Bible Institute, being its principal from 1927-1941. He was the author of several books including '*A Short History of the Baptists in India*', '*Studies in baptism*' and '*Pioneering on the Cauvery*'. Mrs Olive Morling gave considerable assistance in the work of the Bible Institute and in training Biblewomen. She wrote '*Light in Hindu Homes*'. A considerable amount of Tamil literature was produced during this period.[13]

David Thrower (1900-85) completed sixty-three years of missionary work in India and gained such high regard as an authority on the Tamil language that he served on examination boards in that capacity. He was also a keen botanist and was regarded by the Royal Botanical Gardens, Kew, as a principal source of specialist information on plant-life of the sub-continent. He and his wife, née Martina Watts, were both members of the Courland Grove baptist church, Clapham in SW London. They shared a common love for the people of India which kept them there as residents to the ends of their useful lives. David Thrower produced a great deal of Tamil literature but his magnum opus was a Bible Concordance in Tamil which has seen five editions and is the only work of its kind ever produced. The Indian pastors and congregations loved them both, knowing well that they held first place in the affections of these two utterly devoted christians who had long since ceased to be 'foreign missionaries' but had merged completely into the Indian scene and culture.

Burma and **Assam** were among the early fields of baptist witness in South-East Asia. The commencement of work in Burma has been told already in the course of reviewing the missionary work of Judson. His greatest impact was in the northern lands and it is in Assam that most baptist churches are to be found today. Altogether in Burma there are thirty-two thousand baptised believers gathered in nearly three thousand baptist churches today.[14]

China

China has the largest population of any country in the world
and boasts an ancient civilisation. The Christian missionaries first
reached Peking in the mid-sixteenth century and were Jesuits
who established a relationship with the Emperor for
residence and limited opportunities to teach. Matteo Ricci
was the best known of the various French, Spanish,
Portuguese and Italian priests who laboured to build up a
catholic church there. A Chinese bishop was appointed to the
see of Nanking in 1680 when it was claimed there were three
hundred thousand converts. In 1773, partly as a result of
strife between the Pope and the Jesuits over their accommodation of Chinese ancestor worship; the Jesuits were
disbanded and persecution occurred. The Manchu emperors
adopted a hostile attitude to all westerners and their religions
and in the eighteenth century passed edicts forbidding
christian worship entirely. All western presence was restricted
to the port of Canton and it was here that the first protestant
missionaries entered China. Robert Morrison, a Scot of the
London Missionary Society, was the pioneer. The Netherlands Missionary Society was next, followed by English
workers of the undenominational societies.[15] The first baptist
missionaries were the Americans **J. L. Shuck** and **I. J. Roberts**
who were followed by **William Dean** in Hong Kong. Others
established a station at Ningpoo after baptising their first
Chinese convert at Maçao. The British Baptist Missionary
Society began work in China in 1859 at Chefoo.[16] The first
group of missionaries were struck down by disease and in
ten years the last survivor died of typhus.

Dr **Timothy Richard** (1845-1919) was the son of an
ardent baptist Welsh farmer. He trained as a schoolmaster
and talked his way into theological college. He sailed for
China as a baptist missionary in 1869 arriving about the
time of the Tientsin massacre. He found himself the sole
baptist on the field and lacking any knowledge of the
language or experience of life in China. He travelled,
listened and studied intensely until he was thoroughly
conversant with every aspect of Chinese life. His remarkable natural gifts and open-mindedness led him to most
sectors of life. He gave himself to the Chinese in pursuit of

every kind of social and economic improvement and engaged in educational activities, opening an English school. Missionary colleagues accused him of neglecting the prime purpose for which he had come to China and said that he was not preaching the gospel. His unorthodoxy led to a breach with the Baptist Missionary Society and to his lonely mission to bring help to China's millions, but few evangelicals saw his work as furthering the cause of Christ. Richard lived long enough to see a Chinese University of Western Studies established at Tai Yuan Fu in Shansi province, scene of a dreadful massacre of christians.[17] B.M.S. workers had entered Shansi province in 1890 whilst the Americans had reached Szechwan and Han Yang in Central China. In 1892, some baptists formed an independent mission for indigenous work in an endeavour to break the idea of a 'western religion' and called it the Gospel Baptist Mission.[18]

It was Marshman, the baptist missionary in India, who gave the Chinese their first bible in Mandarin in 1822 and followed this with the New Testament and other literature in Cantonese.[19] These were produced initially for distribution to Chinese nationals abroad but proved ready-made tools for actual missionary work in China proper.

American baptists, from their beginnings in Maçao, Hong Kong and Canton in the 1830s, spread the network of ministry west and north,[20] despite the massacres during the Boxer Revolution and subsequently in the years following the Sino-Japanese War and World War Two, when several persecutions of christians took place. Their losses were great and ultimately the communist revolution suppressed christianity forcing it to become at best a tolerated and controlled movement. These long years with little news of christian churches in China have recently come to an end. It now appears that true, spiritual christianity has prospered as an indigenous work of God throughout the oppression of it. Once again, Chinese christians can meet publicly for worship and there is growing evidence of the vast extent of a virile christianity in the land. The resultant church seems to be entirely indigenous and peculiarly Chinese and its emergence from the shadows is awaited with great expectancy.

Hong Kong, a British colony on the mainland for almost a century, has a vast population. American missionaries first landed and commenced work there in 1832, before they began to work elsewhere in mainland China. There are said to be thirty thousand baptist church members in the colony, which is to lose its British colonial status and revert to China before the end of this century.

Taiwan, which used to be called **Formosa**, has been evangelised by American baptist missionaries during the past hundred years. Since World War Two, the presence of a substantial American business community has strengthened the influence of baptist witness in this Chinese island. There are about one hundred baptist churches there having a membership of about fourteen thousand.

Japan has three hundred and forty baptist churches with thirty-three thousand members but growth is slow. Baptist churches are seen as part of the 'Americanisation' of their country by the Japanese since World War Two and they attract a certain strong nationalistic resistance as a consequence.

The most aggressive evangelism since the Second World War has taken place in **South Korea** where christian expansion has been phenomenal. The present six hundred baptist churches in the country have about fifty-two thousand members.

Thailand, or Siam as it was called formerly, was evangelised by missionaries from the United States who commenced their labours in 1833. It is thought that there are at least a hundred baptist churches there today in a war-stricken country where communications and regular endeavours are impossibly difficult. One authority gives a total church membership estimated at eight or nine thousand believers.

The **Philippines** were colonised by the Spanish and the Roman faith imposed upon the people. As amongst South American Indians, so the primitive animist philosophies of the native people were accommodated in the catholic system in order to make it more attractive as the established religion of the islands. The Americans took the colony at the end of the nineteenth century and it became their colony until independence in 1940 since when it has been an independent republic. The first baptist missionaries came to the Philippines in 1900 being sent by the North American Convention Missions Board.[21] The leader in this baptist pioneer ministry was a Spanish speaking Swedish missionary whom the baptist churches of Sweden had sent to evangelise in Spain and who had established a baptist work in Barcelona. The American Missionary Union took over responsibility for him and in 1900 sent him to the Philippines where Spanish was still the administrative language. His name was **Eric Lund** and he began work in the Philippines with the N.A.C.M.B. supporting him. He took with him a Filipino engineer, who had been among his converts in Barcelona, as a fellow worker.[22] From the commencement of American rule, the Philippines had religious freedom though the catholic faith dominated and still does. There are today eight hundred baptist churches throughout the islands, mostly in the urbanised areas, and they claim ninety thousand members. The Baptist Bible churches of the United States have large numbers of workers in the country which forms one of their main mission fields. The British independent baptist churches have also commenced a work in Metro-Manilla since World War Two, which is of distinctly 'Particular Baptist' type. A growing number of churches adhering to the old London Confession of 1677/89 is resulting.

Australasia

Following the discovery of **Australia** by Captain Cook in 1770, British emigrants have made it their home. Inevitably they brought with them their British traditions and planted their churches in the new country. **Dr John**

Saunders (c1790-1859) was born in Camberwell, London, and joined the Denmark Hill church at the age of 17 years. He rejected the opportunity to become a Member of Parliament and gave himself to the christian ministry. After planting two new churches in London, he set out for Sydney to pastor a baptist church begun two years earlier by **John McKaeg**, a Scottish baptist layman. He quickly became a popular preacher and founded the Bathurst Street baptist church, remaining its pastor until his health broke up and he died in 1859.[23] Baptist work in the antipodes has always been strongest in New South Wales.

By 1840, there were baptist churches in Launceston and Hobart, in Tasmania, in Sydney, Adelaide and Melbourne. The pastor of the Adelaide church was **David MacLaren**, the father of the eminent Manchester preacher, **Alexander MacLaren**. During the Gold Rush, which commenced in 1851, the expansion of churches into the new areas took place as they opened up. The churches which developed in Victoria were principally open communion churches designed to accommodate the mixture of immigrants entering the country. South Australian churches developed along the same lines. The churches in Tasmania had strong links with Spurgeon who sent them students from Pastors' College to plant churches. These were distinctly 'Spurgeonic', reflecting the moderate calvinism of their mentor. The pioneer of baptist work in Tasmania was **Rev H. Dowling** who came from Colchester, England in 1834.[24]

More recently, the Australian baptist churches have formed associations and have tended to link more closely with the American churches of The Southern Convention. They reflect their methodology in evangelism and 'revival' campaigns. Some churches which have adhered to the older confession, with their sovereign grace doctrines, have separated and maintain an independent existence as traditional Particular Baptist churches of an English type. They have links with the English Strict Baptists. The last to bring baptist churches to birth was Western Australia where they are still few in number for so large an area. Altogether, there are about seven hundred baptist churches in Australia with about fifty thousand members.[25]

New Zealand has been called more British than Britain herself and reproduces the ecclesiastical situation as it is in the mother country. The early colonists planted their national church which became the establishment, enjoying some degree of state protection.The growth of Free Churches was consequently very slow. However, today there are baptist churches in all the main cities and many of the provincial townships. The first baptist church in New Zealand was founded in 1851 at Nelson in the South island on the Tasman Sea. Many students from Spurgeon's College settled into churches in New Zealand and the church life of those reflected the moderate calvinism of the Spurgeonic tradition. Despite their closeness to the Australian baptist churches, they owe little to them and have not imbibed the American influence which that country's churches has done. In New Zealand the classical British style of baptist church life prevails. There are 154 baptist churches in the dominion with eighteen thousand church members. Most are in the national baptist union though there are some independent churches having a strong 'reformed' emphasis, which have emerged during the past two decades.[26]

   Polynesia, with which we embrace all the Pacific Islands, includes many areas which were subject to the earliest missionary endeavours of the modern movement. This was largely undertaken by the Presbyterians and undenominational missionary societies and there is not a large baptist presence throughout these island nations. **Indonesia** has seen some influx of baptist workers from North America and from the Philippines but the baptist presence is still minimal.

14
The doctrine of the church

The upsurges of 'baptist' protest against the departure of so-called 'mainstream christianity' from the biblical simplicity of christian faith and practice has been reviewed in previous historical chapters. In these baptist movements a strong and single-minded appeal was consistently made to the scriptures as the sole source of authority in the churches. This is a prime characteristic of the baptist of all times. He submits willingly to the scriptures, taking them as his only rule. The baptist is a scripture-ruled believer.

Furthermore these 'baptist movements' have been distinctly aware of bible doctrine and vitally concerned for the preservation and implementation of the 'faith once delivered to the saints' in the Word of God. Modifications, accommodations and departures from plain biblical teaching have always galvanised true baptists into protest. Revealed truth is binding for him. The baptist is a doctrinally concerned believer.

Any closer examination of the baptist's heritage reveals him as the representative of biblical, truly mainstream christianity rather than the mass movements which claim that description. It has been the baptist role to be 'the voice crying in the wilderness', rebuking, correcting and calling back christians everywhere to return to God's Word as the sole arbiter of christian fidelity. It must be contended therefore that the baptist is the true, orthodox christian and the bible-motivated witness against persistent apostasy. In no area is this to be seen more plainly than in the vital doctrine of the church, by which is meant the bible's plain teaching on what constitutes a true, christian church.

The Doctrine of the Church

The Doctrine of the Church as set out in scripture is the prime characteristic of the baptist and not his mode of baptism, as is so frequently asserted.[1] Indeed it is the baptist definitions of 'What is a christian?' and 'What is a church?' which actually separates him from ever changing christendom. This has been the cause of baptist protest from the fourth century until now. This is the reason today for the separation of the baptists from the modern ecumenical movement; and it will be that which will divide ultimately bible-disciplined baptists from tomorrow's 'World-Church'.

Furthermore, it is the baptists' insistence on the biblical doctrine of the church, with their unqualified submission to the Word of God, which becomes the test of 'What is a Baptist Church?' It is that which disqualifies large numbers of christian congregations which retain the designation 'baptist' quite improperly. In principle, all christian congregations, not adhering to this biblical doctrine in both creed and practice, are no churches in the New Testament sense. A correct mode of baptism does not make for a correct church order. The New Testament doctrine of church is more fundamental than that.

The baptist makes this definition of the church, 'The church of Christ, in its largest signification, is the whole company of regenerate persons in all times and ages, in heaven and on earth'[2] In the various confessions of their faith, baptists have amplified the key word 'regenerate' by speaking of the total number of the elect of God, redeemed, called, repentant, believing, baptised and finally glorified people of God.[3] In this comprehensive sense the 'church' is identical with the 'kingdom of God'; both terms signifying that redeemed humanity in which God in Christ exercises actual spiritual dominion. The scriptures distinguish between this 'universal' or invisible church and the 'individual' or 'local' church in which the former takes local and temporal form in a district and in which the characteristics of the 'church' as a whole are commonly exhibited.[4]

The baptist defines the 'local church' as that smaller

company of regenerate, repentant, believing and baptised persons who, in any given community, voluntarily gather themselves together and unite in accordance with the teaching of Christ in the scriptures, for the purpose of securing the complete establishment of the kingdom of God in themselves and in the world.[5]

This 'local church' is God's basic unit on earth.[6] All discipline and service as set out in scripture, is related to this unit and not to any larger grouping of churches. Therefore the existence of any other intermediate grouping, such as regional, national or denominational 'churches' is totally outside the order laid down in the scriptures. The baptist recognises the total independence of such a local church under Christ the Head, to whom each is finally responsible for its administration, stewardship of the gospel, discipline of the membership, appointment of its officers and the ordinances.[7] The prevailing use of the word 'church' in the New Testament is in its local sense and therefore the baptist usage of the word 'church' relates to the local church. The baptist rejects the use of expressions such as 'The Catholic Church', 'the Church of England', 'The Presbyterian Church of Scotland', 'The Reformed Church of France'. The baptist rejects in one sense the name by which he is customarily described, 'The Baptist Church' because this implies by its use that it is an organised grouping of churches, that is a 'denomination', whereas the proper usage for every christian church should be 'The baptised church of Jesus Christ' or just 'christian church'. When bible-ruled baptists speak of 'an association' or 'a convention' of churches, they retain in the fullest sense the local independence of the local churches and are expressing the plurality of such churches in any stated area, as the scriptures do in Acts 9:31; Phil.3:6 and 1 Timothy 3:15.[8]

Accordingly, when they refused to be bound to the State by an hierarchical decision in the Constantinian marriage of the Church to the Empire, the Donatists were scripturally correct and fully justified. The authority to take such an overall decision does not exist in the New Testament. Indeed, the Donatists were expressing their baptist convictions as we have seen previously. The same became true of other later protest groups.[9]

In the same sense, the Donatists and others to which attention has been drawn in earlier chapters, together with the sixteenth century anabaptists in particular, were biblically correct and characteristically 'baptist' in rejecting the practices of christendom which added unregenerate or unbelieving members to its churches. The cleverly devised argumentation of Augustine and others that the New Testament churches were comprised of a 'mixture of wheat and tares' and that for that reason it was normal and biblical for such a mixture of believers and unbelievers to form churches here on earth must be rejected. Unbelievers cannot be consciously and deliberately added to the churches, according to the scriptures. Augustine's justification of the suppression of the Donatists on that basis is without any biblical support. Their rejection of the baptising of unregenerate infants (or adults) as unbiblical, and their conclusion that all such 'baptisms' were totally worthless, were entirely correct. They were also correct in declaring that all such rites were not in any sense christian baptisms. The opponents of the Donatists called them 'Anabaptists', the first use of this term. In no sense was baptism as a believer a re-baptism because the rite administered whilst they were unbelievers was null and void. The historic baptist doctrine must be emphasised here, namely, that the church of Christ should be a pure church comprised of regenerate believers only and that that is the true biblical standard.[10]

Church Discipline

The English word 'discipline' as used by christians, has tended to modify its meaning so that frequently it means corrective punishment. The word came into English use from the latin for a scholar, pupil and adherent (*discipulus*) being derived from the word which means 'to learn' (*disco*). It came to be used for that way of life characteristic of the teaching of a philosopher or a military leader, for example, the discipline of army life. Its use for the 'way of life' taught by Jesus to his followers, and submitted to by them, is 'christian discipline' and these followers are properly called 'disciples'. It should always be taken in this positive sense when related to church life. Christians are 'Christ's disciples' because they have learned of him the true and living way and walk in it.[11]

The earliest protest movements, such as the Montanists, Novatianists and Donatists demanded that all the churches' members should live a godly life.[12] Augustine of Hippo sneered at them, calling them 'spotless saints'[13] and Luther did the same ten centuries later.[14] The sixteenth century baptists were constantly abused by their opponents on account of their desire to live godly lives. Those same opponents again and again were forced to bear testimony that the despised anabaptists lived lives above reproach. They criticised Luther for his strident emphasis on 'salvation by faith alone' because it tended to lead to carelessness about the christian's life. The anabaptists affirmed constantly the saying of James, 'Faith without works is dead.'[15] They insisted that saving faith was always accompanied by the 'spiritual fruits of righteousness'[16] actually seen in the believer's daily life in the world. Neander says of the Novatianists that 'they maintained that purity and holiness of life were essential marks of the true church' and 'Every church neglecting discipline ceases to be a true church'.[17] Ten centuries later, the anabaptist set the same biblical standards; for example the Schleitheim Confession 1527 which makes it a major tenet, saying in its Preamble, 'We... who have been and shall be separated from the world in everything and completely at peace...', adding later, 'a very great offence has been introduced by certain false brothers... They have missed the truth...are given over to lasciviousness and self-indulgence of the flesh. They think faith and love may do and permit everything since they are believers'.[18] In setting this out, that confession speaks of the imposition of excommunication, or the 'ban' as they termed it, whereby a member who has 'slipped', and has rejected first and second admonitions to repent, is banned according to the command of Christ.[19] The 'ban' became a major concern with the anabaptists as they strove to maintain 'pure churches, and ultimately occasioned divisions among the Netherland assemblies.[20]

It is a baptist characteristic that the church members submit themselves one to the other in love and accept rebuke, correction and instruction towards the realisation of a clear testimony before the world of the redemption in Christ. They insist that following Christ imposes upon them this submission to his Word and that failure to accept such admonition breaks fellowship and compels the separation of the unrepentant.

Local Church Government

The local church is a gathering of the regenerate believers submitting themselves to Christ as Head and to one another as members of equal standing in the fellowship. For the good order and effective discipleship, each local church is provided with elders and deacons by the sovereign gifting of the Lord. These gifted persons are recognised and set apart for their ministries by the church. The elders, sometimes referred to as overseers or presbyters, are entrusted with 'the spiritual ministrations of the church, watching over the souls of the members as those who must give an account'.[21] The pastors are included among the elders in the church; indeed, baptists have often seen all elders as pastors. Deacons are entrusted with the business management of the affairs of the church and the caring financially for the elders, widows and poor. The appointment of these 'officers of the church' is solely a matter for the local church itself and not a concern for other churches. There is no jurisdiction of one church over another but all are equal and independent of interference or control by other churches or groups of churches. The baptist recognises the plurality of the gifts bestowed upon their churches, believing that each and every member has a God-given capability to contribute to the total ministry of the fellowship to its own members and to the world in proclaiming the gospel.[22] The baptist rejects all authoritarianism other than that exercised by Christ the Head through his Holy Spirit and by the Holy Scripture but persists in the simplicity of the biblical order. The tendency of the modern 'house group' churches, and those associating in such movements as 'Restoration' is to reinstate echelons of power similar to the hierarchical systems of the catholics and others. This distinguishes them from the historic baptist practice of scriptural simplicity.

Liberty of Conscience and the Voluntary Principle

The baptists have 'the singular and distinguished honour to have repudiated, from their earliest history, all coercive power over the consciences and actions of men with reference to religion. They were the proto-evangelists of the voluntary principle'. This relevant statement comes from the pen of Dr H. E. Skeats in his 'History of the Free Churches', in which he adds a footnote reading, 'The author is not connected with the baptist denomination; and has therefore, perhaps greater pleasure in bearing testimony to undoubted historical fact'.[23] Hubmaier had been explicit in this teaching, 'A Turk or a heretic is not convinced by our act, either with the sword or with fire, but only with patience and prayer; and so we should await with patience the judgement of God'.[24] Indeed, in their early days the reformers had tempered their view, as for instance the Memmingen Resolutions 1531, 'It is contrary to the right of christian government to force faith upon the world with the sword and other violent compulsion... evil should be resisted alone with the mighty Word of God and the person erring in faith should not be knocked down suddenly but should be tolerated in all christian love as a harmless person'.[25] However, this was not to last long and the protestant reformers became as coercive as ever the catholics had been.

Not only does the baptist allow his brother man a liberty of conscience and eschew all use of force to convert to christian faith but he also insists on the voluntary nature of saving faith which is consistently affirmed in scripture. Augustine had argued that the New Testament gave the 'church' its authority for forcing men against the natural will to conform, quoting Luke 14:23 and John 15:6 for instance.[26] Ferdinand and Isabella of Spain had utilised these same scriptures for establishing the Inquisition whose main purpose was to coerce men to catholic faith.[27] This violence to the individual conscience was continued by Zwingli and Luther in edicts enforcing the christening of infants upon pain of penalty in default, as mentioned previously.[28] It must amaze twentieth century christians to learn that the Congregationalists of Boston, New England, made the same demand by law upon all its citizens.[29]

President Roosevelt's declaration of the Four Freedoms of 6 January 1941 gave as the second, 'We seek to make secure... the second freedom... of every person to worship God in his own way everywhere in the world'.[30] The Helsinki Agreement 1975 affirmed this for all men, though it is barely implemented by all its signatories. The Anabaptists accorded that freedom to Turks and Jews in the sixteenth century and it ever remains a baptist principle.[31] They also excluded the possibility of baptists ever taking over secular government by the explicit statement in the 'Martyrs' Synod at Augsburg 1527.'[32] Though many anabaptists, from Michael Sattler and Hans Denck of Southern Germany to Menno Simons in the Netherlands, excluded civil service for practising christians, and in the same way refused military service too, both Hubmaier and Marpeck, their outstanding theologians took a different view. According to Williams, Hubmaier says, 'The magistrate may be expressly christian precisely in the manner of his discharging of his office. If the magistrate puts to death justly without any hate... in his heart, he is more than a magistrate... he is fulfilling his God-ordained duty in this world, which must never be identified with the kingdom.'[33]

The baptist believes that the free action of the will is involved in saving faith by the enabling grace of God and not divine coercion. Neither can human coercion produce true saving faith in any person. Similarly, christian discipleship is voluntary yielding of the body and soul by the believer to the rule of Christ as Head as his reasonable service. This principle contributes to his rejection of infant baptism because 'sponsors' cannot believe on the behalf of the child. Indeed it is only as men make their confessions of faith voluntarily that we can be sure that their religion is real. As Milton said, *'Truth to be true must be conscientiously arrived at...'*[34] The Baptist World Alliance reiterated this in its declaration of 27 June 1939, 'Voluntariness in personal and corporate worship, institution and service is essential to vital religion... no man, nor government, nor institution, religious or civil, social or economic, has the right to dictate how a person may worship God'.[35]

There is one aspect of liberty of conscience in which the baptist is frequently misunderstood and sometimes baptists themselves have failed to grasp it. Whereas baptists have always claimed total liberty of conscience for all men so that the 'Turk and the Jew' should be afforded freedom to practise their faiths uncoerced by civil or clerical powers, yet within the christian church the baptist has both affirmed and enforced a strict discipline of conformity to scriptural faith and practice. Hence, any toleration of heresy or deviation from biblical standards is utterly abhorrent to the baptist. He expresses his understanding of biblical standards in detail and with great care, as for instance, in the seventeenth century confessions of faith.

The evacuation of doctrinal content from the bases of fellowship during the nineteenth century by 'baptist' churches and the 'Baptist Union' was a violent departure from the historic baptist position and could not be justified under the cloak of 'liberty of conscience'. Herein lies the conflict of conviction between the two baptist stalwarts of that century, Spurgeon and Clifford, great friends though they were. Spurgeon was bound by the credal discipline of the scriptures in everything and believed that to discipline the local church fellowship accordingly had nothing to do with the baptist doctrine of 'liberty of conscience.' Whereas according to Underwood, 'Clifford took the attitude he did during the Downgrade Controversy' because 'it was impossible for him to bind himself, or any other, by a creed'. Spurgeon was not claiming authority for any man-made creed, but for the absolute authority of the Word of God. By this the christian must be bound; and this is historic baptist teaching.

The Baptist and Church State Union

The Donatists, says Frend in his classical study of that christian movement, looked on the church 'as a small body of the saved surrounded by the mass of the unregenerate and they insisted that the independence of the church had to be upheld at all costs.'[36] It was inevitable that they rejected as unthinkable any union between the Church and the Empire as was brought by Constantine the Emperor and the power-seeking church dignitaries. The Donatists held a high doctrine of the church based upon personal faith and voluntary discipleship and rejected the concept of the 'church' comprised of 'all citizens in a given locality,'. and to this heretical notion they made their unqualified protest. Dostoevsky says, 'a compromise arose... the Empire accepted christianity and the church accepted the Roman law and state. A small part of the church retired into the desert and there began to continue its former work'.[37]

That 'small part in the desert' was not permitted a quiet withdrawal but was suppressed with all the force of Roman arms. Indeed Verduin says, that the Donatists were not the least surprised when troops were sent to quell their protest.[38] Their rebellion was against the marriage of 'church' and 'state', an act of apostasy which is known as the Sacralist Heresy. This heresy has characterised all the catholic churches, the orthodox churches of Eastern Europe, the State Churches of Western Europe and many British dominions and even Free Churches (!) in the United States up to about 1840. Although the Donatists' rebellion against sacralism was repressed, similar baptistic protests against this heresy have occurred in wave upon wave of dissent ever since[39] Harnack said in 1886, *'In the twelve centuries before the Reformation, it has never lacked for attempts to get away from the State-Church priests' church and to reinstitute the apostolic structurisation. That is to say that throughout medieval times there has never been a moment when Constantine stood unchallenged. Wherever the New Testament is held in high honour, its concept of the Church of Christ will continue to challenge. There a church based upon personal faith will challenge the concept of a Church embracing all'.*[40] Even Luther, with his principle of 'Sola Scriptura' seemingly promising hope of a New Testament church, soon fell for the blandishments of the Protestant princes, the perpetuation of the sacral system of Rome and the security it offered him and his followers. In a very little while 'Donatists' were born again as 'Baptists'! The separation of Church and State remains an exclusively baptist principle to this day. Yet baptists always endeavour to be good citizens.

When a little later, baptists spilled over into Britain and eventually the first Baptist church was founded here by Thomas Helwys in 1611, the same baptist principle held good for its membership. The classical statement of Helwys in his amazing book entitled, 'The Mystery of Iniquity' published in London in 1612, states, *'The King is a mortal man and not God, therefore hath no power over the immortal souls of his subjects to make laws and ordinances for them and to set spiritual lords over them. If the king have authority to make spiritual laws and lords then he is immortal God and not mortal man. O king, be not seduced by deceivers to sin against God whom thou oughtest to obey, nor against thy poor subjects, who ought and will obey thee in all things with body, life and goods, or else let their lives be taken from the earth. God save the king.'*[41] He further says, *'Our lord the king is but dust and ashes as well as we; therefore let not the king be angry with his servants... though he should kill us, yet will we speak the truth to him'.*[42] Helwys continues, *'We do freely profess that our lord and king is but an earthly king and he hath not authority as a king but in earthly causes; and if the king's people be obedient and true subjects, obeying all human laws made by the king, our lord the king can require no more; for men's religion is betwixt God and themselves; the king shall not answer for it, neither may the king be judge between God and man; let them be heretics, Turks, Jews or whatever, it appertaineth not to earthly power to punish them in the least measure...'*[43]

In concluding this section of the consideration of the Doctrine of the Church, it is necessary to record the progress in the thought of those christians committed to the sacralist heresy in moving away from all coercion in conversion of pagans or heretics and the severance of their church-state unions. Many of the established churches have ceased to preserve the Constantinian link, though retaining the doctrinal concept most often expressed in the retention of the Head of the State as the Head of the Church, as in Wales, Ireland and Canada and in the Episcopal Church of Scotland, The status of the Roman Catholic church in France changed when the republic became a secular state at the Revolution in 1789. There are many who anticipate the dis-establishment of the Church of England and the dismantlement of 'state-religion' in England.

15
The baptist and church ordinances

Christian Baptism

The baptists understand from scripture that Christ has
established two ordinances, or continuing commanded
practices in his church for all time, namely, Christian
Baptism and the Lord's Supper. These are sometimes
called 'sacraments' but because of the origin of this word
and the consequential overtones of meaning that its usage
tends to imply, a preference for the simple term
'ordinance' exists among them. There have been some who
would speak of the command to 'Preach the Gospel' as a
church ordinance which in the ordinary use of the word it
clearly is. In common with the rejection of the other five
'sacraments' of the catholic church by the reformers in the
sixteenth century, baptists hold baptism and the Supper to
be binding on all New Testament churches.

Whereas the catholic churches, and some protestant
churches, hold that these ordinances communicate special
grace to those that partake, as for instance, that salvation is
assured to the person baptised (baptismal regeneration),
the baptists affirm that the ordinances are acts of obedience
which set forth the central truths of the gospel, particularly
the death and resurrection of Jesus Christ. The ordinances
are therefore symbolic declarations of the Gospel and not
in themselves channels of special grace to the obedient.[1] In
this they share the reformer Zwingli's view rather than that
of Luther. In the sixteenth century 'radical reformation'
there were those who ceased to practise the ordinances.
They rejected the keeping of the 'letter', holding that the

237

commands of Christ were spiritual matters not to be literally retained in the churches. They were reacting against the abuse of the ordinances as powerful means of grace in themselves as the catholic church taught. Meditation on the death and rising of Jesus was an adequate obedience. These were called 'Spiritualists' and were not in reality 'anabaptists' though often so-called by their opponents. The successors of these 'spiritualists' are found today among the Quakers. The historic baptist position is that these two ordinances of Christ are to be literally kept in obedience until the Lord returns.[2]

In arriving at their understanding of these two ordinances, the baptist is ruled by his characteristic submission to the Word of God, rather than the traditions of men, and by his high doctrine of the church. He is characteristically meticulous in his obedience of scripture and in this way stands out against all other streams of christian practice. From the Donatists, through most of the protest movements whose history we have already outlined, the Petrobrussians and Waldenses down to the Anabaptist and their contemporary successors, baptist submission to the biblical order is evident to all. Before plunging into the study of the ordinance of baptism, it must be understood that the baptist view of it derives from the two pre-eminent doctrines of Word and Church.

The ordinance of baptism is commanded in scripture as the first act of a believer's discipleship and it is a once for all act of obedience which, provided that it was obeyed in faith, is never repeated. The practice of baptising believers, who have reputedly been 'baptised' as infants before coming to faith, after their coming to faith has been called a 're-baptism'. This is a false deduction to be rejected. Only immersion after coming to faith can be scripturally called baptism and all else is a meaningless rite.

The baptists define christian baptism as the immersion in the name of the Trinity of a person who, having heard and received the gospel of Jesus Christ, repents of his sins before God and believes in the Lord Jesus Christ for salvation, bearing witness to both the gospel and his own salvation in that act of obedience, his first step of discipleship in which he proclaims Jesus his Saviour and

Lord. The baptists hold that by baptism is meant immersion and that no other meaning can be properly given to it, an argumentation for which follows later.[3] It is held also that the preaching of baptism is an inherent part of the fulfilment of Christ's Great Commission to the churches and that preaching the gospel without it is defective.[4]

The Proper Subject for Christian Baptism

In baptism, the baptist emphasis is not on the mode of baptism as has so often been stated, but on the spiritual status of the person being baptised. It is evident from the Great Commission of Matthew 28:19 that the proper subject of baptism is one who has had the gospel preached to him and the Holy Spirit has made him spiritually alive to his state as a sinner and to the good news God proclaims of the forgiveness of sins and he has accordingly responded, becoming a disciple of Jesus Christ. A disciple is one who has been taught, has learned from the teaching and commits himself to follow in its way. He is therefore evidently a regenerate man who by grace is aware of sins and has turned from them, believing in Jesus Christ for salvation as proclaimed in the gospel. He has been 'born from above' and is indeed a newly made disciple. In no sense can this 'required-status-for-baptism' be attained by an unregenerate person, infant or adult, whether sponsors or the church make promises on his behalf or not. The Great Commission itself rules out the validity of infant baptism and so does the first documented fulfilment of that Commission recorded in Acts 2 which reflects the evidence of regeneracy in the felt need for forgiveness of sin and the response to the gospel in repentance and obedience in baptism.[5] Hence baptists demand that the subjects of baptism must be regenerate.

Baptism in the scripture is said to declare the gospel and the subject's salvation by reason of his union with Christ Jesus by faith in his death, burial and rising again.[6] Hence it follows that the subject of baptism has personal union with Christ Jesus in that way and so must be regenerate. The proper subject of baptism is therefore a sinner who is born again of the Holy Spirit, repentant, believing and obeying the gospel, and no one else should be given christian baptism.[7] The pre-requisite of faith for baptism is not peculiar to the baptists. Luther, early in his ministry said, 'If you receive sacraments without faith, you bring yourselves into great difficulty, for we oppose against your practice the saying of Christ, 'He that believes and is baptised shall be saved'. Luther concludes that *'Baptism helps no one, it is also to be given to no one, except he believe for himself, and without personal faith no one is to be baptised'*. Luther declared baptism worthless without the personal faith of the person baptised.[8]

The Proper Mode of Baptism

The baptist, in his definition of christian baptism as quoted above, states that the proper mode of baptism is immersion of the believer in water. The following reasons establish this practice as biblical:

a. The actual word, used by the Holy Spirit, always means immersion and not anything else;

b. The recorded instances of baptism in the scriptures demand such a meaning;

c. The significance given to baptism in scripture cannot be satisfied by the use of any other mode;

d. The practice of the early church, and of most christians since, indicates immersion as being the scriptural mode.

Eminent christian scholars, who are not baptists, give ample evidence that the meaning of the bible word for 'to baptise' (i.e. *baptizein*) is to immerse. The father of the reformed churches, Calvin says, 'It is evident that the term 'baptise' means 'immerse entirely' and this was the form used by the early church... I wish that the genuine institution of Christ had been maintained...'[9] Thomas Goodwin, the Congregational Puritan, says, 'In the sacrament of baptism we are said to be buried with him in baptism... (Romans 6:3,4; Colossians 2:12)... buried with him..., risen with him... the baptised being first buried under water and then rising out of it'.[10] Martin Luther says, 'The minister dips the child in water signifying death; that he brings it out again signifies life as Paul explains in Romans 6. Being moved by these reasons, I would have those that are baptised to be entirely immersed as the word imports and the mystery signifies.'[11]

The American baptist scholar of Rochester Theological Seminary, Dr T. J. Conant, has provided a masterly examination of the greek word *'baptizein'* in both sacred and profane literature and shows that it always means 'dip' or immerse. He gives 168 examples from Greek writers from the third century throughout the New Testament period to the early fathers. He shows that that is the correct use of the word. He also examines the Greek version of the Old Testament. *'The Septuagint'*, which reaches the same conclusion.[12] The recently deceased American paedobaptist, John Murray also adds his contemporary and non-baptist testimony to the same effect in his book on christian baptism.[13] The baptist case for immersion only is set out in A. H. Strong's *Systematic Theology,*[14] John Gill's *Complete Body of Doctrine,*[15] Abraham Booth's *Paedobaptism Examined*[16] and Alexander Carson's classic work *'Baptism'*. For those who want to study the attempts made by paedobaptists to contradict this view, the reading of the classic *'History of Baptism'* by William Wall[18] or the more modern book by Pierre Marcel which is available in an English translation are the strongest cases made, although falling short of their task![19] The weight of evidence, beyond all doubt rests with the baptist when he says that the bible word for baptise means to immerse or dip.

Furthermore, the bible's recorded instances of baptism in Matthew and Mark indicate that there was a coming up out of the water which presupposes immersion as having first taken place. (Matthew 3:16; Mark 1:10). The choice of Enon for baptisms on account of there being 'much water there,' indicates that immersion, rather than sprinkling or pouring, was practised. (John 3:23). Then both 'Philip and the eunuch went down into the water' indicating immersion again. (Acts 8:38); The meaning of the word used together with its emblematic usage demand immersion. For instance, Jesus speaks of his death as a baptism (Mark 10:38; Luke 12:50). Believers' baptism is described as burial and a rising again in the scriptures. (Romans 6:3,4; Colossians 2:12). Even Israel's 'baptism' in the Red Sea is expressed as 'being under' the cloud, i.e. immersion (1 Corinthians 10:1,2). These latter emblematic or metaphoric usages of baptism demand that immersion be understood.

It is stated above that the practice of the early church and those since shows that immersion is the commonly understood and accepted practice. Bishop Cyril of Jerusalem was immersing in the fourth century.[20] The first immersion of the anabaptists of the sixteenth century has been described previously.[21] The reformers Luther and Calvin have been quoted in favour of immersion.[22] The Roman Catholic Council of Trent, overhauling their whole faith and order in a thorough reformation in the same century, confirmed that immersion was the proper mode.[23] In 1577, Paulicians and the Swiss Brethren met to review common areas of teaching and they agreed that baptism was immersion.[24] The usage of the Church in England from 1085 to 1549, known as the 'Salisbury Use', required immersion in anglican churches.[25] The 're-formed' Church of England in its 1549 and 1662 Prayer Books stated with great plainness that the priest shall 'dip'![26] Anglican bishops Handley Moule and J. B. Lightfoot of the last century define baptism as immersion.[27] Sanday and Headlam, in the *'International Critical Commentary'*, and also Professor R. T. Knowling, in the *'Expositors' Greek Testament'*, take the same stand.[28] In the current *'Lion Handbook of the Bible* 1977, Dr Donald Guthrie speaks of baptism as *'a going down into the water and a coming up again...'*[29] The classical work on baptism by the Anglican, William Wall, whose life's work was to defend christening as practised in his own church, says *'the ordinary way was to baptise by immersion'*.[30]

In Britain, the practice of the baptists was by sprinkling or pouring until 1611 when Thomas Helwys denounced sprinkling and insisted on immersion.[31] Particular Baptists did not re-introduce immersion among themselves until 1642.[32] It follows that Dr J Clarke, the founder of the first baptist church on Rhode Island in 1639, having been a member of Spilsbury's Particular Baptist church in London before emigrating, was not immersed.[33] This London church is still in existence and practises believers-only baptism by immersion having done so from that date.[34] In 1644, the Particular baptist churches of London produced their (first) London Confession and in it insisted on immersion.[35] British baptist churches of both streams have continued to practise immersion from that time until today. During the present century there has been a rebellion against traditional churchmanship and the mainline denominations of christianity which has spawned multitudes of 'house churches'. Despite many novelties introduced, these adhere to immersion for baptism. During this twentieth century there has also been a progressive move away from sprinkling towards immersion among the traditionally paedobaptist churches too. The former anglican vicar of St. Paul's, Cambridge, referring to Christ's baptism in Matthew 3:5 and Mark 1:5 at the Carey Conference in 1971, said *'The plain implication is... that he was immersed... Incidentally, one can see the absurdity of translating 'baptizo' here as 'sprinkle' or 'pour'. You can dip someone into water but you cannot sprinkle them into water unless you have used a mincer beforehand.'*[36] The reader will recall the baptism of Wolfgang Ulimann by the anabaptist Grebel in the Rhine in 1523. Ulimann said that he would not be *'sprinkled out of a dish but drawn under and covered with the waters of the Rhine'.*[37]
Baptism is immersion.

The early church had some controversy over the validity of a baptism in which the status of the administrator was in question. The baptist believes that he derives the validity of his baptism directly from the New Testament and that, provided the requirements there are being met, then the ordinance of believer's baptism cannot be questioned. Quoting the American baptist theologian Strong, '*It is the erroneous view that baptism is the act of the administrator which causes the anxiety of 'High Church Baptists' to deduce their baptist lineage from regularly baptised ministers all the way back to John the Baptist, and which induces... We have no need to prove a baptist apostolical succession. If we can derive our doctrine and practice from the New Testament, it is all we require'.*[37a]

The first instance of baptism by immersion among the anabaptists is carefully preserved and detailed by Kessler. It was the baptism of Wolfgang Ullmann in February 1525 by Conrad Grebel. Ullmann in requesting baptism asked that it be '*not out of a platter*' but by immersion. Grebel and Ullmann went down into the River Rhine, near Schaffhausen, and Grebel, according to Kessler, '*put him under the waters of the river and covered him over*'. Thereafter the Swiss brothers practised baptism by immersion and no longer by affusion. Furthermore, another interesting aspect of this historic baptism is that the baptiser, Conrad Grebel, was not an 'ordained minister' but a 'layman' which examples the baptist understanding of the ordinance, namely, that the 'rite' draws nothing from the person who baptises but its validity rests in the person being baptised. Again, the baptist insists that 'an ordained minister' is not essential to a proper baptism.

The Significance of Baptism

For the baptist, baptism signifies the previous entrance of a believer into communion with his Lord and Saviour Jesus Christ, both in his death and his resurrection, by which means newness of life has come to a formerly spiritually dead sinner. It declares that regeneration has taken place through union with Christ and he is now alive to God. It is therefore a symbol...

a. of the death and resurrection of Jesus Christ as stated in Romans 6:3, '*all of us, who were baptised into Christ, were baptised into his death*',

b. of the purpose of that death and rising again, namely, to atone for sin, delivering sinners from its penalty and power and bringing them into newness of life in order *'that we may live a new life'* (v 4) and *'count yourselves dead to sin but alive to God through Christ Jesus'*. (v11).

Coneybeare and Howson, not baptists, say that Romans chapter six cannot be understood without remembering that the primitive method of baptism was by immersion.[38]

Two further points of the symbolism of baptism must be added, namely, it is a symbol of...

c. the accomplishment of the work of grace in the person baptised who thus professes his own death to sin and his rising to spiritual life (Galatians 3:27).

d. the union with Christ, and with all baptised believers in Christ, for there is *'One Lord, one faith, one baptism'*, (Ephesians 4:5). *'All baptised by one Spirit into one body whether Jews or Greeks, slaves or free, we were all given the one Spirit to drink.'* (1 Corinthians 12:13)

Despite his practice of sprinkling or pouring being against his biblical judgement, yet Luther says, *'Baptism is a sign of death and resurrection, being moved by this reasoning I would have those baptised to be altogether dipped in water as the word and the mystery signifies'*.[39] The central significance of baptism is the death and resurrection of Christ Jesus. The believer's death to sin and resurrection into new life are also set forth. The baptised person declares his confession of sin and repentance therefrom, his trust in Christ's death and resurrection alone for his salvation and the new life he now has in Christ under whose rule he resolves to live. Immersion alone can signify that union with Christ in his death as it alone signifies the radical change effected from spiritual death to spiritual life. To omit burial in baptism is to omit all reference to Christ's death and would be tantamount to holding the Lord's Supper and making no reference to his death there.[40]

Infant Baptism

The baptist rejects the baptism of infants primarily for the reasons set out in their definition of christian baptism and of the proper subject of baptism. There is no ground for thinking that infants were included in any of the baptisms recorded in the New Testament, as will be established in the following paragraph dealing with Household Baptisms. Even so the practice of baptising infants has existed to a lesser or greater extent from the third century onwards. It arose from the growth of a heresy that baptism, in some mystical manner, communicated spiritual life to one baptised. Once the doctrine of original sin became established, the rite of baptising infants as soon after birth as possible became an urgent matter in order to prevent them dying before being saved. Baptism had become a saving sacrament communicating eternal life regardless of the exercise of faith or the fact of regeneracy. Indeed, the child was deemed to be regenerated by baptism despite absence of any biblical support for it. This belief remains embedded in all the catholic churches to this day. For instance, the Church of England 1662 Prayer Book, in the rubric of the Service of Public Baptism, expresses such a heresy, saying *'Seeing now... that this child is regenerate and grafted into Christ's church, let us give thanks...'*[42] It is true that many evangelical clergy of the Anglican communion insist that they have a mental reservation and that they do not believe in 'baptismal regeneration.' Others argue that they rely on a pre-requisite exercise of faith by either (1) the parents or god-parents in the name of the child, or (2) by the church itself, adding that such exercise is a sufficient ground scripturally to see the infant as a 'believer' potentially. The baptist can find no such grounds in the scriptures for baptising anyone who is not already a believer as has been set out above.[43]

Tertullian wrote the first known christian work on baptism entitled *'De Baptismo'*. Using latin, for baptism he used the verbs *'tingere'*, *'mergere'*, *'immergere'* and *'mergitere'* with their derivatives, all conveying **'immerse'**. Describing baptism as then practised, he speaks of *'entering the water'* and *'coming up out of the water.'*[44] Bishop Barlow, writing of infant baptism in the sixteenth century, said '*there was not any just evidence for it for about two hundred years after Christ*'.[45] The historian Neander says, '*baptism was not administered at that time without the conscious participation of the person baptised. We have every reason for holding infant baptism something foreign at that stage of christian development*'.[46] The Waldensians rejected infant baptism[47] as did the anabaptists after them.[48]

Tertullian, the Donatist, also rejects the use of 'sponsors' or 'god-parents', as they are usually called today, saying '*What necessity is there to expose sponsors to danger since they cannot guarantee that the little one is, or will be, spiritually-minded?*' He adds, '*faith alone secures salvation*'. As a Donatist, Tertullian speaks with the strong conviction of those who rejected religious innovations and adhered to strict scriptural practice in traditional baptist manner.[49] Speaking of that early period, Schleiermacher says, '*The Roman Apostolical practice thoroughly agrees in demanding beforehand a beginning of faith and repentance, as all traces of infant baptism men have wished to find in the New Testament must first be inserted there!*'[50] Peter de Bruys and the Paulicians restored the baptism of believers only in the twelve century campaign for purifying the church.[51] The sixteenth century anabaptists rejected infant baptism but that section in the following century bearing the name of Mennonites tended to return to it. The baptist finds no place for infant baptism in the scripture and rejects it out of hand.

Infant baptism can be traced to many pagan practices in which the newborn child was admitted into nationhood, by the Romans, Greeks and some Germanic tribes; rites involving washings on his seventh, eighth or ninth day.[52] When the Constantinian apostasy came about, in which membership of the Church and citizenship of the Empire became synonymous, the way was opened up for infant baptism to be the primary rite of initiation into both the church and the nation. In closing this section, let the last words on this subject come from the eminent Scottish historical theologian, Professor Cunningham, a presbyterian, who writes '*It* (that is infant baptism) *tends greatly to introduce obscurity and confusion into our whole conception of baptism, that we see it ordinarily administered to infants and very seldom to adults. This leads to insensibly form a defective and erroneous conception of its design and effect...*' and he goes on to say that there is no scriptural warrant for infant baptism in its general doctrine. The pre-requisite qualifications required for baptism, namely, faith and repentance, an infant cannot meet. The proper subjects for baptism are persons who have come to years of understanding. The Professor calls them 'adults' but the baptist does not insist on full adulthood but 'believers only'.[53]

Household Baptism

There are some christians who insist that the scriptures record the baptisms of entire households and that this presupposes the inclusion of infants and provides a bibilical case for the baptism of children of christian parents before they come to an age when they are able to believe for themselves in Jesus Christ for salvation. Such views have found a hearing among some baptist type movements including a section of the Christian Bethren. The biblical baptist rejects this as contrary to fact. A brief examination of the households claimed to include infants can be given here to show that there is no such support for that view.

a. Cornelius	Acts 10	All whom Peter baptised had received the Holy Spirit.
b. Lydia	Acts 16	Her house was composed of 'brothers' not 'infants'.
c. Jailor	Acts 16	All baptised were filled with joy in believing.
d. Crispus	Acts 18	All believing were baptised and no others.
e. Stephanus	1 Cor.1	All the baptised were converts actively serving the Lord.(cf 1 Corinthians 16:15)

So that all the baptised were those who had heard the Word, believed and became active disciples and no incapable infants were among them. Baptists accept the clear evidence of scripture and reject the imagined deductions of the paedobaptists who claim silent inference to support their non-existent case for baptism of infants on the strength of other people's faith. No such evidence exists in scripture.[54]

To quote the presbyterian scholar, Professor Cunningham again, '*The fundamental spiritual blessings on the possession of which the salvation of men universally depends i.e. justification and regeneration by faith - are not conveyed by the instrumentality of the sacraments, but that, on the contrary, they must already (his emphasis) exist before even baptism can be lawfully or safely received. The general tenor of scriptural language on the subject of baptism applies primarily and directly to the baptism of adults and proceeds upon the assumption that the profession implied in the reception of baptism, the profession that is, that they have already been led to believe in Christ and to receive him as their Saviour and Master, was sincere or corresponded with the real estate of their minds and hearts*',[55]

The baptism of households, or even a whole nation, when the head thereof believes, must be rejected, as all baptists have taught. The only exceptions have been small sects of baptistic brethren. Hence the baptist asserts that the supposed conversion of Britain, by Augustine of Canterbury in 598 AD was not christian conversion.

Baptists have also rejected the many non-scriptural ceremonies and elaborations which some have added to the rite of baptism, such as the anointing with oil, renunciation of the devil, the imposition of hands, giving of milk and honey and forbidding of baths for seven days afterwards. Whilst resisting all innovations, baptists concede that some of the early fathers did practice some of these addenda though without scriptural grounds. The view that baptism washed away sins has been rejected by baptist voices ever since Tertullian said, '*We are not washed in order that we may cease from sinning but because we have ceased, because we have already been washed in heart*'.[56] Baptists understand the pentecostal scripture of Acts 2:38 not to imply that baptism procures the forgiveness of sins but that it is the sign of that remission, indeed the visual declaration of the means of it, namely, the death, burial and resurrection of Jesus Christ.[57] Wyclif succinctly put it in these words, *'Baptism does not confer but only signifies the grace which was given before'.*[58] In his warning against putting confidence in ceremonies, the Anabaptist Denck says, *'ceremonies are not sinful in themselves but he who hopes to secure heaven through Baptism or the Lord's Supper has a superstitious form of faith'.*[59] From the Swiss Brethren at Zürich in 1525 in a *'Declaration of Faith and Defense'*, probably from the joint hands of Grebel and Manz in the Neumarkt in the city, comes this final note, *'It is clearly seen what baptism is and to whom, baptism should be applied, namely, to one who has been converted by the Word of God, has changed his heart, and henceforth desires to walk in newness of life... From this I have clearly learned and know assuredly, that baptism means nothing else than the dying of the old man, and the putting on of the new, and that Christ commanded to baptise those who had been taught'.*[60] 'Go and make disciples of all nations, baptising them in the name of the Father and of the Son, and of the Holy Spirit, and teaching them to obey everything that I have commanded you; and surely I will be with you always to the very end of the age'.[60a]

The Lord's Supper

The Baptist has always recognised that the second ordinance of Christ, which he has commanded his church to keep, is the Lord's Supper. Unlike baptism, which is an ordinance to be kept once, and that at the beginning of the believer's discipleship,[61] the Supper is to be repeated regularly by the church. Its frequency is not set down in scripture although examples are given of a daily and a weekly celebration.[62] Every such occasion is to be well ordered by the scriptural principles set out plainly in 1 Corinthians chapters 10 and 11. The command of the Lord Jesus to his people, to commemorate his death continually until he comes again, by regular and orderly participation in the Supper, is not in doubt among baptists. Indeed it is accepted by the greater part of christendom.[63]

The Lord's Supper is a celebration of the Lord's death

for the believer's sins and his rising again for his
justification, that is for his right standing with God. In
Christ's death, God reconciled his people to himself
completely and in this glorious reality believers rejoice as
often as they gather together at the Table of the Lord.
They declare their total dependence on their once
crucified Lord, who is now risen and ascended on high, as
the sole source of all spiritual life. They rejoice also in the
continuing communion with the Lord by which the life
begun in their new birth, is continually sustained and
ultimately perfected.[64]

The Supper is to be celebrated by the assembled local
church and not in any private way. It cannot be properly
administered in any gathering, large or small, which is not a
disciplined local church. It is a festal occasion declaring the
completely finished work of the believers' redemption in
Christ and declares this good news to the world.[64]

Baptists use common bread and wine in the Supper and
they claim no change in the substance of either during it.
For baptists the Supper is commemorative and symbolic
and in no sense a sacrifice; neither does it become a
communicator of grace. The obedience of faithful discipleship in keeping the Supper, the exercise of a living faith
in remembering the Lord's death and the setting forth of
the oneness of the 'body' of the gathered church, bring to
the proper participant abounding blessing. This has led
many baptists to say, as does **Dr E. F. Kevan** for instance,
that '*the Lord's Supper is a special means of grace but not a means
of special grace*'.[65] Which is to say that the communicant does
not receive any special grace peculiar to the Supper which
he cannot receive at other times of real communion with his
Lord. In terms of reformation theology, this means that the
baptist rejects the teaching of both Rome and Luther and
stands close to Zwingli, who learned his doctrine from the
baptist theologian, Balthasar Hubmaier and from the
baptist pastor in Zürich, Wilhelm Reublin.[66]

Balthasar Hubmaier laid a foundation for succeeding
generations of baptists when he provided for believers in
his beloved Waldshut to have '*Eighteen Dissertations concerning the Entire Christian Life...*' in 1524, among which he set
out the place of the Lord's Supper in the local church.

Numbers 5 and 6 declare the '*Mass is not a sacrifice but a memorial of the death of Christ. Therefore it may not be offered, either for the living or dead;*' and '*As often as such a memorial is celebrated, shall the death of our Lord be preached, as each one of us finds in his heart and on his tongue*'. Apart from the denial of traditional catholic doctrine, his teaching affirms these factors of which baptists have never lost sight. The Supper is a memorial, a remembrance, that it is a celebration and setting forth of Christ's death for his church and that a sharing equally by all in it should express the total oneness of the local fellowship. This oneness was from the first a high ideal of the anabaptists. In the Schleitheim Confession of three years later, the Third Article reads, '*In the breaking of bread we are all of one mind and are agreed. All those who wish to break one bread in remembrance of the broken body of Christ, and all who wish to drink as a remembrance of the shed blood of Christ, shall be united beforehand by baptism in one body of Christ which is the church of God and whose Head is Christ.*' At this point communion in churches of any other character is excluded and it continues, '*Whoever has not been called by one God to one faith, to one baptism, to one Spirit, to one body, with all the children of God's church, cannot be made into one bread with them, as indeed must be done if one is truly to break bread according to the command of Christ*'.[67]

In the seventeenth century confessions from 1610 onwards the requirements match the ancient statutes of their fathers; to the disciplined local church the baptised believer is added and that church received both bread and wine as one body in memory of and in a declaration of the Lord's death.[68] During the Commonwealth, baptist strength in Britain lay in the Midlands. The churches of that area issued confessions which invariably required baptism of believers by immersion for membership, enforced a strict discipline in each local church and set the Lord's Supper within its fellowship.[69] John Myles built up similar churches in Wales, beginning in the Gower and published a first Welsh baptist confession in May 1656.[70] Other areas gathered in associations and declared their faith in similar terms but towards the end of the seventeenth century there was a sizeable body of baptists in the land demanding and practising open communion at the Table even though most still demanded baptism before membership. The inconsistency of this double standard does not seem to have concerned them. They argued for the two separate practices. When the 1689 London (Second) Confession was published it failed to speak to the issue, as the churches were by then divided by it.[71] Since that time English baptists, as distinct from both continental and American baptists, have largely divorced admittance to the Lord's Table from membership of the local church, and membership from baptism, except in those churches known as Strict Baptist and the majority of those in Wales.

The baptist understands the Supper to symbolise the Lord's death as a substitute Saviour for his sins and it declares his own personal participation in the benefits of that death through his spiritual union with Christ. In the memorial, the believer acknowledges his need of sanctification through a reproduction in himself of dying to sin and rising to life eternal, reflecting the Calvary sacrifice. It declares the union of all disciplined believers in Christ's body, the church, together with their joyous expectation of perfect union with him at his appearing.

As with baptism, participation in the Supper presupposes a previous experience of saving grace though it has no saving or sanctifying power in itself. The necessary qualifications for participating in the Lord's Supper are the same as those for local church membership, the ordinance being part of the continuing communion or sharing of it. These qualifications are, therefore, regeneration displayed in repentance and faith, and a discipleship expressed initially in baptism and thereafter in being added to the local church, together with a continuing in full submission to its discipline by the Word of God. Those disorderly or disobedient disciples, whose indiscipline breaks fellowship, have no place at the Lord's Table within the church. Furthermore, in the sense that the Supper expresses the unity of the local church fellowship in the Lord, all disorderly and disobedient acts such as immoral conduct, neglect of the commands of Christ, heresy, stubborn unwillingness to accept correction exclude from the fellowship and therefore from the Table of the Lord. Neither is there any individual right to the Table, just as there is no biblical example of a totally independent christian. All submit themselves first to the Lord and then the one to the other for his sake. The practice of discipline in this manner was very rigid among the anabaptists, as we have seen when referring to the use of excommunication, called by them the 'ban'.[72] The exercise of this strict biblical discipline at the Lord's Table is often referred to as 'strict' or 'closed communion.' In Britain it has led to those baptists adhering to it being called 'Strict Baptists'.[75] Similarly, the failure to practise such a biblical discipline has led to many baptists being called 'Open' baptists.[74]

The practice of 'Open Communion' among baptists is almost entirely limited to England and those areas of the world that have been evangelised by English baptists. The greater part of the world's baptists hold and practise restricted communion. The concept of receiving the unbaptised first arose in England in 1640 when the question arose in London's first Particular Baptist church about the propriety of inviting 'unbaptised' godly ministers to preach occasionally in the pupilt. Spilsbury and his church decided against the liberal suggestion and barred all ministers who could not heartily accept the faith and order of the church. Kiffin left Spilsbury and formed London's second church in Devonshire Square and of which he became the pastor.[75] It was a further twenty years before the question of admitting unbaptised believers to the Lord's Table arose.

When Charles II was given the English throne, he restored the Church of England to its established position and evicted about two thousand godly ministers from their parishes, that is all who would not accept the imposition of the Book of Common Prayer and conform to anglican standards. This brought many former ministers into the congregations of the dissenters. Those that were 'congregational' or 'independent' had no problems in receiving such persons into their fellowships. The position of baptist churches was different. If the ejected ministers had confessed their faith in believer's baptism, the way into church fellowship was open to them as the 'Particular Baptists' and the 'Puritan' ejected ministers would be virtually at one in doctrine. Where they refused to submit to baptism as believers, rejecting the teaching of the Bible and insisting on retaining their heretical views of infant baptism, their position was entirely different. No truly baptised church could receive them. This led to controversy among the baptists. Kiffin and others stood firm for the biblical position but John Bunyan took a deviant course; he would receive them to the Lord's Table and ultimately into membership. Here lie the roots of the baptist controversy between the exponents of 'Strict' and 'Open' communion. So sharp was the difference among the ministers and messengers assembled in London in 1689 to agree and authorise the publication of the new Confession of Faith, that the addendum on the communion of the Lord's Supper was omitted entirely. In our chapter six the views of John Bunyan have been set out and in this current chapter the biblical case is presented in favour of strict communion.

In the following century, the controversy arose again. The pastor of Spilsbury's church was Abraham Booth and he firmly stood for 'strict' communion along with Carey, Fuller and others. The Rylands were the propagandists in favour of 'open' communion at this time. At the beginning of the nineteenth century, Robert Hall raised the issue again and entered into controversy with Joseph Kinghorn of Norwich, who took Booth's position in favour of 'strict' communion. Kinghorn was minister of St. Mary's baptist church, Norwich, among whose members were Jeremiah Coleman of the famous mustard firm. Robert Hall wrote at that time, 'Strict Communion is the general practice of our churches, though the holders of the opposite opinion are rapidly increasing in numbers and respectability'.[76]

The churches in northern England tended to adhere more tenaciously to the 'strict' position than their southern brothers. When they established their Baptist College, first in Bury in 1866 and then later moving it to Manchester, they laid its foundation firmly on the historic baptist principles, stating, '*The President and the Professors shall hold substantially such doctrinal views as are enunciated in the Baptist Confession of Faith adopted... London 1689; and shall also maintain baptism on a profession of faith as necessary to church fellowship and communion at the Lord's Table*'.[77] In the south, the open communionists predominated and formed their London Baptist Association in 1865 on clear open communion lines. However, the strict communionists did form an association in 1841 and a more stable body in 1871 which continues until this day as a strong fellowship and is reported elsewhere.[78]

At the beginning of this current twentieth century, Charles Williams wrote, '*Charles Haddon Spurgeon, with the majority of British baptists, invited all who loved the Lord Jesus Christ to commemorate with them his love in dying for them.*' It is Dr H. Wheeler Robinson who reports this in this book published in 1927. He adds this comment, '*It would be a curious result if the practice of 'open membership' should become predominant amongst baptists as open communion has done. Our dictionaries might have to define a Baptist Church as the only one which did not make baptism a condition of admission*'.[79] Incredibly, that tragic decline in church discipline is already a hard fact amongst baptist churches less than sixty years later. Not only is the Table not disciplined, but the church fellowship is open too. Historically, baptists have stood for the 'strict' position and have seen the 'Table' as an integral part of the church's fellowship. Inevitably, the two stand or fall together. Alas! very little biblical 'baptistness' remains in so many churches still calling themselves 'baptist'! Some, still recognised by their national unions have united with paedobaptist churches, congregational, methodist and even anglican, as the things that divide count for so little today. In this ecumenical climate of today this departure from the rule of truth is viewed by man as 'spiritual progress' towards that oneness that is the biblical ideal. However, for those who believe that the unity of all christians cannot be realised by the sacrifices of truth or principle, it appears quite otherwise. True spiritual unity can only be attained by a total submission to the Word of God and not by the neglect of its teaching. Baptists are despising their heritage and bringing greater reproach on the Lord's name than the apparent fragmentation of christianity occasions. Even Spurgeon was not without fault in this matter, taking a position of strict baptised membership but allowing the unbaptised to take communion at the Lord's Table.

The largest concentrations of baptist churches today are to be found in the United States of America and in the Union of Socialist Soviet Republics in Russia. Both these large bodies of baptist churches adhere to the historic baptist discipline of strict communion at both the Lord's Supper and in admission to church membership. Indeed they rightly insist that there are not two levels of communion, one at the Table and another for membership but rather that the Lord's Supper is a church ordinance to which those who share fellowship alone may rightly commune.

16
The baptist and gospel mission

'**Go and make disciples of all nations**, baptising them... teaching them...' said Jesus to his followers just before leaving them. The baptist is bound by the Word of God. The baptist submits literally to this **'Great Commission'** placed on him by his Saviour and Master. He counts himself under orders to proclaim the Good News of salvation to all he can reach with his voice or his life, regardless of whether he is appointed to any special office in the church or not. As the baptist understands scripture, to be a christian is to be a missionary. He knows that there are some in the church with special gifts and these are set-apart by it for special service. Some are set apart for special 'missionary service' but these are not the only persons to whom the common missionary task is given. All believers are to be missionaries.

The story of the first three centuries of christianity is remarkable and exciting because the early christians lived to tell others of the Christ who receives sinners, setting man right with his Maker. Their own lives were transformed by the gospel which they shared with others and, for that very reason, they themselves were testimonials to the validity of the message they proclaimed. Christ Jesus saves to the utmost all who come by him to God. Within three hundred years their witness had shaken the Roman Empire, challenging the Emperor himself to come to terms with it. The baptist certainly rejects the Constantinian marriage of church and state and declares it a master-stroke of the Devil, designed to weaken the witness and destroy the mighty worldwide surge of christianity. Yet he also recognises that the evil actions of prelates and emperors have been overruled to bear evidence to the divine blessing that rests on the simple obedience of all believers in spreading the news of the grace of God. One of the first fruits of that dreadful compromise was seen in the first major upsurge of baptistic testimony against apostasy in the professing churches of Christ. The subsequent story of how 'the wrath of man' has brought 'praise to God' has been traced in the historical chapters of this book.

Adolf Harnack, in his book, '*The Mission and Expansion of Christianity*' says, '*The most numerous and successful missionaries of the christian religion were not regular teachers but christians themselves, in virtue of their loyalty and courage... Everyone who seriously confessed the faith proved to be of service in its propaganda. Christians are to let their lights so shine that pagans see their good works and glorify their Father in heaven... they could not be hidden... they could not fail to preach their faith plainly and audibly... the great mission of christianity was accomplished by means of informal missionaries*'.[1]

The Donatists maintained an effective missionary ministry and spread the gospel widely throughout Mediterranean countries. This same missionary witness was also to be found in their spiritual successors. The Paulicians, protesting against the worldliness of the priesthood, spread the simple gospel into the Balkans and through southern Europe, being found in France as late as the twelfth century, still preaching Christ.

The itinerant ministry of men like Peter of Bruys, and Henri of Lausanne and many others has the same hallmark of biblical authenticity. Robert Linder writes, '*The hallmarks of apostolic christianity were simplicity, community, evangelism and love*', as already noted.[2] The deterioration of mainstream christianity through the centuries is marked by the erosion of these 'hallmarks' and, specifically in the decline in 'the mission of the individual believer' to evangelise. Paul the apostle puts that duty eminently well, saying, '*You yourselves are our letter... known and read by everybody. You show that you are a letter from Christ... written not in ink, but with the living Spirit of God...*'

The anabaptist believers of the sixteenth century expressed their total submission to the scriptures in this same missionary manner of life. Gladly they set aside the things of this life in order to be more free to move around testifying to Christ and his gospel. It is said, 'The Hutterites carried the gospel to every part of German-speaking Europe. They spoke with power of the kingdom of God, showing all men that they must repent, be converted and turn from the vanity of this world and its unrighteousness, from a vile and sinful life, to God their Creator and Jesus Christ their Saviour and Redeemer. To all such work God gave his blessing and grace, so that it was carried on with joy.' This Hutterite missionary work was costly, to quote Estep, 'Eighty percent of them died a martyr's death.'[5] Speaking of this characteristic commitment of the anabaptists to missionary work, Williams says, *'The radical reformers turned with vehemence to the pentecostal task of converting the world to christianity'.*[6] In their first generation, every anabaptist believer was *'a responsible disciple of Christ ready to propagate his faith by martyrdom. This new christian was not a reformer, but a converter to Christ'.*[7]

The baptist belief is that every christian is commissioned to live to make Christ known with intense urgency. Their confidence in the second coming of Christ gave the anabaptist such an urgency. Indeed evangelism ought always to be seen as an immediate task, controlling and often overriding life's normal course. This is in contrast to the 'magisterial reformers' whose concern was to reform the churches. The baptist gives priority to striving for the salvation of perishing sinners.[8] This is of relevance to this second-half of the twentieth century in which greatest concern has tended to centre on reform of the erroneous in the churches. Whilst not neglecting the one, the supreme call must not be depressed to a secondary place.

'To be a christian was not child's play but to be commissioned for life', Williams comments on the anabaptist fathers.[9] They regarded themselves as apostolic emissaries commissioned from on high to *'proclaim good news to the poor, freedom to the prisoners, recovery of sight to the blind, release for the oppressed, to proclaim the acceptable year of the Lord's favour,'* just as their Master had said in Nazareth fifteen centuries previously.[10] They strove to make the local church's whole fellowship into a *'royal priesthood, a holy nation, a people belonging to God'*,

a lay apostolate with everyone a missionary.[11]

The Mennonites continued to see the christian's daily life as a missionary commission long after the other anabaptists. During the sixteenth and seventeenth centuries, they penetrated the countries bordering the Baltic Sea and into inland Russia and planted churches or rather christian communities. Some residual presence continued into the middle nineteenth century when the German baptist and English 'Brethren' evangelisation of Russia had got under way. Dutch Mennonites formed their **'Association for the Spread of the Gospel'** in 1847 and sent missionaries to Indonesia, which work was strengthened by the sending of help from the Russian churches in 1888.[12]

The stories of Carey and Judson have been told, with accounts of the commencement of baptist work in India and Burma as well as of other pioneers such as Paul Besson, the founder of baptist work in Argentina. Baptists, faithful to their doctrine of mission have given the world the modern missionary movement. In some sense non-baptist churches have taken into their system the essentially baptistic concept of 'living to make Christ known'. All contemporary groupings of baptist local churches have an emphasis on evangelism which is frequently underlined in their confessions of faith as an obligatory principle to evangelise the world. Regrettably by many it is seen in a non-baptist sense as the ministry of the whole body of churches fulfilled by a few 'specially gifted people' rather than in a work out of the baptist concept of 'every believer a missionary'.

The Baptist Bible Union of America 1923 said in its Article XIII, *'We believe that the true commission of the church is found in the Great Commission, first to make disciples...'*[13] Whereas the Article XI of the Southern Convention 1963 says, *'It is the duty and privilege of every follower of Christ.. to endeavour to make disciples of all nations'*.[14] The Swedish baptists say, *'We believe the gospel should be preached to every creature...'*[15] French baptists, *'It is incumbent on the local congregation to declare the gospel...'*[16] Australians make a similar declaration of christian duty to evangelise.[17] Despite the severe penalties imposed by an atheistic state for all *'unlawful propaganda'*, the Russian baptists in the

1963 confession of the All-Union Conference of Evangelical Christian Baptists make the same principle clear, saying, '*It is the purpose of the local church to declare the kingdom of Christ to its members and to propagate it to the world*'.[18] Many of them languish in prison or labour camp because of their faithfulness to their calling as christians. The English Strict Baptists, often charged with inertia because of their alleged 'calvinism', but who have a long and honourable record of missionary commitment, say in their 'Affirmation of Faith' 1966, '*It is the duty of the church to provide for... the proclamation of the gospel throughout the world*'.[19] It is even more interesting to note that the English Baptist Union, whose progressive neglect of its heritage we have chronicled in chapter seven, and whose confessional statement is reduced to but three principles, still declares in the last, '*That it is the duty of every disciple to bear witness to the gospel of Jesus Christ and to take part in the evangelisation of the world.*'[20] The instrument of the Union's churches, The **Baptist Missionary Society**, remains one of the world's principal missionary outreach bodies, although the independent baptist churches of Britain have been said to send out more missionaries pro rata of their church memberships through their **Grace Baptist Mission**, to which reference has already been made; whilst American baptists provide the largest body of missionaries, probably outnumbering all others taken together. Both American and British independents operate their mission work as totally church-based and not as national societies. Each missionary is answerable solely to his own home church; whilst the home churches collectively strengthen each other through common service units, like Grace Baptist Mission referred to above. This form of outreach is closer to the biblical concept of local churches being the divinely chosen unit rather than national or denominational organisations and structures.

Looking back over the centuries, baptists of all periods have fulfilled their gospel calling and the message has been preached to almost all nations. Churches have been planted in almost all countries and peoples from all kindreds, tribes and tongues have come to faith in Christ. In recording the development of baptist churches throughout the world in earlier chapters, constant reference has been made to baptist evangelisation. The baptist responsibility today remains the same. The baptist must enter into the heritage his fathers have left him and keep the Great Commission of his Lord constantly before him until the whole world is evangelised in these last days to the praise and glory of the Father and his Son, Jesus Christ.

17
The baptist – good works and grace

'**They live on earth, but their citizenship is in heaven**', said Diogenes of the Donatists[1], bearing testimony to their constant desire to reflect the holiness of the Christ who lived in them. Throughout the early centuries the baptistic witness of succeeding groups testified against the godlessness of the professing priests and bishops of christendom and demanded that the people of God should be seen to be his people in the purity of their lives. Augustine of Hippo may have jeered at the Donatists as **spotless saints** and Luther despised the anabaptists of his day with similar jibes, but the testimony of contemporaries constantly bears out the fact that these witnesses of the holy God bore that witness with consistently holy lives.[2] Personal piety and godly lives were the hallmarks of the humblest believers of these early 'baptists', their enemies frequently bearing testimony to them.

However, the decline of godliness in professing christendom, particularly after the infamous marriage to the Empire, led to the evolution of 'The Christian Church' as a national religious organisation in which 'simplicity and spontaniety' were replaced by a 'despotic institutionalism', 'salvation by faith' by the practice on unconscious babes of a 'standard mechanical rite', the 'ordinances of the gospel' by 'magical rites' and a truly spiritual 'life in Christ' was debased into 'submission to priestly authority'.[3] One consequence of this was the emergence of religious 'good works' as part of a system of 'merit' whereby the benefits of God's grace were mediated by the priest-ridden church to its subservient communicants according to its own arbitrary decisions. 'Good works' became the key to the church's treasury of benefits both for this life and that to come. The infamous 'indulgence system', to which Luther took violent exception, was a typical example. The theology of such a 'commercialised' system was the antithesis of the New Testament's salvation by grace.

The reformers' initial attack on the papal monolith was the declaration of **justification by faith alone**. This theme became the **battlecry of the Reformation**. That it should so dominate the reformers' re-statement of bible truth is perfectly understandable from our distance. They were so determined to reform 'The Church' (Note - not 'the churches') on a thoroughly New Testament basis that they overlooked the consequence of preaching salvation by faith alone. At all costs, they intended the world to understand that 'good works' had no part to play in the getting right with God but that it was a work of God alone and totally unrelated to any supposed merit of the sinner being saved. A man's salvation rested totally on God's grace and the works of man played no part whatsoever. This had to be emphasised in order to destroy the trust in 'good works' which Rome had built up. However, there was an inherent weakness in this approach which was quickly brought to light, not by the catholic priests but by those reformers who insisted in taking the reformation to the full limits demanded by a total submission to scripture.

The anabaptists quickly reduced Luther's battlecry 'sola fide' (by faith alone) to a meaningless shibboleth. They insisted that 'saving faith' could never exist alone! '**Saving faith**' was certainly a work of God in his grace within the man he saves and without it there could not be any true experience of salvation. In that they agreed with the reformer but they went on to say that which Luther was loth to acknowledge, lest it should weaken his attack on Rome, that '**saving faith was always accompanied by good works**'. **Whilst Luther denounced James's letter as an** '*epistle of straw*', the anabaptists insisted with James that '*faith without works is dead*'. They insisted that saving faith does not and cannot exist without works. Furthermore they accused Luther of jeopardising the moral life of christian communities by his incomplete teaching.[4] The anabaptists also highlighted the irreconcilable contradiction between the theology of 'justification by faith' and the Lutheran theological support of infant baptism which proclaims justification without faith. Denck, the evangelical anabaptist, *'declared that saving faith can never be the inherited belief, inculcated by one's parents, otherwise salvation would itself be hereditary.'*[5]

The peril of Luther's inadequate statement of salvation by faith alone has tended to give rise to the antinomian characteristic of the Galatian church, with its technical righteousness. Lutheranism proclaimed a forensic justification, a juridical declaration of discharge from the penalty of sin, and this is certainly an essential part of the biblical doctrine. The anabaptists insisted that the legal fact would be accompanied by a practical outworking in the believer of the fruitful works of righteousness and that, without such evidence, the reality of the 'saving faith' must be called into question. They emphasised the moral and ethical content of a declared righteousness and did it so strongly that their pre-eminent theologian, Hubmaier, speaks of justification as the *'holiness realised through faith.'* For him the object of faith is the 'grace of God made available and effective through the incarnate, crucified and risen Christ.'[6]

Hubmaier, in the first three of his *'Eighteen Dissertations'* 1524, states that;

1. Faith alone makes us pious before God;

2. This belief is recognition of the mercy of God, since he has redeemed us by the sacrifice of his only-begotten Son, and this excludes all nominal christians who have only an historical belief in God;

3. Such faith can not remain passive but must **break out** (German-*ausbrecken*) to God in thanksgiving and towards mankind in all kinds of good works of brotherly love.[7]

The translation of Estep in article three rightly emphasises the dynamic outburst of the new-born inner-creation which cannot but break out and be seen explicitly in the outward life of the believer, that is in the fruits of the Spirit, the good works that inevitably accompany a saving faith. The consequence was that the baptist places a continuing emphasis on the disciplining of believers in the church.

Menno Simon, writing twenty years later in his 'Foundation of Christian Doctrine', states: '*The whole heart casts itself upon the grace, word and promises of the Lord, since it knows that God is true and that his promises cannot fail. In this the heart is renewed, converted, justified and becomes pious, peaceable and joyous... and so becomes a joint heir with Christ and a possessor of eternal life.*'[8]

Pilgram Marpeck said similarly, '*Justification by faith was far more than a legal transaction in the heavenly court. It meant a new life, a life of discipleship in obedience to the risen Lord*'.

The baptist challenges all christians with this moral and ethical content of the reformed doctrine of justification, and he does so without resorting to a works-righteousness soteriology. His challenge is to show 'living saving faith' by 'living good works' in lives totally yielded to declaring the beauty and glory of the Redeemer. Felbinger, the Hutterite anabaptist, said '*A christian does not receive his name from his baptism but from the conduct of the whole of his life*'.[10]

Staying with the anabaptists a little longer, we note that they enforced the strictest discipline on their church members, rigidly applying the teaching of Jesus in Matthew's Gospel.[11] Article two of the Schleitheim Confession states: '*The ban shall be employed with all those who have been baptised into the one body of Christ, who are called brothers and sisters, and yet who slip sometimes and fall into error and sin, being inadvertently overtaken. The same shall be admonished twice in secret and the third time openly disciplined or banned according to the command of Christ in Matthew 18. But this shall be done according to the regulation of the Spirit (Matthew 5) before breaking of bread, so that we may break and eat one bread with one mind and in love and drink one cup.*'[12] Most baptist churches have some such rule but many do not enforce it, locking away the big stick so well that they have forgotten they have it and for what reason. Looseness of conduct and failure to bring forth the fruits of righteousness by the membership results. The testimony of the church fails to validate the gospel it proclaims because the lives of its membership call it into question. This is none other than the consistent testimony of scripture and no new doctrine of the baptists. Good works must accompany faith.

The anabaptists succeeded so well in their witness that they were accused of teaching sinless perfection, a charge which Hubmaier felt obliged to refute, saying, 'The charge is a monstrous injustice, for we know that both before and after baptism, we are poor and miserable sinners'.[13]

Contemporary critics of the fourth century Donatists said, '*The manner of conduct which they display is wonderful and confessedly beyond belief...*'[14] The twentieth century church historian, Latourette, traces the same discipline and chaste conduct in the Donatists' baptistic successors, the Bogils in the Balkans and Bulgaria, the Arnoldists of France and Switzerland, the Waldenses of Piedmont and Savoy down to our friends and fathers, the anabaptists of the sixteenth century.[15] Of one group he quotes the comment, '*their most caustic critics bore witness to their high moral characters.*'[16] Zwingli, the Swiss reformer, attacked the Swiss anabaptists saying that such high standards of practical christian living were impossible to apply and ought not to be attempted because the church of God was invisible. They replied, '*True, the saints elect of God are only known to God, and the true church is invisible but we can deal explicitly with our members and maintain a pure church by discipline in its local visible expression*'.[17]

Those same Swiss brothers took a strong line against antinomianism, saying that the conduct of the believer is always a vital concern of the church because it impinges on the honour of the Head, the Lord Jesus Christ. The catholic writer, Jerome Verdassen quoted by Armitage, said of our baptist fathers, '*In the sight of the authorities, they lived as peaceful citizens, obedient and noted for uprightness, honesty, conscientiousness, temperance and godliness.*'[18] The Lutheran writer, John Anastatius, comments, '*The anabaptists are elevated above the other protestants on account of their peace-loving disposition, strength of faith and godliness of life.*'[19] Latourette sums up the testimony to the godly living of our fathers and the impact of their good works on the world around them, saying, '*Even among their severe critics were those who admitted that they were honest, peaceable, temperate, eschewed profanity and harsh language, and were upright, meek and free from covetousness and pride. They endeavoured to live up to the ethical demands of the sermon on the Mount. The catholic way of striving for perfection was that of the monastery, communities of celebates apart from the world.*'[20] The anabaptists sought perfection, but out in the world where it would testify effectively for the glory of their Lord. The people of God were seen to be the very people of God indeed and God was known by the world, out there in the world, by his living presence in the lives of his people. Since when, in this twentieth century, has an unbeliever, coming into our assemblies for worship, been convinced, and falling down, said, '*Indeed God is really here among you!*'? [21] Our Saviour, Christ did not pray that the Father would take his people out of the world but that he would keep them from the evil, in order that by their good works, their holy and loving oneness, a oneness in the Father and the Son, the world may believe... that the world might know...[22] Here surely is the apex of godly conduct, the fruits of the Spirit, the bearing of all good works, out in the world to validate the gospel of Jesus Christ out there, that men might know and that men might believe.

The baptist forefathers showed their oneness with each other by their tender care and concern for each other just as the Lord commanded his followers to do. They set an example so far above anything apparent in contemporary times. Pre-eminently, their love bloomed most beautifully in their forgiving and tender love towards those terribly misguided church leaders, who persecuted them with outrageous brutality. Consider the forgiveness Hubmaier showed towards his brother in Christ, Zwingli, whose colleague and instructor in the faith he had been. Zwingli could imprison his brother in the dampest dungeon in Zürich, the Wasserturn out in the river Limmat, and permit him to be tortured on the rack, yet Hubmaier could forgive and pray for his perfidious colleague. Again, when Lord Liechtenstein, whom Hubmaier had led to the Lord, handed him over to be tortured and burnt in Vienna, Hubmaier could love and forgive.[23]

Capito called, Hans Denck 'the Pope of the Anabaptists',

though history has called him 'The Apostle of Love.' Listen
to Denck's last letter as he lies dying at thirty years of age
worn out with his evangelistic endeavours, *'It gives my heart
pain that I should stand in disunity with many men whom I cannot
help but call my brothers because they pray to the same God, to
whom I pray, and give honour to the Father, for the same reason I
honour him, namely, because he has sent his Son, the Saviour of the
world. Therefore, as God wills, and so much as in me is, I will not
have my brother as an opponent and my Father as a judge; but in
the meantime will attempt to reconcile all my adversaries with me.'*
Dr Keller, in his Life of Denck, says, *'No one has been able to
discover even the smallest spot in his character.'*[24]

The reformer, Bucer, said of Michael Sattler, whom he
banished from Strassburg, *'No doubt he was a dear friend of
God'*.[25] Zwingli detested Felix Manz and was fully party to
the drowning of that faithful servant of God. Indeed he
said of Manz, *'Let him who talks of going under water* (baptism),
go under!' Yet Manz could write to his executioners, *'Love to
God through Christ shall alone avail and subsist; but boasting,
reviling and threatening shall fail. Charity alone is pleasing to
God; he that cannot show charity has no part with God. It is
incumbent on him who will be an heir of Christ to be merciful, as
the Father in heaven is merciful. Christ hated no man; his true
disciples are likewise devoid of hatred; this following Christ is the
true way, as he went before... I will now conclude my memorial... I
hereby resolve that I will remain faithful to Christ and put my trust
in him who knows my every distress and is mighty to deliver.
Amen'*.[26]

The sixteenth century anabaptist fathers lived under
acute pressures yet maintained the evidences of being truly
the children of God. The issues that divided christians in
that fateful age were no less than those that fragment
believers today. The godly conduct and loving spirit that
they manifested should challenge baptists in these days to
be mindful of the Lord's command to love one another. Let
love temper the judgements we pass on the Lord's servants
from whom arminianism, antinomianism, Amyraldianism
or anything else divides. Let love temper our judgements;
let love restrain our blanket condemnations; let love stir up
our hears in honest prayer for all who love our Lord and
Saviour in sincerity and truth.

Not only did the fathers show such love towards those brothers from whom they differed, they showed true Christlike love towards one another within their fellowships. Listen to the Hutterites giving their biblical grounds for their community life, which Williams calls '*the strong longing for sharing, togetherness and unity, even as with the Father and the Son.*'[27] Peter Riedemann, their second generation leader, says, '*Community is naught else than that those who have fellowship have all things common... even as the Father has nothing for himself, but that he has he has with the Son, and again, the Son has nothing for himself, but all he has he has with the Father and all who have fellowship with him. Thus all those that have fellowship with him have nothing for themselves but have all things with their Master and with all those that have fellowship with him, that they may be one in the Son as the Son is in the Father. It is called the communion of the saints because they have fellowship in holy things, yes, in those things whereby they are sanctified, that is in the Father and in the Son, who himself sanctifies them with all that he has given them. Thus everything serves for the betterment and building up of one's neighbour and to the praise and glory of God the Father.*' It is evident that Riedemann is writing an exposition of John 17 and related texts.[28]

The baptist begins by total submission to the Word of God and the result is as Paul told Timothy, '*so that the man of God may be thoroughly equipped for every good work.*' He also prayed for the Colossian believers that '*you may live a life worthy of the Lord and may please him in every way, bearing fruit in every good work...*'[29]

The final section of this chapter must return to the doctrine of grace among the baptists. Firstly, we must repeat that their emphasis on good works being an essential evidence of true salvation, and their insistent demand for godliness in the christian daily life, did not move our fathers from their conviction that salvation was of grace. The biblical baptist does not rest his doctrine of salvation on works, as the catholic theologian has done. Neither has he over-reacted against the romanist's dependence on merit so as to weaken his concern for holy living, as the reformers tended to do. Salvation, among baptists, is always of grace. However, baptists have not always agreed on those issues concerning the sovereignty of God in salvation which came to a head among the reformed churches in the early years of the seventeenth century. It is needful that we take some note of these variations before leaving this subject.[30]

Early baptist ancestry, among the Donatists, Bogils and Albigenses, takes little note of Augustine's classical definitions of the doctrines of grace and of predestination. They were concerned with his abuse of scripture in attempting to defend the union of church and state and justify infant baptism. They rejected his defective exposition of the parable of the **'Wheat and Tares'** and his deduction that the church of Christ would always remain a mixture of the regenerate and unregenerate until the judgement day. They rightly claimed that this aspect of Augustine's teaching would lead inevitably to low moral standards throughout christendom.[31]

The Waldensian churches held salvation by grace and not of works, together with a clear doctrine of justification by faith. When, under Farel's influence, they drew closer to the reformed churches, they revised their confessional position to bring it into line with the genevan standards, acquiring a distinctively calvinistic emphasis.[32]

As we have seen, Balthasar Hubmaier, the sixteenth century anabaptists' greatest theologian, sympathised with those views of God's sovereignty in grace which afterward became called 'calvinist.' This is reflected, says Williams, in Hubmaier's exposition of the Pauline epistles in the course of his polemical works. Hans Denck, on the other hand, advanced the view that the atonement was sufficient for all men, though limited in its efficacy to the elect.[33]

Progressively, anabaptists of that period took a universal view of the extent of the atonement, arguing that man was delivered from the bondage of original sin and his will was set free to choose good or evil. Melchoir Hofmann is typical of these but over against them the clear, biblical teaching of Pilgram Marpeck stands out insisting that '*a sinful proclivity in man remained.*'[34]

Two factors were to polarise the doctrine of salvation as held by all evangelicals, whether baptist or reformed, namely, the publication of Calvin's '*Institutes of the Christian*

Religion' together with Beza's elaborations, and the Synod of Dort (Dordrecht) of 1618-19. At Dordrecht the reformed churches from several countries examined and rejected the assertions of the Remonstrants, led by Arminius, who had set out five points of objection to the traditional reformed confessions. They opposed **Total Depravity of Man** since the Fall, **Unconditional Election**, a **Limited Atonement**, the **Efficacious Call** of Grace and the **Perseverance of the Saints**. The rejection of these tenets of orthodox religion became known as the '*Arminian Heresy*'.[35]

Dutch baptists had planted churches in Kent and Essex during the previous century, bringing their universalism with them. When Thomas Helwys brought his émigré English church to London 1611, it also brought the same general view of the atonement. Lumpkin says of *Helwys 1611 Confession of Faith* that, '*It shows... signs of its author's calvinistic background. It is anti-calvinistic on the doctrine of the atonement and anti-arminian in its doctrines of sin and the will...*'(!)[36] The next significant confession of faith from these churches was published in 1651, and of this Lumpkin says, '*No consistently arminian system is revealed; rather, some traditional emphases of calvinism are set forth.*'[37] The *Standard Confession of Faith* of these General Baptist churches dated 1660, whilst being more clear on its universality of the atonement (see Article III), it is explicit in declaring its conviction that '*God's election to eternal life of such as believe is of his grace alone*', saying, '*yet confident, we are, that the purpose of God according to election, was not in the least arising from foreseen faith in, or works of righteousness done by, the creature, but only from the mercy, goodness and compassion dwelling in God...*'[38] (Article VIII). The reader will remark how close this comes to the reformed doctrine of unconditional election which was held by Particular Baptist churches and expressed in their confessions.

Later confessions of the General Baptists reveal stronger anti-calvinist sentiments but retain an insistence on the electing grace of God. The 1770 confession of the New Connexion General Baptists states its view of universal atonement most succinctly but still adheres explicitly to salvation by grace (see Article 3)[39] As stated in Chapter 7 of this book, there has been a progressive reduction in the doctrinal content of the Basis of the Baptist Union of Great Britain and Ireland. Today, it says *'Christ died for our sins'* in its only reference to atonement and the word or idea of 'grace' finds no place.[40] Though the Union drew its origin from Particular Baptist churches, who always stated their doctrinal position in explicit confessions, making special reference to atonement and grace, this is forgotten in the interest of the admission to membership of New Connexion and other churches into its fellowship without doctrinal test.

The marriage of baptist churches with the reformers' doctrine of salvation in the Particular Baptist churches has been an uneasy alliance. The development of *'convenantal theology'* into the extra-biblical theory of 'Federalism' by the Princeton theologians[41] has had to be rejected firmly by the baptists. See, for example, its refutation in Strong's Systematic Theology.[42]

Similarly, with the revival of reformed theology in this second half of the twentieth century, baptists object to the use of the Covenant of Grace by paedobaptists in attempting a defence of infant baptism. As also baptists reject the reformed insistence on interpreting the New Testament by the Old, the New Testament church by Israel, christian baptism by circumcision. Particular baptists firmly take their stance with Paul as stated in Galations 3:7. *'They which are of faith, the same are the children of Abraham'*. David Kingdon has produced an excellent discussion of this issue in his book entitled, *'The Children of Abraham'*.[43]

Particular Baptist churches have indeed declared themselves without ambiguity in their historic confessions. Lumpkin says of the First London Confession 1644, that it reflects, 'calvinism of a moderate type' yet that 'moderation' does not prevent a clear statement that salvation is altogether of grace.[44] Its Article V says *'the elect, which God hath loved with everlasting love, are redeemed, quickened and saved, not by themselves, neither by their good works, lest any man should boast himself, but wholly and only by God of his free grace and mercy through Christ Jesus...'*[45] This same emphasis on salvation being of God's grace has persisted throughout succeeding generations until the latest Particular Baptist

confession, that of 1966, which remains explicitly clear
These same confessions have retained the historic emph
ases on the necessity in every christian, of a godly life and of
good works, and take these two together, grace and good
works, asserting no antimony nor tension between them
This is characteristically baptist and a vital component of
his biblical heritage.

18
The baptist – today and tomorrow

The baptist's heritage is an immensely rich record of the grace of God in preserving a biblical church witness throughout the centuries of the christian era. The early churches of the first two centuries were recognisable as biblically based churches of baptised believers only and it was only as this period began to close that there were serious departures from those standards. As biblical standards waned and the lives of christians, and particularly of those holding office in the churches, ceased to reflect the fruits of righteousness, so a witness against such departure arose having distinctive characteristics which have been labelled 'baptistic'. With the marriage of church and state, broader issues of erroneous doctrine demanded sharper testimony against apostasy and that 'baptistic' protest became more strident in the Donatists, the first christians to be called 'anabaptists'. The Paulicians and other groups maintained a repetitive testimony against the prevalent evils in the 'catholic' churches throughout the Roman Empire. These upsurges of 'baptistic' witness were constantly calling christians back to a biblical standard of faith and practice. The Waldensians and the sixteenth century anabaptists brought this sequence of protest for the truth down to the time of the Reformation, and thence by means of the modern baptist movement, into the current time. In this historical review, the emerging characteristics of **'The Baptist'** have been identified and listed in the course of this study and must now be summarised.[1]

First, the baptist believes in the Bible as being God's authoritative and inerrant Word and that the christian must give total submission to it in everything. He does not add tradition to the Word as does the Papist. Nor does he stop short of the absolute sufficiency of scripture as did the protestant reformers of the sixteenth century, who evolved the dictum that *'whatsoever is not prohibited in scripture is permissible'*. Hence their opinion that infant baptism is permissible as it is not explicitly prohibited; whereas the baptist position is that *'that which is not commanded is not required'*. Further, the protestant reformers developed a theory of *'necessary consequences'* by which they divided between what is *'explicitly stated'* in the scripture and what is *'implicitly taught'*.[2] Kenneth Good has called attention to the striking contrast which is evident in a comparison of the Westminster Confession (presbyterian) and the Second London Confession (baptist). This contrast stands out the more strikingly when the reader takes account of the fact that the baptists in the latter were endeavouring to show themselves at one with Puritan positions wherever their consciences would allow. Hence it is by the differences that remain that the baptist position is identified as distinct from that of the presbyterians; such as the deletion in Chapter I section vi in the London Confession of the words, *'good and necessary consequence may be deducted from scripture'*, as in the Westminster, and the substitution of *'or necessarily contained in scripture'*. The baptists here reject an idea deduced from theology and not from scripture.[3]

Secondly, the baptist insists that the Church is the gathered company of regenerate persons in any locality, each of whom has evidenced his spiritual life by his personal repentance and faith in the Lord Jesus Christ for salvation and who has begun his voluntary discipleship in believer's baptism by immersion in the name of the Trinity.[4] Unlike both catholic and protestant, the baptist rejects the false statement that 'the visible church of Christ consists of all those throughout the world that profess the true religion, together with their children,'[5] to quote the exact words of the Westminster Confession. Indeed the baptist rejects the division of the church into 'visible' and 'invisible' but instead believes that the word 'church' means 'the local church' and that the total number of the glorified saints is the only other use for the word 'church' in a biblical sense.[6]

In speaking of the 'local church', the baptist believes that it is God's basic unit for the outworking of his purpose to glorify himself in his church on earth and is careful to define it in precise biblical terms as have been examined and presented earlier. On these principles the baptist must take his stand today and tomorrow:

1. A regenerate, believing church;

2 A baptised church membership;

3. A church entirely free from the state;

4. A church practising local autonomy;

5. A church of voluntary disciples;

6. A church of godly disciples whose lives are holy and righteous;

7. A church believing and practising the priesthood of all believers;

8. A church engaged in evangelising the world;

9. A church requiring nothing but what the scriptures express explicitly;

10. A church sitting loosely to material things, anticipating the coming of her Lord in glory.

In previous chapters, these principles have been seen in part or in whole, earnestly propagated by Donatists, Paulicians, Bogomils, Albigenses and Waldenses during the Middle Ages of papal dominance. The Waldenses, and their successors the anabaptists, at extreme cost, bore their

testimony to these biblical principles of scripture and
church both against the apostasy of Rome and the 'half-way
reform' of the Protestants during the sixteenth century. In
the midst of today's apostasising ecumenism, the Word of
God demands that the same stand be taken for those same
principles lest the light of truth be dimmed and darkness
fall upon mankind again.

**Thirdly, the baptist insists on the necessity of a godly life
both holy and righteous**. The earliest upsurge of baptistic
protest was against the toleration in the churches of a
progressively worldly life, taken up with material things
and particularly among priests and bishops. The studies
have shown that there was a constant need for this
testimony to be borne in successive periods of church
history. The Albigenses, Peter de Bruys and Henri of
Lausanne are examples. The Lollards in Britain raised the
same call to reformation of life among the clerics. Even the
catholic mystics cried out in the same way, Savonorola and
Tauler, for examples. When the protestant reformation
dawned, the leaders were as vocal on this issue, as were the
anabaptists Hubmaier and Denck; but soon only the baptist
protest was to be heard. Indeed the baptists found it
necessary to rebuke Luther for his neglect of the necessity
for the believer to show his faith by his works, as has been
seen in earlier chapters.[7] The shortest life of any man
justified by faith, the dying thief in the gospels, revealed
the change in his inner life and the evidence of the fruit of
the Spirit in his altered attitude to his fellow malefactor as
he remonstrated with him.[8] The world is to see the
believer's good works and glorify the Father in heaven.

Furthermore, the baptist demands a strict discipline in
the churches.[9] Every member's life is to be open before his
fellow and they each are to submit themselves to one
another. Churches must discipline themselves faithfully so
that the Redeemer's name is jealously guarded. The
preaching of the pure gospel demands a holy church to
back its divine authority in addressing the world. The
baptist fathers urged their people to live a life of mutual
edification and encouragement to that purpose. Successive
generations of their persecutors bore testimony that the

lives of the baptists were beyond rebuke. [10] Whilst catholics sought perfection in cloistered isolation, the baptist lived a pure life out in the world where it validated the gospel they preached. This principle must be taken to heart in today's conditions, if the gospel is to be effective. The quality of life that God expects of his people must be spelt out clearly. Since when has an unbeliever come into our assemblies and been convinced and falling down said, *'God is in you of a truth.'*[11]

The baptist seeks to fulfill his christian life within the local church and not apart from it. He is not, nor can he be, an individualist. The variety of the natural gifts, as well as of the special spiritual gifts, of the individual members of the local church provide for its completeness as the unit designed in God's grace to declare effectively his purpose of salvation to the world of sinners. The baptist cannot view himself alone but always as a part of the unit, or body, as the scripture calls the church. This is no other than should be the biblical norm among christians and, as far as it is so, the 'baptist' desires no separate 'baptist' assembly. He neither desires nor claims any special 'local church' but delights to be one with all those who gather in his Master's name, ruled by his biblically given principles and striving solely for his glory under his headship.

Fourthly, the baptist is in the world to preach the gospel to every creature. He lives to lead men to Christ.[12] He is not in the business of promoting 'baptist churches' as a structured denominational organisation among others, nor to compete for the world's favour for his cause. Indeed the baptist view of the world in any sense is always secondary to his priority commitment to lead sinners to Christ as individual persons. The baptist is supremely concerned with preaching the gospel to the world that sinners might be saved. His priority is essentially for persons, because God's plan of salvation is individual and personal. Election, redemption, calling, hearing the Word, conviction of sin, repentance and saving faith are such and all matters in which God deals with men one by one. This is illustrated from the supposed 'conversion' of the Anglo-Saxons by Augustine of Canterbury in 597. The sprinkling

of Ethelbert and his minions might have made them
'catholic vassals of Rome' but did nothing towards bringing
them to Christ as the Celtic christians of that day in Wales
so clearly stated in their rejection of the persecuting
Augustine.[13] This is the reason why baptistic Donatists of
the fourth century rejected the empire-wide religion of
Constantine; and it accounts for the rejection of the
half-way reform of the sixteenth century by the anabaptists, also for the rejection of the national church by British
baptists in that and the following century, as well as the
rejection of all establishment churches, anglican, congregational, presbyterian and catholic by the American baptists
in both the colonies and in the constitution of the United
States subsequently. Today's world-wide spread of baptist
churches should be still addressing themselves to the
conversion of persons throughout the world's population.
In so far as some may have become structured, self-
perpetuating bodies striving for denominational pre-
eminence, they have rejected Christ and their own
heritage. In so far as the Great Commission is still being
honoured and holding first-place in the commitment of
those churches, the baptist heritage is being honoured and
God is being glorified in his churches by Christ Jesus.[14]

This is not to say that baptist christians have no concern
for the social well-being of their fellow men. Indeed, the
preaching and practice of the gospel has always occasioned
a broad-based ministry to the needy from the days of
Pentecost, through the centuries of baptist history which
we have traced and down to our own times. The
community caring of the Hutterite Brethren of the
seventeenth century stands as an excellent example.
Indeed the American first baptists of Rhode Island colony
laid down an even broader concern for the liberty of the
consciences of their fellows. Where in the world were Jews
able to worship more freely than in 'baptist' Rhode Island
which set the pattern for the new Republic's constitution?
The baptist, **Thomas Guy**, endowed the foundation of the
famous teaching hospital in London. Another London
baptist **Charles Spurgeon**, established sixty-six charitable
institutions during his pastorate at the Metropolitan
Tabernacle.[15] But with them all, the priority commitment

was to preach Christ to sinful men and that is still the baptist commitment to the world today.

Our fathers challenge us to take the Great Commission seriously because they held it to be binding on all true disciples of Christ in every age. There is a tense strain between the systematised theology of state-related churches and the simple urgency to win men to Christ in a living church. Williams said, *'our fathers turned with vehemence to the pentecostal task of converting the world to christianity.'*[16] They applied themselves to their evangelistic task with urgency, believing that the Lord's coming was near. The anabaptist's ruling passion was his missionary obligation.

Those anabaptist forefathers held that the *'teaching and pastoring gift'* belonged to the set-apart minister of the Word, just as Paul taught, and the reformers in their day. But the baptists grasped something which the reformers seemed to miss and which the twentieth century baptists are in danger of losing, namely, that it is the Christ-given task of every believer to *'proclaim the gospel to every creature'*. *Estep says, 'They believed that the Great Commission was binding on all true disciples of Christ and they felt obliged to obey it... and obey it they did. Into all German-speaking Europe they went with their Bibles and tracts, their hymns and sermons, to preach, to teach, live, suffer and die for Christ's sake.'*[17] They paid a terrible price for their obedience, as has been noted, about 80% of the Hutterite missionaries dying for their faith.[18] Their commitment appears unparalleled in history. They formed, in the crucible of suffering, one of the most aggressive missionary movements of all times.[19] Pastors and people, they were all committed to the preaching of the gospel to all who could be reached. Williams comments, 'In all parts of the anabaptist movement in the sixteenth century, one is impressed with the mobility, the purposefulness and the testimonial missionary urgency of every convert, whether he be commissioned elder or a steadfast wife of a weaver evangelist. In the stress of personal accountability and explicit faith, the whole of the Radical Reformation pushed the Lutheran doctrine of the priesthood of all believers in the direction of a universal lay apostalate'.[20] Those baptist forefathers challenge the twentieth century baptists to demote everything else to a

secondary place and make the supreme priority the
preaching of Christ to every creature, 'to present our
bodies a living sacrifice' in order that the gospel may be
sounded out to earth's remotest bound.

   The Baptist must consider seriously his relationship with
other christian churches. Baptists in the twentieth century
live amidst a plethora of professedly christian churches,
denominations and societies and he is compelled to
recognise and do his duty towards them. The plurality of
christianity is necessarily an embarrassment but the baptist
may not bury his head in the ground and ignore the hard
facts of today's situation. His forefathers were dutiful in all
situations and always without regard to the consequences.
They faithfully protested for the truth and rebuked every
kind of departure from it. The baptist task today is no
different. He must remind himself that he is not here for
his own health but for the saving-health of the perishing.
He is not here to engage in his own aggrandisement, to
make a name for baptists or to glory in his conquests. His
task is to preach Christ and gather believers into orderly,
well-taught churches that God may be glorified in them.

   The second half of this century saw a revival of the
'reformed doctrine of salvation' largely through the republica-
tion and careful study of the writings of the protestant
reformers and their puritan followers. For baptists, this has
meant a revival of the study theology of their seventeenth
century 'Particular Baptist' forefathers. Similarly, paedobaptists have also been strengthened and their 'Westminster' theology re-installed amongst many spiritually
awakened churches. There has been much mutual enjoy-
ment of this 'neo-reformation' among both types of
churches to whom the doctrine of grace is precious. Almost
unnoticeably, baptist churches have taken into their system
a 'regard' for reformed churches in spite of the latter's
continued adherence to the paedobaptist heresy. This is
undermining the testimony of the baptists as a consequence. It cost our forefathers dear to stand apart from those
adhering to that heresy in their day; similarly, today's
baptists must be prepared to be 'out-of-step' and even
persecuted for the truth's sake. It is as important today to
expose and condemn the infant-baptism error as it ever

was in the fathers' day and baptists must not shirk their total submission to scripture in this matter of truth nor hesitate to stand separated from those who persist in this heresy. Here the previously stated insistence to reject all but solid biblical evidence must again be made.[21]

Similarly, the baptist must enforce a strict biblical discipline in the church and not tolerate any accommodation pleaded on 'charitable' grounds. Biblical standards must be set out clearly and they must be enforced. Inevitably this means the making of a clear witness against the laxity and looseness in other churches and refusing to accommodate baptist order in the interest of maintaining outward harmony among 'christians.' The baptist cannot allow changing standards to 'match the times', because he remains convinced that God's Word stands as an unchanged and absolute authority in all church matters. The baptist cannot acknowledge as true churches of Christ any that compromise their doctrine or order by failing to maintain a membership of disciplined baptised believers only.

The baptist recognises the benefits which fellowship among churches will bring but must reject fellowship which compromises the truth. In this respect he rejects as unbiblical the structured institutions which exist in the world in the name of christianity but which contradict the simple biblical principle that God's unit is the local church. Hierarchical organisations among churches with tiered offices of authority and regional, national and international centres of administration and government have no place in the plan of God as the baptist understands scripture. In so far as such structures have been built up in the name of baptist churches, the biblically disciplined baptist disowns them entirely. He believes they introduce a 'third force' into the simplicity of local church autonomy in which believers submit themselves to the rule of Christ as Head as a direct rule through the Word and by the Holy Spirit. The baptist adheres to the main truths of the christian faith, and is not a schismatic, and acknowledges that such truth is often common ground with those in other assemblies which are not called baptist. But, as has been shown in detail previously, the baptist distinctively holds certain bible truths to which he calls all christians everywhere to return.

The baptist is an uncomfortable bedfellow, as has been said earlier, because he cannot biblically express church unity with those in error who hold another doctrine of the gospel or of the church.[22] Ecumenical union, or church-to-church fellowship, which crosses such doctrinal frontiers is not permissible for him. Similarly, ecumenical evangelism is not possible. The Great Commission of Christ is the biblical basis for all christian evangelism. In the Master's words, the gospel is to be preached together with a response required, namely, believers' baptism.[23] Modern ecumenical evangelism demands a compromise at this point because not all participating churches and preachers are willingly ruled by the scripture in this particular. This compromise results in the omission of the preaching of the believer's duty to be baptised on coming to faith in Jesus Christ. That is error. It is a blatant departure from the commandment of scripture. Furthermore, the scripture demands that the new convert be taught to obey everything that Jesus has commanded. The baptist finds that both the separation from the gospel of baptism, and the sending of converts to their nearest church, or the one that they claim to have some link with, is a wholly unacceptable practice and bars baptist participation in united missions for evangelism.

There is another, frequently over-looked, result of these differing convictions governing evangelism, held by the baptist on the one hand and the ecumenical co-operator on the other. Ecumenicals can cheerfully divide up potential fields of mission into spheres of service with a view to not trespassing upon another's working-district. In doing this, they recognise as valid the work of all kinds of professing christians, regardless of unbiblical doctrines or practices. The baptist is not free to make such compromises whether at home or on the overseas mission field. He is obliged to preach the whole counsel of God, not only to the obviously pagan, but to the unsaved nominal christian. Compromising ecumenical churches count such separation 'unchristian' but it is no more than biblical simplicity, that pre-eminent baptist characteristic which makes the baptist stand out in today's society as the true non-conformist that he is. He remains the recurring witness to unchanging truth by which the Holy Spirit still rebukes apostasy and calls churches to repentance, to more than reform, to an unqualified return to New Testament christianity.

Our baptist fathers set an example to follow in loving one another, even as our Lord commanded. Recall the forgiveness shown by Hubmaier towards his persecuting brother in Christ, whilst suffering the tortures of the rack at Zwingli's hands, and again, the love shown to Lord Liechtenstein, whom he had led to the Lord, when he had him handed over to be tortured and burnt in Vienna by the catholics.[24] Remember the tender heart of Hans Denck, dying worn out in his thirtieth year, who wrote in his last testament, 'It gives my heart pain that I should stand in disunity with many men whom I cannot help but call my brothers because they pray to the same God to whom I pray, and give honour to the Father for the same reason that I honour him, namely, because he sent his Son, the Saviour of the world. Therefore, as God wills, and so much as in me is, I will not have my brother as an opponent, and my Father as a judge, but in the meantime will attempt to reconcile all my adversaries with me'.[25] Does the world see in today's non-conforming baptist such tender love for others that it will say, as it did of Denck, *'no one has been able to discover even the smallest spot in his character.'*[26] To love the brothers who stand at one with us is one thing, but to love the brothers from whose compromise we separate, is another. Such love should temper the judgements made on other christians from whom baptists divide in their stand for the truth. In nothing is this more necessary than in the condemnation of godly paedobaptists who persist in the blasphemous heresy of infant baptism which the fathers called 'the highest and chief abomination'. Baptists must expose this scandalous barrier to the salvation of multitudes for what it is; but that exposure must be made in Christ-like love.[27] To fulfil his mission, the baptist must maintain a life above rebuke himself otherwise how can he correct effectively the errors he sees in others or help them to set their lives right with scripture. It is no part of a baptist's way of life to be tolerant of wrong but he must fulfil his ministry in love.

Baptists historically reject a dependence upon the ordained ministry, whether of priest or pastors, for the understanding and interpretation of scripture, or for the proper administration of the ordinances of baptism and the Lord's Supper, believing in the universal priesthood of believers, a doctrine which the reformers brought to light but failed to practise in their church systems. Every believer is individually indwelt by the Holy Spirit and he stands before God without need of any earthly mediator of the Word or grace of God. In this matter his relationship with other christian assemblies and denominations must be in tension. In this matter also the baptist needs to show a gracious spirit, remembering that the scriptures also give pastors and teachers a specially gifted ministry which even they must accept and be seen to be submissive to biblical precept. The baptist must show unconditionally a willingness to see all other churches submit to the Word of God and to Jesus as Head with the consequential elimination of any separate baptist witness! Herein is seen his honesty in commitment to his heritage.

The baptist has to check constantly his relationship with his fellow baptists in a church to church sense. As has been shown in the course of previous chapters and explicitly stated in the first, not all churches called 'baptist' are baptist in fact.[28] Some churches still call themselves 'baptist' because such was their origin but they have jettisoned the heritage of their fathers to a greater or lesser extent. They may no longer submit to the scriptures entirely as the Word of God, authoritatively governing the church's profession of faith and practice. Some have even called the scriptures into question and rejected their authority outright. Such are no longer baptists. Some have ceased to preach the whole counsel of God and accommodated themselves to society's changing fashions. Some have ceased to demand a credible evidence of regeneration and faith in Christ as necessary for membership and even dropped believers' baptism as required for admission to the church fellowship. Such have ceased to be baptist churches. The fact that national or international 'baptist unions, conventions or alliances' ignore such departures from truth and still allow such erroneous churches to remain in their membership lists, does not alter one whit the fact that such are not baptist. Some 'baptist' churches have amalgamated with 'Anglican', 'Congregational', 'United Reformed' or 'Methodist' churches and condoned the unscriptural doctrines and practices of those bodies. Such churches have ceased to possess any claim to the name 'baptist'. The baptist is compelled to stand apart from all such and deny church to church fellowship with them. Yet his stand must be compassionate, whilst firm, that God may be honoured and a clear biblical witness made.

Many baptist churches have neglected biblical simplicity and adopted an authoritarianism not much different from that which characterised Rome and was rejected at the Reformation in the seventeenth century; although presbyterian elders and synods soon re-acquired an over-ruling authority which cannot be found in scripture. From the first they adopted a structured hierarchy obnoxious to baptists at the time. It is easy for baptists to reject such hierarchical government in all those churches which follow in the catholic tradition, though called protestant. It is not so easy for baptists to spot and reject those evidences of incipient unbiblical authority which their own groupings have installed to act and speak on their behalf. What about the installation of Area Superintendents by the Baptist Union in England and Wales in 1915? Are they much different from anglican sees and bishops, or indeed, the catholic equivalents?[29] What of the subtle insertion into British baptist trust deeds of a necessity for the supposedly independence local church to belong to a specified union and to call as pastor only such ministers as are listed by that union?[30] What kind of independence is that? More pertinently, where did this authority come from? It is not to be found in the scripture and by this token it is not baptist.

Most astonishing is the recent evolution of 'renewed baptist churches' which are certainly rejecting the overlordship of the Baptist Union in Britain but have installed a new hierarchy all their own! These churches in many cases have experienced a real spiritual revival, having previously been spiritually dead. For this, the biblical baptist must be thankful to God and therefore the more careful when he comes to take a separatist line against the unbiblical aspects of these particular churches which frequently belong to nationwide structured hierarchies connected with the magazine 'Restoration'. They too have divided up the country into 'dioceses' and they too have adopted an unbiblical pyramid of authority over the churches, with 'apostles' at its apex! They too have turned their backs on the true baptist doctrine of the local church as God's basic unit. They cannot be acknowledged as fellow bible baptist churches. In this case the tender spirit of the separating baptist is more necessary in view of the evidences that exist of a work of God among these charismatic assemblies.

The bible baptist applies the rule of scripture to the local church's fellowship literally. He must not accommodate the traditions of men, the pressures of the times nor the susceptibilities of those christians who find meticulous regulation by scripture irksome. Hence his church is maintained as a fellowship of baptised believers and the Lord's Supper is placed well inside the disciplined control of the local church as in the scripture. There may well be churches which are so regulated by scripture and are seen to be truly biblical churches though not called by the name 'baptist' and the bible baptist will readily recognise such as sister churches because the nature of a gospel church is seen, not in its name, but in its biblical practice. Some Fellowship of Independent Evangelical Churches in Britain would come under this head.

The need for true christian brotherly love has been emphasised when looking at the baptist's relationship to christians in other than baptist groupings. Here it is vital to emphasise that such love of the brothers is most essential when the bible baptist is considering his relationship towards those others who are known as baptists but whose failures require him to separate from and to rebuke. Let such love temper all the judgements which the bible baptist makes upon his fellows from whom he is divided by Arminianism, Antinomianism, Amyraldianism, or any other abnormality. Let love temper our judgements; let love restrain our blanket condemnations; let love stir our hearts in honest prayer for all who love the Lord Jesus

Christ in sincerity and truth. The baptist forefathers not only showed love towards brothers in the larger sense, but they showed it in an exquisite manner within the local church fellowships. They spoke of their *'strong longing for sharing, togetherness and unity, even as the Father with the Son.'* [31] Many of the older British baptist churches have a church covenant which runs like this, *'Having first given ourselves to the Lord by grace and then to one another for his sake, we covenant together...'* In its spirit let today's baptists love one another.

In this book, the story of the baptist has been traced with a view to identifying his biblical characteristics and observing his place in the purposes of God during the course of the christian era. To this has been added an outline study of his distinctive doctrine and church order with an examination of its biblical basis as well as its historical development. The reader will have concluded, that the baptist movement is *'a resurgence, a reiteration, a restatement'* of a constant theme in which God addresses his churches with a challenge to return to a total submission to scripture in doctrine and practice, as was quoted from Professor L. Verduin earlier.[32] There should be no need for a baptist witness and no need for baptist churches if only christians would unreservedly submit themselves to God's Word in everything. It was a baptist who said that *'if other denominations saw the light about baptism and followed it, then the baptist denomination would disintegrate'*[33] Certainly that aim should always activate the baptist's reforming ministry. However, the need has been seen to be much larger than the question of baptism alone. Indeed, study has shown that this is not the main issue that activates the baptist's testimony, but rather the whole area of submission to scripture and a right understanding of the nature of a christian church. It is encouraging to find a contemporary trend to renounce the catholic conception of the church among anglican clergy and a strong movement towards a living, regenerate local church fellowship, witnessing for Christ in its own district. The virile charismatic upsurge of this century, with the birth of house churches, has shown a similar acceptance of the simplicity of local church witness in biblical terms. The revival of the doctrines of grace in post-Second World War years has turned many nascent puritans into bible baptists as churches have come into being. Doubtless this is an appropriate period for the baptist to take note of his heritage and give attention to his own God-given place among the churches and *'do the first works'*.[34]

This study will have achieved little if it fails to excite the christian reader to submit himself wholly to the Word of God and establish himself in the fellowship of those who do the same by whatever name they may be known. The baptist's challenge to his fellow christians remains as ever, to be fully such a disciple of Christ as shall fully conform to the scripture. His desire is not the adoption of a name nor of a new mode of baptism, but no less and no more than a total submission to the rule of the Word of God.

Equally, the author will fail if he does not challenge his fellows baptists to look well to their spiritual well-being. They have more than *'a name to live!'*[35] They must hear what the Spirit is saying to the churches in the inerrant scriptures of truth. Wholly disciplined by the Word they must live to make Christ known to all men everywhere. They must live such lives as make his gospel credible by all around them. Equally well, should **'The Baptist'** be addressing an unbeliever, he would beg of you to hear the gospel of God's grace proclaimed in His Word and 'be reconciled to God.'

'The Baptist' would remind himself that all the seven churches, addressed by the Living Lord in the opening chapters of the last book of the bible, were baptised churches. Lest he thinks *'too highly of himself'*, he needs to take to his heart those very same scriptures because **'The Glorious One'** still walks among the lampstands today. Do not his solemn words sound in our ears? *'I know your deeds, your hard work and your perseverance. I know that you cannot tolerate wicked men; that you have tested them that claim to be apostles and are not and found them false. You have persevered and have endured hardships for my name and have not grown weary. YET I hold this against you, you have lost your first love... He that has an ear let him hear!'*[36]

Notes

Notes

Introduction

1. *The Trail of Blood*, J.M. Carroll, Lexington, Ky, USA 1931.
2. *A History of English Baptists*, A.C. Underwood, Kingsgate, London 1947 p 45; *A Pocket History of the Baptist Movement*, G.O. Griffith, Kingsgate, London undated, pp 60, 63-75.
3. *Baptist History and Succession*, Chas. B. Stovall, Kentucky USA 1945, pp 129, 130; *Baptist Succession*, D.B. Ray, Lexington, Ky, USA 1870 together with an *Appendix* to it published by Prof. A.S. Worrell, also of Lexington; the whole thesis argues for Baptist Succession.
4. Some are disinclined to make use of this mode of description; therefore please note:—
   The adjective 'baptistic' is used here and elsewhere in this book, to indicate that which is typical of baptists in doctrine and/or church practice, without there being a full commitment to baptist teaching in all particulars.
5. *The Reformers' Stepchildren*, Professor L. Verduin, Wm. Eerdmanns Publishing Company, Grand Rapids USA, 1964; English edition quoted throughout, Paternoster Press, Exeter, UK.

Chapter 1

1. *Lettera Apud Opera*, Stanilaus Hosius, Trento c1530, pp 112, 113.
2. *The Anatomy of a Hybrid*, Prof. L. Verduin, Eerdmanns Publishing Company, Grand Rapids USA, 1964.
3. *ibid* p 153n.
4. *History of the Baptists*, Thos. Armitage, Bryan Taylor, New York USA 1870, pp 327, 328.
5. *Baptist Confessions of Faith*, W.L. Lumpkin, Judson Press, Valley Forge Va USA, 1969 ed, pp 174, 175.
6. *ibid* p 203.
7. *ibid* p 241, 250.
8. *Concern for the Ministry*, T.F. Valentine, P.B.F. London 1967, p 4 etc.

9. see Chapter 14 p 225fs.
10. Lumpkin op cit pp 248-252.
11. Griffith op cit p 124.
12. *The Baptist Story*, E.A. Payne, B.V. Press, London 1978, p 15.
13. *The Religious Denominations of the World*, V.L. Milner, Garretson, Phila. USA, 1871, pp 41, 42.
14. *Stepchildren*, Verduin, op cit pp 277-279.
15. *Baptist Distinctives*, Dr. J.M. Stowell, Regular Baptist Press, Des Plaines, Ill, USA, 1965.
16. Whitley op cit p 4.
16. *Matthew 22:21; Mark 12:17; Luke 20:25;*
18. see Chapter 14 p 255fs.
19. *idem* pp 226-229.
20. see Chapter 15 pp 239-240.

Chapter 2

1. *New Park Street Pulpit*, Vol VII, C.H. Spurgeon, Passmore, London p 225.
2. *Metropolitan Pulpit*, C.H. Spurgeon, Passmore, London 1881 Vol 27 p 249.
3. *A History of the Baptists*, J.T. Christian, Southern Baptist Convention Publications, 1922.
4. Carroll op cit.
5. *The Baptist Heritage*, J.M. Halliday, Bogard Press, Texarkana USA 1974.
6. Armitage, op cit p lfs.
7. Underwood op cit p 27.
8. *The Life and Faith of the Baptists*, H. Wheeler Robinson, Methuen, London 1927.
9. *The History of British Baptists*, W.T. Whitley, Griffin, London, 1923.
10. Hosius op cit.
11. *Stepchildren*, Verduin op cit p 14.
12. *Acts 11:26.*
13. *Acts 20:28.*

Chapter 3

1. *The History of Christianity*, ed T. Dowley, Lion, Tring UK, 1977 see Introduction p xii.
2. Griffith op cit pp 12, 17.
3. *ibid* p 18.
4. *ibid* p 28.
5. Armitage op cit pp 155-164.
6. *ibid* pp 158, 159.
7. *History of the Christian Religion and Church*, J.A.W. Neander, Berlin 1826; English ed p 203.

8. *Ecclesiastical History*, J.L. von Mosheim, Göttingen 1755, Eng. ed.
9. Armitage op cit pp 182-184.
10. Griffith op cit p 28.
11. *2 Corinthians 11:3; cf Romans 12:8;16:19; 2 Corinthians 1:12 KJV.*
12. Griffith op cit p 27.
13. see Chapter 14 pp 234-236.
14. or Cassivelaunus, King of the Catuvellauni or South Britons, see *History of Britain*, Prof. G.M. Trevelyan, Longmans, London 1926, 3rd ed 1945 p 16.
15. *Welsh Baptists*, J. Davis, 1835, American rep. Hogan, Pittsburg 1976 pp 1-7; see also *Church History*, Andrew Miller, Pickering & Inglis, London 1875, pp 254-256; *The Celtic Church*, J.T. McNeill, University of Chicago Press, 1974 p 10.
16. *Exposition of the New Testament*, John Gill, London 1763, rep 1853 Vol ii p 647; McNeill op cit p 16.
17. *Exposition of the Old Testament*, John Gill, London 1761, rep 1852 Vol i p 56.
18. *Bye-Paths in Baptist History*, J.J. Goadby, Stock, London 1871, p 1.
19. Armitage op cit p 227.
20. *Baptist History*, J.M. Cramp, Stock, London 1868; quotes Fuller's *Church History* i;13.
21. says they *"watched, prayed, fasted, preached having high meditations under a low roof and large hearts betwixt narrow walls"* adding *"it is now generally acknowledged to be a fable."* p 26.
22. Trevelyan op cit pp 14, 28.
23. Davis op cit p 8; *Acts and Monuments*, J. Foxe, London 1563, p 104; *Treatise on Baptism*, H. D'Anvers, London c1672 pp 60, 61.
24. Davis op cit pp 9, 10.
25. *Encyclopedia of Religious Knowledge*, Schaff-Herzog, Grand Rapids, Mich, USA, 1949 vol ii p 468; McNeill op cit p 23.
26. The region of North-west/Central Turkey; see *Acts 2:10; 13:14fs; 16:6.*
27. *A History of Christianity*, K.S. Latourette, Harpur, New York 1953 pp 128, 129; *A History of the Christian Church*, F.J. Foakes-Jackson, Cambridge 1891 pp 184-187.
28. *The Pilgrim Church*, E.H. Broadbent, Pickering & Inglis, London 1931 p 12.
29. Foakes-Jackson op cit p 208.
30. Latourette op cit p 129.
31. Foakes-Jackson op cit pp 223-225.
32. Latourette op cit p 138; for Hubmaier see Chapter 4 pp 53-58.
33. *ibid* pp 137-139; Neander op cit vol i p 343.
34. Mosheim op cit (quoted by Armitage op cit p 203).
35. *A Handbook of Church History*, S.G. Green, R.T.S., London 1907, p 331; Armitage op cit p 213.
36. *Stepchildren* Verduin op cit pp 21-62; Armitage op cit pp 201, 283, 316.
37. *ibid* p 34.

38. Griffith op cit pp 29-33.
39. Armitage op cit p 201.
40. *A History of the Christian Church*, W. Walker, T & T Clarke, Edinburgh 1918, p 235; Neander op cit Vol V pp 361-363; Broadbent op cit pp 45-48.
41. Latourette op cit p 299; Green op cit p 388.
42. *idem*; Green op cit p 46.
43. Green op cit p 387.
44. *ibid* p 388; Latourette op cit p 299.
45. Latourette op cit p 299.
46. *ibid* p 300.
47. *idem*; Green op cit p 424. (Their leader in Bulgaria was Jeremiah, surnamed Bogomil, meaning *Friend of God*.)
48. Gk *cathari* means *the pure ones*, or *puritans*; Latourette op cit pp 299-301.
49. Latourette op cit pp 453-455.
50. *idem*.
51. Davis op cit p 17.
52. Latourette op cit pp 177-182.
53. *Historical Theology*, Wm. Cunningham 1862, Banner ed London 1960 vol 1 pp 472-482.
54. Goadby op cit p 8.
55. *Milner's Church History*, J. Milner, Hogan & Thompson, London 1835, Vol iii p 459; Goadby op cit pp 8, 9; *One Snowy Night*, Emily Holt, Shaw London c1875 Historical Appendix pp 380-384.
56. *A Short History of the Baptists*, H.C. Vedder, American Baptist Publications Society, Philadelphia USA 1897, pp 49-54; Latourette op cit p 455.
57. Latourette op cit p 450; Broadbent op cit p 45.
58. Broadbent op cit pp 85, 86; Green op cit pp 507, 508; Miller op cit pp 454, 455; *Notices Historiques du Cinquantière de l'Association Evangélique des Eglises Baptistes*, F. Buhler, Mulhouse France 1971 p 7n.
59. Broadbent op cit pp 86, 87; Latourette op cit p 450; Miller op cit pp 455, 456; see also Chapter 10 – 'France', pp 159-165.
60. *idem*.
61. *idem*; Lion *History*, op cit pp 314, 317, 319, 320.
62. Broadbent op cit p 91.
63. *The History of the Evangelical Churches of the Valleys of Piedmont*, S. Morland, Henry Hills, London 1658, rep CHRA Gallantin Ten. USA, 1982 pp 30-34.
64. Broadbent op cit pp 91, 92.
65. *idem*; cf *History of Protestantism*, J.A. Wylie, Cassel, London, Vol 16 for a fuller account of the Waldenses.
66. Latourette op cit pp 751, 760, 761.
67. *idem* pp 451, 452; Broadbent op cit pp 92-94; Williams op cit pp 520-526; Lion *History* op cit p 315; Vedder op cit pp 66-74.
68. Latourette op cit pp 450-453, 761-766, 1289; Williams op cit pp 519-529, 559fs.

69. *ibid* pp 539-545.
70. *ibid* p 707; *Patterns of Reformation*, G. Rupp, Epworth, London 1969 p 255 and note.
71. Broadbent op cit pp 106-111, 116, 142, 282; Walker op cit pp 280-281; Lion *History* op cit pp 356, 357; *Imitation of Christ*, Thomas á Kempis (1380-1471); for influence on John Wesley see Latourette op cit pp 649, 1023.
72. *Christian Dogmatics*, J.J. van Oosterzee, Eng tr Hodder, London 1874, p 34.
73. *Itinerary*, J. Leland, London 1533-39; John Wyclif, L. Lechler, Vienna, Eng tr entitled *John Wyclif and his English Precursors*, Lorimer/Green R.T.S. London 1904, p 86.
74. Lechler op cit p 123.
75. *ibid* p 139.
76. *ibid* pp 149, 150, 193.
77. *ibid* p 198.
78. *ibid* pp 209-212.
79. *idem.*
80. *ibid* p 219; cf *Isaiah 58:1*.
81. *History of English Baptists*, J.M. Crosby, London 1738, Vol i p 8.
82. Lechler op cit pp 255fs.
83. *ibid* p 453; Broadbent op cit pp 117-121.
84. Broadbent op cit pp 123-125; Lechler op cit pp 497-505; Walker op cit pp 304-306;
85. *ibid* pp 126, 132-135.

Chapter 4

1. *The Radical Reformation*, G.H. Williams, Westminster Press, Philadelphia USA 1962, pp 159, 162; Broadbent op cit pp 96, 112, 162.
2. *Luther*, J.M. Todd, Hamish Hamilton, London 1982, p 371; *Martin Luther*, E.G. Rupp, Arnold, London 1970 pp 9-16, 29, 33; Latourette op cit pp 703-705.
3. *The Anabaptist Story*, W.R. Estep, Eerdmanns, Grand Rapids Mich USA 1975, pp 145-147; see Chapters 14 and 15 for fuller treatment.
4. Latourette op cit pp 708, 709.
5. *ibid* 710; Rupp op cit p 67.
6. Mosheim op cit.
7. Williams op cit pp 839fs.
8. A fuller treatment of these points is found in Chapters 14 and 15.
9. Armitage op cit p 397.
10. *ibid* p 304; Robertson's *History of Charles V* Vol ii pp 353-356; Milner op cit p 840.
11. W.E. Neff quoted by Estep op cit p 79.
12. *Hans Denck Schriften*, W. Felmann, Bertelsmann Verlag, Gütersloh Germany 1956 quoted by Estep op cit p 79.
13. Williams op cit pp 149-155; Estep op cit pp 73-79.

14. Armitage op cit p 388; *History of Augsburg*, Wagenseil, Augsburg 1822, Vol ii p 67.
15. *ibid* p 388; Lumpkin op cit p 167.
16. Estep op cit p 75, 87n4; Latourette op cit pp 781, 782.
17. *ibid* p 40-50.
18. Lumpkin op cit pp 22-31; Williams op cit pp 181-185; Estep op cit p 41.
19. Estep op cit pp 42, 43.
20. *ibid* p 42-48; Williams op cit pp 185-188.
21. *idem* quotes *M. Sattler's Trial and Martyrdom* 1527, G. Brossart.
22. Estep op cit pp 40-50.
23. Williams op cit pp 44-46, 75-79, 81; also see Estep's (op cit) index; Vedder op cit p 95.
24. *ibid* pp 362-368, his whole chapter is devoted to the Münster tragedy; Vedder op cit p 95.
25. *Balthasar Hubmaier*, Torsten Bergsten, Eng tr W.R. Estep, Judson 1978.
26. *ibid* pp 25, 48-66.
27. *ibid* pp 68-78.
28. *ibid* pp 90-121.
29. *ibid* pp 124-132.
30. *ibid* pp 123fs.
31. *ibid* pp 134.
32. *ibid* pp 137-141.
33. *ibid* pp 155-159.
34. *ibid* pp 228-271.
35. *ibid* pp 216fs; Latourette op cit p 781.
36. *ibid* pp 288-311 (see whole of his chapter 13).
37. *ibid* p 304; Vedder op cit pp 83, 84.
38. *ibid* p 323.
39. *ibid* p 39-40.
40. *ibid* pp 379, 380.
41. *ibid* pp 397, 398.
42. see illustration; *ibid* p 391.
43. *ibid* pp 347-380 for review of Hubmaier's theology.
44. Latourette op cit pp 719, 735, 780; Williams op cit pp 38-44, 57-59, 69-75, etc.
45. Williams op cit p 78; Estep op cit pp 65, 80-82.
46. *ibid* p 676.
47. *ibid* p 680.
48. *ibid* p 253; Estep op cit pp 83-87.
49. Armitage op cit p 385.
50. Williams op cit p 273; Estep op cit p 84; Broadbent op cit pp 194-196.
51. *Pilgrim Marpeck*, J.J. Kiwiet, J.G. Oncken Verlag, Kassel 1957, pp 94-122; Estep op cit pp 132, 88n24.
52. Estep op cit pp 86, 87; Williams op cit p 274.
53. Williams op cit pp 274, 891.

Chapter 5

1. Williams op cit pp 119-121; Estep op cit p 27; Armitage op cit p 336.
2. see previous chapters.
3. *History of the Reformation*, D'Aubigny, London 1843, Vol II, pp 364fs; Latourette op cit p 747; Miller op cit pp 678, 679.
4. The house stands in Neumarkt No 5, in the old city of Zürich. It bears a commemorative tablet reading (in German) *"In this house lived Konrad Grebel who, together with Felix Manz, founded the baptist movement"* and the legend, *"Rebuilt 1752"*. It stands opposite the National Archives office and is now used for a theatre club being close by the old city theatre. A photograph appears on back cover.
5. Latourette op cit pp 747-749; Williams op cit pp 90, 91.
6. Williams op cit p 65.
7. *ibid* pp 145, 146.
8. see previous chapter pp 53-58; Vedder op cit pp 84-87.
9. Williams op cit pp 145, 146.
10. Estep op cit pp 8-14; for a fuller account *Conrad Grebel and the Emergence of Anabaptism*, E. Huser, FEBE Symposium, Mulhouse 1970 Part III; *Chronicles of the Hutterite Brethren*, Eng tr J.F. Zieglschmid, New York 1943; Williams op cit p 123.
11. Estep op cit pp 10, 11; Williams op cit pp 119, 120.
12. *ibid* p 27, 38 n12; *Sabbata mit Kleineren Schriften und Briefen,* J. Kessler rep Huber, St. Gallen 1902 p 144.
13. Estep op cit pp 27-30; Rupp op cit p 371.
14. *ibid* pp 28-30; Armitage op cit p 314.
15. *ibid* p 31; Williams op cit pp 120-148.
16. Verduin op cit pp 217.
17. Estep op cit p 32.
18. *ibid* p 33; Armitage op cit pp 335, 336; Warns op cit p 193.
19. *ibid* p 34.
21. *Der Stark Jorg*, J.A. Moore, Oncken Verlag, Kassel 1955 p 46; Estep says that this book provides an excellent biography together with two hymns of his composition.
22. Estep op cit pp 33-37; Armitage op cit p 336; Williams op cit pp 120-126; 679; and index.
23. *ibid* pp 72, 73.
24. Mark 16:20.
25. Williams op cit pp 147, 88, 121; Estep op cit p 82.
26. *ibid* p 88.
27. *ibid* p 96; Estep op cit p 82.
28. *ibid* p 121, 181.
29. *ibid* p 186; Estep op cit p 83.
30. *ibid* pp 251.
31. *ibid* p 185.
32. *ibid* p 187.
33. *ibid* p 419.
34. *ibid* p 421; Estep op cit p 83.

35. *Calvin*, François Wendel, Paris 1950, Eng tr P. Mairet, Fontana London 1965, chapter 1; Williams op cit pp 750-752.
36. See chapter 14; Williams op cit pp 756-760; *The Church through the Centuries*, G.C. Richardson, Rel. Bk. Club, London rep New York 1938 p 61.
37. See chapter 15 pp XXX.
38. Williams op cit 606.
39. *ibid* p 607.
40. *ibid* p 614.
41. *ibid* p 622; Verduin op cit 50-57; Estep op cit p 15 n28.
42. *ibid* pp 12-26, 529-537, etc.
43. *ibid* p 5.
44. *ibid* pp 19, 20; Latourette op cit pp 672-674; Miller op cit pp 598-601; Walker op cit pp 256, 319, 320.
45. Williams op cit pp 639-653, 733-757.
46. *ibid* pp 749-762; Latourette op cit pp 792-795.
47. *ibid* pp 425-429, 670-681; Estep op cit pp 97-103.
48. Latourette op cit pp 785, 786; Lion op cit p 402; Estep op cit pp 114-129.
49. *The Story of the Mennonites*, C.H. Smith, Mennonite Pub, Newton USA 1957 pp 85, 86; Williams op cit pp 387-391; Estep op cit pp 114, 115.
50. Williams op cit p 387; Estep op cit p 116.
51. *ibid* p 390; Estep op cit pp 117, 118.
52. Estep op cit pp 118, 119.
53. *ibid* p 120; Smith op cit pp 90-92; Williams op cit pp 392-394.
54. Smith op cit pp 94-99.
55. *ibid* p 110; Estep op cit p 126.
56. *ibid in toto*;
57. Goadby op cit p 8.
58. J. Milner op cit Vol iii p 459; Goadby op cit pp 8, 9. *One Snowy Night*, E. Holt, Shaw London 1875, see Historical Appendix pp 380-384.
59. Armitage op cit p 447.
60. *idem*; Cramp op cit p 205.
61. *William Tindale*, R. DeMaus, R.T.S. London 1904, a Biography.
62. Williams op cit pp 799fs; Walker op cit pp 401-408; *Documents Illustrative of Church History*, Gee & Hardy, London 1896, pp 178-252.
63. Estep op cit p 209; see also Horst in Esteps notes p 233.
64. Williams op cit p 403.
65. Foxe op cit pp 278-286; Williams op cit p 403.
66. Armitage op cit p 407.
67. *idem*; Foxe op cit p 323; Crosby op cit pp 46-51.
68. Williams op cit p 780.
69. Gee & Hardy op cit p 275; Walker op cit pp 406, 407.
70. Latourette op cit see chapter 36 pp 788-796.
71. *ibid* p 406.
72. *ibid* pp 809, 810; Walker op cit p 412.
73. Walker op cit p 413.

74. *ibid* pp 413-415.
75. Williams op cit p 701; Crosby op cit pp 79, 80.
76. *ibid* p 784; Armitage op cit p 452; Lumpkin op cit pp 79-81.
77. *ibid* pp 781, 782.
78. *ibid* pp 784-787; Lumpkin op cit pp 97-99; Wall op cit Vol ii p 106.
79. Underwood op cit pp 32-46; Armitage op cit pp 455-460; Cramp op cit pp 255-262 & pp 80-87.
80. *Baptism Anatomised* Wm. Wall Oxford 1704, p 107; Crosby op cit p 95.
81. Crosby op cit pp 95fs.
82. Underwood op cit pp 46, 47.

Chapter 6

1. *The English Baptists of the Seventeenth Century*, Dr. B.R. White, Bpt. Hist. Soc. London 1983 p 21.
2. *ibid* p 22.
3. *ibid* p 23.
4. *idem*.
5. Schaff-Herzog op cit Vol 1 pp 456, 457.
6. Estep op cit pp 219-223.
7. Underwood op cit pp 46-48; Lion Hist, op cit p 389.
8. Technically the term *'arminian'* had not then come into use. (Synod of Dordrecht was 1618.)
9. Underwood op cit pp 46, 47.
10. Whitley op cit p 18.
11. Schaff-Herzog op cit p 468.
12. Underwood op cit pp 51-53.
13. *ibid* p 46.
14. *The Mystery of Iniquity*, T. Helwys, London 1612, see Dedication.
15. Underwood op cit pp 46-48.
16. Williams op cit pp 789-791.
17. *ibid* p 787, 788; *Congregationalism*, W.B. Selbie, Methuen, London 1927, pp 14-27; *Dissenting Churches in London*, W. Wilson, London 1808 Vol 1 pp 14-36.
18. Latourette op cit pp 815, 816; Selbie op cit pp 14-41.
19. *London's Oldest Baptist Church*, E. Kevan, Kingsgate London 1933; Underwood op cit p 60; Crosby op cit Vol 1 p 149.
20. Crosby op cit Vol 1 p 102.
21. Lumpkin op cit p 81.
22. Underwood op cit p 69.
23. Whitley op cit p 70; Underwood op cit p 70.
24. Underwood op cit p 70; Robinson op cit pp 148-167.
25. *History of England*, Lord Macauley, Longman, London 1864 Vol 2 p 33.
26. Crosby op cit Vol 1 p 303.
27. Armitage op cit p 441; Underwood op cit pp 66fs.

28. Wilson op cit Vol 1 pp 403-439; see also *Life of Kiffin*, J. Ivimey London.
29. Crosby op cit Vol 1 p 184.
30. *ibid* Vol 2 p 3.
31. *ibid* Vol 3 p 4.
32. *ibid* Vol 2 p 184; Vol 3 p 5.
33. *ibid* Vol 3 p 4.
34. Armitage op cit pp 467-470; Underwood op cit pp 109, 110.
35. *ibid* p 547.
36. See Chapter 6 p 100; Underwood op cit p 109, 110.
37. Whitley op cit pp 132, 133.
38. Lumpkin op cit pp 348-353.
39. Armitage op cit pp 449-450.
40. *ibid* pp 450, 451.
41. *ibid* pp 551, 552.
42. *ibid* p 334; Underwood op cit p 61.
43. *ibid* pp 470fs, 676fs; Underwood op cit p 59fs; Whitley op cit pp 86, 183.
44. Crosby op cit vol 1 pp 334-344; Underwood op cit pp 111fs; Whitley op cit pp 132fs; Armitage op cit pp 547-550.
45. White op cit p 16 quotation from Ivimey.
46. *ibid* p 34 quotation from *To the king's most excellent majesty*, E. Barber London 1641.
47. *ibid* pp 35, 41.
48. for an example see *Association Records of the Particular Baptists-Abingdon Association* Bapt. Hist. Soc., London 1974.
49. Armitage op cit pp 570, 571.
50. White op cit p 40.
51. *ibid* p 104.
52. Robinson op cit pp 148-167.
53. Underwood op cit p 79.
54. *ibid* p 108; *Henry Danvers*, G.E. Lane, Strict Bapt. Hist. Soc., London 1972.
55. White op cit pp 83-86. Lane op cit pp 18fs.
56. *ibid* p 95; Underwood op cit pp 82-84.
57. *Documents of the Christian Church*, H. Bettensen, O.U.P., 2nd ed London/New York 1963 p 293.
58. Whitley op cit p 105; White op cit p 100.
59. White op cit pp 103, 104.
60. Crosby op cit Vol 2 pp 184, 185.
61. *ibid* Vol 2 pp 105, 106.
62. *ibid* Vol 2 pp 185-209.
63. Bettenson op cit p 294.
64. *ibid* pp 294, 295.
65. *ibid* pp 298-300.
66. Crosby op cit Vol 2 pp 355-361.
67. See the following biographical works: *John Bunyan* (i) George Offer, Blackie, London 1890; (ii) J. Brown, Hulbert, London 1928; (iii) A.R. Buckland, R.T.S. London 1928; (iv) an article by T. Dowley,

Hist. Chris. op cit pp 392, 393; additionally Armitage op cit pp 528-539.

68. see Chapter 15 pp 254, 255; Offor Vol 2 pp 602-616.
69. *The Life of Milton*, J. Toland, 1699, rep 1761 pp 145-151; *Milton's Life and Works*, Mitford, Bell London 1886 pp cv-cviii.
70. Mitford op cit p cvi.
71. *Milton's Christian Doctrine*, Vol 2 pp 419-421 quoted by Armitage op cit pp 540-547.
72. Mitford op cit pp 151, 152.
73. Robinson op cit p 159; Macauley op cit chapter 1; Crosby Vol 2 pp 185-193; Underwood op cit p 109; Armitage op cit p 550.
74. Lumpkin op cit p 156.
75. *ibid* pp 235-238 see section B.
76. *ibid* pp 241-295.
77. *ibid* pp 288, 289.
78. *The Beginnings of Quakerism*, Braithwaite, pp 12, 43fs; Whitley op cit p 84fs.
79. *The Records of a Church of Christ meeting in Broadmead, Bristol*, E. Terrill London 1847.
80. White op cit pp 111, 112.
81. *ibid* p 113.
82. Robinson op cit p 158.
83. Underwood op cit p 109.
84. *ibid* pp 110, 111.
85. *ibid* p 109.
86. Whitley op cit p 71.
87. White op cit p 79.
88. *ibid* p 72.
89. *ibid* p 112; Whitley op cit p 134.
90. Whitley op cit p 91.
91. Crosby op cit Vol 3 pp 51, 52; Whitley op cit p 72.
92. White op cit p 74; Underwood op cit p 109.

Chapter 7

1. Underwood op cit pp 116fs; Robinson op cit pp 57-61.
2. Crosby op cit Vol 3 pp 266-271.
3. *Concern for the Ministry*, T.F. Valentine, P.B.F. London 1967.
4. *Galations 3;25*.
5. Ivimey op cit Vol 3 pp 262fs, 272; Underwood op cit pp 135-137.
6. *Hypercalvinism*, P. Toon, The Olive Tree, London 1967.
7. Underwood op cit pp 137-140; Robinson op cit p 214.
8. *ibid* pp 140, 141; Robinson op cit p 61.
9. *ibid* pp 142, 178, 179.
10. *ibid* pp 143-147.
11. *ibid* p 159; *Gill's Body of Divinity*, Baker Book House, Grand Rapids Mich. USA 1978; Toon op cit pp 45, 96fs, 105fs, 119fs; Cramp op cit pp 441-444; *Memoir of John Gill*, J. Rippon London.

12. Wilson op cit Vol 4 pp 141-152, 212-225; Crosby op cit Vol 4 p 272.
13. Underwood op cit pp 149-159; *Free Tradition in England*, E.A. Payne, Kingsgate London p 80.
14. *ibid* p 159.
15. *ibid* pp 160, 178-182; Ivimey op cit Vol 4 pp 606fs, also p 41.
16. *ibid* p 160, 161; Ivimey Vol 4 pp 606fs.
17. *ibid* p 170.
18. *ibid* pp 161-168; *Life and Death of Rev Andrew Fuller*, J.W. Morris, London 1816 pp 37fs; *Life and Works of A. Fuller*, J. Ryland, London 1816.
19. *William Carey*, A. Pearce Carey, Hodder & Stoughton, London 1923; *mss* same author; Armitage op cit pp 579-583; Whitley op cit pp 245-257; Hist. Chr. Lion op cit pp 548fs.
20. Underwood op cit pp 167, 172-174.
21. *ibid* pp 167, 183, 184.
22. *ibid* pp 173fs.
23. *ibid* pp 182-185.
24. *ibid* pp 142, 143, 165, 182.
25. *ibid* pp 168fs.
26. *ibid* p 163; Whitley op cit pp 241, 273, 274.
27. *The Baptist Union* E.A. Payne, Carey-Kingsgate, London 1959 pp 19, 20.
28. *ibid* pp 23-25.
29. *ibid* pp 3, 60, 61.
30. *ibid* pp 3-5, 110-112.
31. *ibid* pp 109, 110.
32. *Pastor C.H. Spurgeon*, R. Shindler, Passmore & Alabaster, London 1892 pp 22-50.
33. *ibid* pp 50-128.
34. *ibid* pp 129-270.
35. *ibid* pp 271-275; Payne BU op cit 127; Underwood op cit pp 127-143.
36. Payne BU op cit p 146.
37. *ibid* p 129.
38. *Baptists Who Made History* A.S. Clement (editor), Carey-Kingsgate London 1955 pp 77-85.
39. *idem; Biography of John Clifford*, C.T. Bateman, Law London 1908.
40. Payne BU op cit pp 2fs.
41. *Spurgeon and the Modern Church*, Rbt. Sheeham, Grace Pub. Trust, London 1985.
42. Clement (essay by Payne) op cit p 128.
43. *ibid* p 131.
44. *The Churches at the Crossroads*, J.H. Shakespeare, Kingsgate London 1918.
45. Payne BU op cit pp 186, 187.
46. *ibid* pp 185, 186.
47. *ibid* p 160.
48. *ibid* pp 184, 12.
49. Clement (Payne) op cit p 135.

50. Underwood op cit p 136.
51. Payne BU op cit pp 200, 219.
52. *ibid* pp 146fs.
53. Lumpkin op cit pp 237-240.
54. *ibid* pp 236, 237.
55. Underwood op cit pp 128-135, 168; Payne BU op cit pp 30, 131.
56. *ibid* pp 60, 61.
57. *Spurgeon*, A. Dallimore, Banner, Edinburgh 1985 pp 209, 212-214.
58. Payne BU op cit pp 109, 110.
59. Dallimore op cit p 205.
60. Payne BU op cit p 142.
61. *ibid* p 146.
62. *ibid* p 160.
63. *ibid* pp 182, 183, 185-187; Clement op cit p 131.
64. Clement op cit p 134.
65. Payne BU op cit p 12.
66. *To be a Pilgrim*, W.M.S. West, Lutterworth, Guildford UK 1983 pp 172-174.

Chapter 8

1. See Chapter 7 p 119.
2. See Chapter 8 pp 145, 146.
3. *Gospel Standard Societies Articles of Faith* London.
4. *The Story of the Suffolk Baptists*, A.J. Klaiber, Kingsgate London 1933 p 108.
5. Underwood op cit pp 109-111.
6. Klaiber op cit pp 70, 71, 81-83, etc; Underwood op cit pp 188, 205.
7. *ibid* pp 81-84; Underwood op cit p 188.
8. Klaiber op cit pp 121, 127-143.
9. *ibid* pp 144-152; Underwood op cit pp 121, 205.
10. Underwood op cit p 208.
11. *idem.*
12. *ibid* p 209.
13. *The Baptists of London*, W.T. Whitley, London, pp 80fs; Payne BU op cit 86, 87; Bapt. Hist. Soc. Quarterly Vol 9 pp 109fs.
14. Underwood op cit pp 246, 247; *Metropolitan Association Centenary Handbook*, London 1971.
15. *ibid* p 105.
16. *ibid* p 246.
17. *Memoirs of Mr. J. Stevens*, anon, Houlston & Stoneman London 1848 pp 88, 89.
18. *A Manual of Faith and Practice*, W.J. Styles, Briscoe, London 1897; *A Guide to Church Fellowship*, W.J. Styles, Briscoe, London 1902.
19. *Affirmation of Faith 1966; Guide to Church Fellowship 1971*; published together as *We Believe* Grace Publ. Trust, London 1983.
20. *Memoir of William Gadsby*, J. Gadsby, London 1845; *Manchester and*

the Early Baptists, Ralph Ashton, Manchester 1916, pp 35-61; Underwood op cit p 185.

21. *Lancashire: Its Puritanism and Nonconformity*, R. Halley, Vol 2 pp 484fs; Underwood op cit p 185.
22. Underwood op cit p 186.
23. *ibid* p 242-246.
24. *The Seceders*, J.H. Philpot, Farncombe, London 1930-32, Vol 2 pp 46fs; Underwood op cit p 243.
25. *Preaching Peace*, P.M. Rowell, Zoar Publ. Trust, Ossett UK 1981 is a sympathetic biography.
26. *The Baptist Times* London, 1929 p 616, Lester Gaunt writing about Strict Baptist churches.
27. Underwood op cit p 105; Whitley op cit p 306.
28. H. Tydeman-Chilvers in Klaiber, op cit p 7.
29. Underwood op cit p 105.
30. *Baptists in the Twentieth Century*, K.W. Clements, Baptist Hist. Soc. London 1983 p 4.

Chapter 9

1. Armitage op cit pp 598-600.
2. *ibid* pp 601-602.
3. *ibid* pp 600-604; Underwood op cit p 84; Whitley op cit pp 78fs.
4. See this chapter; Underwood op cit p 192.
5. *ibid* p 85; Whitley op cit pp 78fs.
6. *ibid* p 96.
7. *ibid* p 102.
8. *ibid* p 129.
9. Armitage op cit pp 607-612; Whitley op cit p 300.
10. *ibid* p 609.
11. *History of the Baptists in Scotland*, G. Yuille, SBUP Glasgow 1926 pp 16-23.
12. *ibid* pp 24-35; Underwood op cit p 72.
13. *ibid* pp 44-54; Underwood op cit p 189fs; Whitley op cit p 294.
14. *ibid* pp 50-52, 60, 61; Underwood op cit pp 194fs; Whitley op cit pp 250, 295-297.
15. *ibid* p 39-44; Underwood op cit pp 194fs; Whitley op cit p 250.
16. *ibid* p 55-65, 69, 72, 73; Underwood op cit pp 194fs; Whitley op cit pp 295-297.
17. *ibid* p 76-88.
18. Armitage op cit p 670; Underwood op cit pp 76fs.
19. *ibid* p 571; Underwood op cit p 195; Whitley op cit p 275.
20. Whitley op cit p 251.
21. *Irish Baptist Handbook*, Belfast, N.I.

Chapter 10

1. See Chapter 3 pp 32, 33.
2. Whitley op cit p 329.
3. Broadbent op cit pp 35-89; Armitage op cit pp 284-287; Latourette op cit p 450.
4. See Chapter 3 p 36; *Notice Historique de Cinquantenaire*, de l'Association Evangélique d'Eglises Baptistes de Langue Française, Mulhouse, France 1971 p 7 (NHC).
5. Broadbent op cit p 87.
6. *ibid* p 96.
7. *ibid* pp 102-106.
8. Wylie op cit Vol 2 p 513.
9. Broadbent op cit pp 226-228.
10. *ibid* pp 208, 209.
11. *ibid* pp 209-211; *Life of Farel* Frances Bevan, Lausanne 1884, Eng tr London 1893.
12. *ibid* pp 221-225.
13. See Chapter 5 pp 72, 73.
14. *The Baptists in Europe*, J.H. Rushbrooke, Carey, London 1923 pp 175, 176.
15. *ibid* pp 176-179.
16. *ibid* pp 177-180.
17. *Sur les Ailes de la Foi*, R. Saillens, Institut Biblique, Nogent-sur-Marne, France.
18. NHC op cit pp 20, 24.
19. Rushbrooke op cit pp 180, 181.
20. *ibid* p 21; NHC op cit p 21.
21. NHC op cit p 23.
22. *ibid* pp 23, 24.
23. *Annuaire de l'Association Evangelique d'Eglises Baptistes de Langue Française*, Mulhouse, France 1982.
24. Rushbrooke op cit p 181.
25. NHC and Annuaire de l'A.E.E.B. op cit.
26. Rushbrooke op cit p 181.
27. *ibid* p 17; *Johann Gerhardt Oncken*, J.H. Cooke, Partridge, London 1908 pp 13-15; Armitage op cit pp 827-830; Clement op cit p 58.
28. Rushbrooke op cit pp 18, 19; Cooke's Oncken op cit pp 16-20.
29. *ibid* p 20; Cooke op cit p 24.
30. *ibid* p 20; *ibid* p 26.
31. Cooke op cit p 27.
32. *ibid* pp 45-61; Armitage op cit p 828; Clement op cit p 61.
33. Clement op cit p 68.
34. Cooke op cit p 72.
35. Rushbrooke op cit p 17; Clement op cit p 58.
36. *ibid* p 26; Cooke op cit p 183; Armitage op cit pp 307-309.
37. *ibid* pp 29, 30; Clement op cit p 63; Cooke op cit p 73, 74; Armitage op cit pp 73, 74.
38. *ibid* pp 29, 30, 75-82; Cooke op cit p 42.

39. *ibid* pp 83-96.

40. *ibid* pp 101-106.

41. *ibid* pp 97-101.

42. *The New Schaff-Herzog Encyclopedia of Religious Knowledge* New York 1949 ed Vol 2 p 210.

43. Rushbrooke op cit pp 48, 49.

44. Annuaire de l'A.E.E.B. op cit.

45. Armitage op cit p 574.

46. Yuille op cit p 46.

47. Rushbrooke op cit pp 48, 49; Clement op cit p 64.

48. see Chapter 11 pp 204, 205.

49. Rushbrooke op cit p 182.

50. see Chapter 5 pp 72-74.

51. Rushbrooke op cit pp 182-185.

52. *ibid* p 185-188.

53. *ibid* pp 49-53.

54. *Missionary Reports* various dates, Grace Baptist Mission, Abingdon UK.

55. See Chapter 4 p 43fs.

56. Smith op cit pp 205, 283, 324, 376-383.

57. *ibid* pp 57, 326, 383; *Out of Great Tribulation* E.A. Payne, B.U.P., London 1974 p 11 (OGT).

58. Broadbent op cit p 305-312; Smith op cit pp 635-637.

59. Payne OGT op cit pp 11-15; Cooke op cit pp 144fs.

60. *ibid* pp 15-24; Broadbent op cit pp 312-333.

61. *ibid* pp 34fs; *Why They Suffered* P. Master, Metropolitan Tabernacle Bookshop, London SE1 1979 pp 2-4 (WTS).

62. *ibid* pp 42fs; *ibid* p 3.

62a. Masters WTS op cit p 1.

63. Payne OGT op cit pp 42fs; Masters WTS op cit p 3.

64. Read: *Faith on Trial*, M. Bordeaux, Keston College, Bromley UK 1971; *Religion in Communist Lands*, also Keston College; *Song from Siberia*, A & P Dyneka, Collins, London 1973 pp 33fs.

65. Visitors to USSR, and other European countries, will find useful *Where is the Baptist Church?*, E. Ruden, E.B.F., Laerdalsgade 7, DK-2300 Copenhagen S., Denmark; also the Annuaire de l'A.E.E.B. op cit.

66. See Chapter 3 p 33.

67. Broadbent op cit pp 57-62.

68. *ibid* pp 93, 94.

69. Rushbrooke op cit pp 167-171.

70. *ibid* pp 157-163.

71. *ibid* pp 164-166.

Chapter 11

1. *The History of the Baptists in Virginia*, R.B. Semple, 1810 rep 1894;

Armitage op cit pp 724-738; Goadby op cit p 460.
2. Armitage op cit p 622.
3. Lion History op cit pp 435, 436.
4. *ibid* p 347.
5. *Baptist Beginnings*, E. Hulse, Carey, 1973 p 51; Armitage op cit pp 653, 654.
6. Goadby op cit pp 404fs; Armitage op cit pp 658fs.
7. Walker op cit p 567.
8. Armitage op cit pp 691, 692.
9. *ibid* pp 658fs.
10. Armitage op cit pp 619-686; Whitley op cit pp 63, 156; Baptist Quarterly 1979/80 Vol 28 p 357; Cramp op cit p 408.
11. Hulse op cit pp 53-56.
12. Armitage op cit pp 715-718; Lumpkin op cit p 347.
13. *ibid* p 729; *The Baptists of Virginia 1699-1926*, Garnett, Ryland USA pp 64-66; Halliday op cit pp 60-66.
14. Armitage op cit p 735 who quotes Abiel Holmes in *American Annals* Vol 2 p 488; Lion Hist. op cit p 441.
15. Lumpkin op cit pp 347-400.
16. Armitage op cit pp 719, 720, 744, 846, 847.
17. *Your Baptist Heritage*, Isaac Backus, Challenge Press, Little Rock, Ark, USA 1844, rep 1976, pp 179-182.
18. Armitage op cit p 779; Backus op cit p 127.
19. *ibid* pp 760-763.
20. *ibid* pp 787-793; Semple see note 1.
21. *ibid* pp 814-818.
22. Walker op cit p 585.
23. Lumpkin op cit pp 377-379.
24. Smith op cit pp 529-835; Estep op cit pp 203, 204.
25. Armitage op cit pp 721-723.
26. Ivimey op cit Vol 3 pp 131-133.
27. Armitage op cit pp 934, 935.
28. Lion Hist. op cit 531-537.
29. Armitage op cit pp 922, 923; Whitley op cit pp 331, 332; Vedder op cit p 284.
30. *ibid* p 920; Vedder op cit p 284.
31. *ibid* pp 920-923; Whitley op cit p 332.
32. *ibid* p 926; see *Baptist History*, J.M. Cramp, Elliot Stock, London 1868.
33. *ibid* p 923.
34. Whitley op cit p 335.
35. *ibid* p 334; Armitage op cit p 923.
36. See Chapter 9 p 155; *ibid* pp 336, 337; *ibid* p 927; Vedder op cit pp 285-292.
37. Armitage op cit pp 933, 934; Vedder op cit p 294.
38. *ibid* p 914.
39. Latourette op cit p 1283; Schaff-Herzog op cit Vol 12 pp 275-281.
40. *ibid* pp 1429, 1430; Underwood op cit pp 199, 200; *The History of the Expansion of Christianity*, K.S. Latourette, Eyre & Spottiswood,

London 1945 onwards, Vol 5 pp 48-61; (When this extensive work is referred to hereafter the abbreviation *Latourette's Expansion* is used; where the one volume *A History of Christianity* is quoted is referenced by his name only, viz: *Latourette*.

41. Latourette's Expansion op cit Vol 5 pp 53, 54.
42. *ibid* Vol 5; Armitage op cit 838.
43. *ibid* Vol 7 pp 174-175.
44. *ibid* Vol 5 p 107.
45. Clement (essay by A.C. Elder) op cit pp 108-116.

Chapter 12

1. Armitage op cit pp 826, 827.
2. *Alfred Saker*, E.M. Saker (his daughter), R.T.S., London 1908.
3. Whitley op cit pp 339-341.
4. Latourette's Expansion op cit Vol 5 p 331; Whitley op cit pp 339-341.
5. *ibid* Vol 5 pp 396, 388, 399.
6. *ibid* Vol 5 pp 423, 424; Armitage op cit pp 826, 827.
7. *ibid* Vol 5 pp 424, 432-434.
8. *Missing Believed Killed*, Margaret Hayes, Hodder & Stoughton, London 1966.
9. Latourette's Expansion op cit Vol 5 p 450.
10. *ibid* Vol 5 pp 440, 441.
11. *ibid* Vol 5 pp 216fs.

Chapter 13

1. Latourette op cit pp 930-933.
2. *ibid* p 932; *Missionary Pioneers in India*, J. Rutherford, Elliot, Edinburgh, 1896 pp 1-33.
3. Rutherford op cit pp 4fs.
4. *ibid* pp 34-56.
5. See Chapter 7 pp 120, 121; Rutherford op cit pp 95-140; Latourette op cit pp 1033-1035.
6. *Other Sheep of the Tamil Fold*, J.K. Thorpe, S.B.M. London 1961; *Into All the World*, E. & J. Appleby, S.B.M., London 1971.
7. Latourette op cit p 933.
8. *Operation World*, P.J. Johnson, S.T.L. Publishers, Bromley UK 1978 pp 100-102, 127-128.
9. Thorpe op cit pp 6-9.
10. *ibid* pp 16-26.
11. *ibid* pp 27-41.
12. *ibid* pp 42-66.
13. *ibid* pp 45-47.
14. Armitage op cit pp 821, 822.

15. *ibid* pp 836, 837; Latourette's Expansion op cit Vol 7 pp 300fs.
16. *ibid* pp 937-939; *ibid* Vol 6 p 312.
17. *ibid* p 939; *A Century of Protestant Missions in China*, D. MacGillivray, Shanghai 1907; Latourette's Expansion op cit Vol 6 pp 318, 319.
18. Latourette's Expansion Vol 6 p 317.
19. See Chapter 7 pp 120, 121; Carey op cit pp 251, 252.
20. Latourette's Expansion Vol 6 pp 302, 306, 317.
21. Armitage op cit p 835.
22. Latourette's Expansion op cit Vol 5 p 270.
23. Armitage op cit p 937-939; Latourette's Expansion Vol 5 pp 143fs.
24. *idem; ibid* Vol 5 pp 143, 148, 151.
25. *idem; ibid* Vol 5 pp 154, 156, 158.
26. *idem; ibid* Vol 5 p 192.

Chapter 14

1. *"Their distinctive feature is the doctrine of the church"*, Whitley op cit p 4.
2. see Matthew 16:18; Ephesians 1:22,23; 3:10; 5:24,25; Colossians 1:18; Hebrews 12:23. *Systematic Theology*, A.H. Strong, Armstrong, New York 3rd ed 1890 p 494.
3. Lumpkin op cit pp 57, 71, 119, 136, 165, 285; We Believe op cit p 21.
4. John 3:3,5; Strong op cit pp 494.
5. Matthew 18:17; Acts 14:23; Romans 16:5; 1 Corinthians 1:2; 4:17; 6:19; 1 Thessalonians 2:14; Strong op cit p 495.
6. Latourette op cit p 782.
7. Strong op cit pp 499fs; We Believe op cit p 21; Lumpkin op cit p 166.
8. Strong op cit p 495 (d); If the alternative reading in the singular of the word *church* in Acts 9:31 is insisted upon, then the baptist understands this to be the collective noun expressing plurality, plus an acknowledgement of the common likeness; that is, all are *independent churches of Christ*.
9. Armitage op cit pp 200fs; Latourette op cit p 139; *Stepchildren* Verduin op cit pp 21-35.
10. *Anatomy* Verduin op cit pp 105-111, 118-121, etc.; Verduin also gives an exposé of Luther on the same error p 165; Note carefully that in the parable of the *Wheat and Tares* in Matthew 13:24-30 & 36-43, Jesus states clearly that the *field* is the *world* and not the church!
11. *An Expository Dictionary of New Testament Words*, W.E. Vine, Oliphants London 1939 Vol 1 p 316 etc; Greek/Latin Lexicons show NT Greek word *matheteuo* to be tr as (L) *disco*.
12. Armitage op cit pp 200fs.
13. *ibid* p 201.
14. See Chapter 4 pp 43, 44; Chapter 17 p 266; Armitage op cit p 201.
15. James 2:26.
16. Philippians 1:11.

17. Neander op cit Vol 1 p 343.
18. Lumpkin op cit p 24; cf *Waterland Confession* see Lumpkin op cit p 57; also pp 101, 110, 111, 121, 186, etc.
19. *ibid* p 25.
20. Smith op cit pp 107-109, 173-177, etc.
21. We Believe op cit p 24.
22. 1 Corinthians 12; Ephesians 4; see Strong op cit pp 500fs.
23. *History of the Free Churches of England 1688-1891*, H.S. Skeats & C.S. Miall, James Clarke, London 1891 p 19 and footnote.
24. Williams op cit p 224.
25. *ibid* p 191.
26. *ibid* pp 4-6; *Anatomy* Verduin op cit p 108fs.
27. *idem.*
28. *ibid* p 144.
29. See Chapter 11 pp 186-190; Ivimey op cit Vol 2 pp 208-211; Armitage op cit pp 686fs; Backus op cit pp 179-182.
30. *What Baptists Stand For*, H. Cook, Carey-Kingsgate, London 1947 p 157.
31. Williams op cit p 255.
32. *ibid* pp 177-185.
33. Lumpkin op cit pp 63, 64; see his article *Waterland Confession of the Mennonites* pp 40-66; Williams op cit p 224.
34. Cook op cit pp 163, 164.
35. *ibid* p 220 giving *Declaration of 27 June 1939* as Appendix II.
36. *The Donatist Church*, W.H.C. Frend, Oxford 1952 quoted by Verduin in *Stepchildren* op cit p 33.
37. Dostoevsky quoted by Verduin *ibid* pp 33, 34.
38. *ibid* p 33.
39. *ibid* p 35.
40. *Didache und die Waldenser* A. Harnack, Leipzig 1886 p 269 quoted by Verduin *Stepchildren* op cit p 35.
41. *The Mystery of Iniquity*, Helwys op cit see Ascription to James I in Facsimile edition p xxv.
42. *ibid* p 42.
43. *ibid* p 69.

Chapter 15

1. *The Lord's Supper*, E.F. Kevan, SBM Kovilpatti India 1960 p 13; (Eng rep available).
2. Williams op cit pp 105-117.
3. See Chapter 16 pp 259fs.
4. *A Paper of Ecclesiology Study Group*, MASBC, London 1985 p 3; *Work of Christ*, W. Berkouwer, Presbyterian & Reformed, ### USA 19## p 199.
5. Further scriptures are Acts 8:12; Romans 6:13; John 3:5; Acts 10:47.

6. see Romans 6:3,4; 1 Corinthians 15:1; Colossians 2:12; cf Strong op cit pp 527, 528.
7. Strong op cit p 530-534.
8. *Baptism*, Johannes Warns, Eng Tr Paternoster, London 1957 pp 140, 145.
9. *Institutes of Religion*, J. Calvin, Eng tr Beveridge, Clarke, London 1962 vol 2 p 524 (#4 xv).
10. *Works* Thos. Goodwin, Nichol, Edinburgh 1861 onwards Vol 4 p 42.
11. *Cat. Minor*, M. Luther Vol 1 p 146.
12. *Meaning of Baptizein*, T.J. Conant 1864 rep Kregel 1977.
13. *Christian Baptism*, J. Murray, Presbyterian & Reformed, Philadelphia, U.S.A., 1972 p 10.
14. Strong op cit pp 522-527.
15. *Complete Body of ... Divinity*, J. Gill, London 1769, Baker rep 1978 Vol 2 pp 640-647.
16. *Paedobaptism Re-Examined*, A. Booth, Palmer, London 1829.
17. *Baptism – Its Mode and Subjects* A. Carson, Houlston & Stoneman, London 1844.
18. *The History of Infant Baptism*, Wm. Wall, London 1702 rep Griffith & Co London 1889.
19. *The Biblical Doctrine of Infant Baptism*, P. Marcel, Paris, Eng tr James Clarke, London 1953.
20. *The Waters Divide*, Bridges & Phypers, IVP London 1977 p 79.
21. see Chapter 5 p 66; Estep op cit p 27.
22. Armitage op cit p 398 quotes Inst. #4 xv and Cat. Minor Vol 1 p 146.
23. *Cat. Trent*, Part II 1545-1563.
24. Latourette op cit p 299; Williams op cit p 678.
25. Armitage op cit pp 426, 427 (quoting Wm. Wall op cit).
26. References to Anglican rubrics use Prayer Book 1662, SPCK No 2092 Cambridge p 221.
27. *Believers' Blue Book*, H. Pickering, Pickering & Inglis, London 143fs.
28. *idem*.
29. *Lion Handbook of the Bible*, Lion, Tring UK 1973 p 584.
30. *History of Baptism*, Wall op cit Vol 1 pp 570, 571.
31. Helwys' *Mystery* Part 3.
32. Underwood op cit pp 58, 59; cf Armitage op cit pp 460-464.
33. If Armitage is correct, rather than Underwood and the British historians, then the contrary could be true.
34. *London's Oldest Baptist Church* op cit Dr. Kevan tells the story of this church.
35. Lumpkin op cit p 167.
36. *Ideal Church*, ed E. Hulse, Carey Publications, 1972 Conference symposium p 25.
37. Armitage op cit p 344; *Sabbata*, Kessler op cit p 144.
37a. Strong op cit p532.
38. *Life and Epistles of St.Paul*,W.J. Coneybeare & J.S. Howson, Longman, London 1862 Vol 2 p184.
39. *Cat.Minor*, Luther, op cit Vol 1 p 146.
40. Strong op cit p 127.

41. Armitage op cit pp 138-146.
42. See note 26 above; Prayer Book 1662 p 222.
43. Strong op cit pp 534-538.
44. *De Baptismo*, Tertullian quoted by Wm. Wall op cit pp 41-50; Conant op cit pp 137-140; Strong op cit p 522.
45. Armitage op cit p 162.
46. *Anti-Gnosticus*, Part II Neander quoted by Armitage op cit p 162.
47. Armitage op cit pp 302, 303.
48. Hubmaier in *Letter to Oeclampadius* November 1524 quoted by Williams op cit p 135.
49. Neander op cit p 436; Armitage op cit p 164, 165.
50. *Der Christliche Glaube*, Vol 2 p 383 quoted by Armitage op cit pp 164, 165.
51. *Baptist Principles*, H. Wheeler Robinson, Carey-Kingsgate, London 1938 pp 55, 56.
52. Warns op cit pp 74, 75 (full references given).
53. Cunningham op cit Vol 2 pp 125, 126.
54. Warns op cit p 60.
55. Cunningham op cit Vol 2 p 144.
56. Neander op cit Vol 1 p 436; Schaff-Herzog op cit Vol 1 p 441; Armitage op cit quotes Cyprian *Epist, LXX Conc. Carth. Ap. Cyp*, p 233; see also pp 162, 302, 303.
57. Strong op cit Sect. 4-B (a) p 531; Bergsten (Hubmaier) op cit p 288; Bergsten's chapter 8 sets out Hubmaier's view in full; Gill's Comm. Vol 1 p 817.
58. Crosbie op cit Vol 1 p 13.
59. *Denck Schriften* p 107, quoted from Estep op cit pp 176, 177.
60. Estep op cit p 152; Matthew 28:19,20.
61. See Chapter 15 p 238.
62. Acts 2:46; 20:7.
63. Luke 22:19; 1 Corinthians 11:23fs; Acts 2:43.
64. Strong op cit pp 538-542.
65. *The Lord's Supper* Kevan op cit p 13.
66. *ibid* p 12; Williams op cit pp 90, 91; see Chapter 4 pp 54-56.
67. Lumpkin op cit pp 18-31.
68. *ibid* pp 102-113.
69. *ibid* pp 174fs.
70. *ibid* pp 216-218.
71. *ibid* pp 235-295.
72. See Chapter 14 pp 228-230.
73. We Believe op cit p 23.
74. Strong op cit pp 546-553 (includes discussion on *Open* and *Closed* Communion).
75. Armitage op cit p 468.
76. *Works* Robert Hall, Holdsworth, London 1839 Vol 3.
77. Underwood op cit p 209.
78. *ibid* p 207.
79. Robinson op cit pp 119, 120.

Chapter 16

1. *The Mission and Expansion of Christianity*, Adolf Harnack, New York 1908 Vol 1 p 348n.
2. Hist. Christ. Lion, ed Dowley, Introduction p xii.
3. *2 Corinthians 3:2,3.*
4. *The Hutterite Brethren*, J. Horsche, Goshen, Ind. USA 1931 pp 7, 8.
5. Estep op cit p 95; see also Williams op cit p 426.
6. Williams op cit pp 844, 845.
7. *ibid* p 844.
8. *ibid* p 861.
9. *ibid* p 863.
10. *Luke 4:18,19.*
11. Williams op cit p 861.
12. Smith op cit p 230.
13. Lumpkin op cit p 388.
14. *ibid* p 393.
15. *ibid* p 409.
16. *ibid* p 415.
17. *ibid* p 420.
18. *ibid* p 423.
19. *We Believe* op cit p 22.
20. *Baptist Union Handbook*, London 1982 p 13.

Chapter 17

1. *Stepchildren Verduin* op cit pp 21-62; Armitage op cit pp 201, 283, 316.
2. Armitage op cit p 209.
3. See Chapter 3 p 26; Griffiths op cit pp 15-18.
4. *ibid* p 152.
5. *ibid* p 153.
6. Lumpkin op cit p 20.
7. Estep op cit pp 145, 146; Lumpkin op cit p 20.
8. *idem.*
9. *ibid* p 149.
10. *ibid* p 96.
11. *Matthew 18:15-19*; see chapter 14 pp 229, 230.
12. Lumpkin op cit p 25.
13. Estep op cit p 186.
14. *Stepchildren* Verduin op cit p 26.
15. Latourette op cit p 450.
16. *ibid* p 455.
17. Williams op cit p 182.
18. Armitage op cit p 408.
19. *ibid* p 409.
20. Latourette op cit p 779.

21. *1 Corinthians 14:24, 25.*
22. *John 17:24.*
23. see Chapter 4 pp 53-58.
24. Estep op cit pp 78, 79; Armitage op cit p 390.
25. Williams op cit p 187.
26. *Stepchildren* Verduin op cit p 217; Estep op cit p 33.
27. Williams op cit p 433.
28. *idem.*
29. *2 Timothy 3:17; Colossians 1:10.*
30. see Chapter 6 pp 85fs.
31. see Chapter 3 pp 25fs. Armitage op cit pp 408, 409.
32. see Chapter 3 pp 25fs.
33. see Chapter 4 pp 43fs.
34. see Chapter 4 pp 43fs; Williams op cit p 839.
35. see Chapter 7 pp 111fs; Latourette op cit pp 764, 765;. *The Articles of the Synod of Dort* Eng tr 1804, rep Sovereign Grace Union, London 1936.
36. Lumpkin op cit pp 114, 115.
37. *ibid* p 173.
38. *ibid* p 227.
39. *ibid* p 343.
40. see Chapter 7 pp 133-135; Baptist Union Directory, BUP London 1981, 82, p 13.
41. *Systematic Theology*, Chas. Hodge, rep J. Clarke, London 1960, Vol 2 p 147.
42. Strong op cit pp 322-325.
43. *The Children of Abraham*, D. Kingdon, Carey Publications, Worthing, UK 1973.
44. Lumpkin op cit p 146.
45. *ibid* p 158.

Chapter 18

1. see Chapter 1 pp 5fs.
2. *The Westminster Confession of Faith* Belfast ed 1933, Chapter 1 section VI; *Commentary on the Confession of Faith*, A.A. Hodge, Nelson, London 1870 pp 37-39; *The Westminster Assembly and its Work*, B.B. Warfield, pp 166, 224-231.
3. *The Baptist Origins*, K.H. Good, published lecture T.B.S. Toronto, Canada October 1983.
4. see Chapter 1 pp 15, 16.
5. *Westminster Confession* op cit Chapter 25, Section II p 86.
6. see Chapter 14 pp 225fs.
7. see Chapter 17 pp 266, 267.
8. *Luke 23:39-43.*
9. see Chapter 17 pp 268, 269.
10. for example H. Denck see Chapter 4 pp 48-50; cf Bergsten op cit pp 78, 79.

11. *1 Corinthians 14:25.*
12. see Chapter 16 pp 259fs.
13. see Chapter 3 p 33.
14. *cf 2 Thessalonians 1:10-12.*
15. see Chapter 7 p 126.
16. Williams op cit p 845.
17. Estep op cit p 84.
18. see Chapter 16 p 260.
19. Estep op cit p 193.
20. Williams op cit p 845.
21. see Chapter 18 p 278.
22. see Chapter 1 p 10.
23. *Matthew 28:19, 20.*
24. Bergsten op cit p 307.
25. *ibid* pp 78, 79.
26. see Chapter 4 p 50.
27. see Chapter 15 pp 246-248.
28. see Chapter 1 p 9.
29. see Chapter 7 p 134 see #12.
30. cf Fairbairn Model Deed of Trust, Baptist Union Corporation, London.
31. Williams op cit p 433.
32. see Chapter 2 p 20.
33. Dr. T.H. Robinson, quoted by Dr. E.A. Payne.
34. *Revelations 2:5.*
35. *Revelations 3:1.*
36. *Revelations 2:2-7.*

Indexes of Persons, Places & Topics

Index – Persons

Index – Places

Index – Topics

Bibliography

Bibliography

ANON. *Affirmation of Faith 1966; Guide to Church Fellowship* 1971 reprinted as *We Believe*, Grace Pub. Trust London 1983. *Annuaire de l'Association Evangéliques d'Eglises Baptistes de Langue Française*, Mulhouse 1982. *Memoirs of J. Stevens*, Houlston & Stoneman, London 1848. *Irish Baptist Union Handbook*, Belfast N.I. *Why They Suffer*, Metropolitan Tabernacle, London 1979. *Religion in Communist Lands*, Keston College, London. *MASBC Ecclesiastical Study Group Paper*, London 1985. *The Centenary Handbook of the Metropolitan Association of Strict Baptist Churches*, M.A.S.B.C. London 1971. *Lion Handbook of the Bible*, Lion, Tring, 1973. *The Baptist Union Handbook*, London 1982. *Savoy Declaration of Faith & Order*, 1658, rep. EP London 1971. *The Articles of the Synod of Dort*, Eng. tr. Oxford 1808, rep Sovereign Grace Union, London 1936. *Westminster Confession of Faith*, Belfast 1933.

APPLEBY, E. & J. *Into All the World*, S.B.M. London 1971.

ARMITAGE, Thos. *The History of the Baptists*, Taylor, New York 1870.

ASHTON, Ralph *Manchester and the Early Baptists*, Manchester 1916.

BACKUS, Isaac *Your Baptist Heritage*, Challenge Press, Little Rock, Ark. reprinted 1976.

BARBER, E. *To the King's Most Excellent Majesty*, London, 1641.

BATEMAN, C.T. *Biography of John Clifford*, London 1908.

BERKOUWER, *The Work of Christ*, Banner of Truth, Edinburgh.

BERGSTEN, T. *Balthasar Hubmaier*, Eng. tr. Estep, Judson 1978.

BETTENSON, H. *Documents of the Christian Church*, O.U.P. London 1963.

BOOTH, A. *Paedobaptism Re-examined*, Palmer, London 1829.

BORDEAUX, M. *Faith on Trial*, Keston College, London 1971.

BEVAN, Frances *Life of Farel*, Lausanne 1884; Eng. tr. London 1893.

BRAITHWAITE, W.C. *The Beginnings of Quakerism*, 2nd ed. London 1955.

BRIDGES D. & PHYPERS, D. *The Waters Divide*, I.V.P. London 1977.

BROADBENT, E.H. *The Pilgrim Church*, Pickering & Inglis, London 1931.

BROSSART, G. *M. Sattler's Trial & Martyrdom 1527* quoted by Estep.

BROWN, J. *John Bunyan*, Hulbert, London 1928.

BUCKLAND, A.R. *John Bunyan – The Man & His Work*, R.T.S., London 1928.

BUHLER, F. *Notice Historiques du Cinquantière de l'Association Evangélique des Eglises Baptistes*, Mulhouse, 1971.

CALVIN, J. *Institutes of Religion*, Eng. tr. Beveridge, Clarke, London 1962.

CAREY, A. Pearce *William Carey*, Carey Press, London 1923.

CARROLL, Dr. J.M. *The Trail of Blood*, Lexington, Kentucky, USA 1931.

CARSON, A. *Baptism in its Mode and Subjects*, Houlston, London 1844.

CHRISTIAN, J.T. *A History of the Baptists*, S.B.C.P. 1922.

CLEMENT, A.S. *Baptists Who Made History*, Carey-Kingsgate London 1955.

CLEMENTS, K.W. *Baptists in the Twentieth Century*, Bap. Hist. Soc. London 1983.

CONANT, T.J. *Meaning of Baptizein, 1864*; reprint Kregel, Gd Rapids, 1977.

CONYBEARE, W.J. & HOWSON, J.S. *Life & Epistles of St. Paul*, Longman, London 1862, vol ii p 184.

COOK, H. *What Baptists Stand For*, Carey-Kingsgate, London 1947.

COOKE, J.H. *Johann Gerhard Oncken*, Partridge, London 1908.

CRAMP, J.M. *Baptist History*, Stock, London 1868.

CROSBY, J.M. *History of English Baptists*, London 1738.

CUNNINGHAM, Wm. *Historical Theology*, Banner of Truth, London 1960.

DALLIMORE, A. *Spurgeon*, Banner of Truth, Edinburgh, 1985.

D'ANVERS, H. *Treatise on Baptism*, London 1674.

D'AUBIGNE, *History of the Reformation*, Walther, London 1843.

DAVIS, J. *Welsh Baptists*, 1835; Reprint, Hogan, Pittsburg, USA 1976.

DEMAUS, R. *William Tindale*, R.T.S. London 1904.

DOWLEY, T. (ed) *The History of Christianity*, Lion, Tring, 1977.

DEYNEKA, A. & P. *Song from Siberia*, Collins, London 1978.

ESTEP, W.R. *The Anabaptist Story*, rev. ed. Eerdmans, Gd. Rapids Mich. 1975.

FAIRBAIRN *Model Deed of Church Trust*, Baptist Union, London.

FELLMANN, W. *Hans Denck Schriften*, Bertelsmann, Gütersloh, 1956.

FOAKES-JACKSON, F.J. *A History of the Christian Church*, Cambridge 1891.

FOXE, John *Acts and Monuments*, Clarke London 1563; Rep. Ward Lock 1880.

FREND, W.H.C. *The Donatists Church*, Oxford, 1952.

GADSBY, John *Memoir of William Gadsby*, Gadsby, London 1845.

GAUNT, Lester *The Baptist Times*, London 1929.

GEE & HARDY *Documents Illustrative of Church History*, London 1896.

GILL, John *Exposition of Old Testament*, London 1761; reprint 1852. *Exposition of New Testament*, London reprint 1853. *Complete Body of Divinity*, London 1769; reprint Baker 1978.

GOADBY, J.J. *Bye-Paths in Baptist History*, Stock, London 1871.

GOOD, K.H. *The Baptist Origins*, (published lecture) TBS Toronto 1983.

GOODWIN, John *Works*, Nichol ed. Edinburgh 1861.

GREEN, S.G. *A Handbook of Church History*, R.T.S. London 1907.

GRIFFITH, G.O., *A Pocket History of the Baptist Movement*, Kingsgate London.

HALL, Rbt. *Works*, Holdsworth, London, 1839.

HALLEY, R. *Lancashire – Its Puritanism & Nonconformity*.

HALLIDAY, J.M. *The Baptist Heritage*, Bogard Press, Texarkana, USA 1974.

HARNACK, A. *Didache und der Waldenser*, Leipzig 1886. *The Mission and Expansion of Christianity*, tr New York 1908.

HAYES, M. *Missing Believed Killed*, Hodder, London 1966.

HELWYS, Thos. *The Mystery of Iniquity*, London 1612.

HODGE, A.A. *Commentary on the Confession of Faith*, Nelson London 1873??

HODGE, Chas. *Systematic Theology*, rep. J. Clarke, London 1960.

HOLT, Emily *One Snowy Night*, Shaw, London 1875.

HORSCHE, J. *The Hutterite Brethren*, Goshen Ind. USA 1931.

HOSIUS, Stanilaus *Lettera apud Opera*, Trento.

HULSE, E. *Baptist Beginnings*, Carey Publications, London 1973. *The Ideal Church*, Carey Publications, London 1972.

HUSER, Etienne (ed) *Conrad Grebel & the Emergence of Anabaptism*, Mulhouse, 1970.

IVIMEY, J. *The History of the Baptists*, London 1811-1830. *Life of Kiffin*, London.

JOHNSON, P.J. *Operation World*, S.T.L., Bromley, London 1978.

KESSLER, J. *Sabbata mit Kleineren Schriften und Briefen*, reprint Huber, St. Gallen 1902.

KEVAN, Ernest *London's Oldest Baptist Church*, Kingsgate, London 1933. *The Lord's Supper*, S.B.M., Kovilpatti, India 1960.

KINGDON, D. *The Children of Abraham*, Carey Publ., Worthing 1973.

KIWIET J.J. *Pilgram Marpeck*, Oncken Verlag, Kassel 1957.

KLAIBER, A.J. *The Story of Suffolk Baptists*, Kingsgate, London 1933.

LANE, G. Eric *Henry Danvers*, Strict Baptist Hist. Soc., London 1972.

LATOURETTE, K.S. *A History of Christianity*, Harpur, New York, 1953. *The History of the Expansion of Christianity*, Eyre & Spottiswood, London 1945 onwards.

LECHLER, L. *John Wycliffe & his English Precursors*, R.T.S. London 1904.

LELAND, *Itinerary*, London 1533-39 reprint Oxford 1710-12.

LUMPKIN, W.L. *Baptist Confessions of Faith*, Judson, Valley Forge, USA 1969.

MACAULEY, Lord *History of England*, Longman, London 1864.

MacGILLIVRAY, D. *A Century of Protestant Missions in China*, Shanghai, 1907.

McNEILL, J.T. *The Celtic Churches*, University Chicago Press, USA 1974.

MARCEL, Pierre *The Biblical Doctrine of Infant Baptism*, Univ. Press Paris, 1950; Eng. tr. James Clarke London, 1953.

MILLER, Andrew *Church History*, Pickering & Inglis, London 1875.

MILNER, J. *Church History*, Hogan & Thompson, London 1835.

MILNER, V.L. *Religious Denominations of the World*, Garretson, USA 1871.

MITFORD, *Milton's Life and Works*, Bell, London 1886.

MORLAND, Samuel *The History of the Evangelical Churches of the Valleys of*

Piedmont, Hills, London 1658, reprint CHRA Gallatin 1982.
MOORE, J.A. *Der Stark Georg*, J.G. Oncken Verlag, Kassel, 1955.
MORRIS, J.W. *Life and Death of Andrew Fuller*, London 1816.
MOSHEIM, J.L. von *Ecclesiastical History*, Helmstedt 1727, Göttingen, 1755.
MURRAY, J. *Christian Baptism*, Presbyterian & Ref. Philadelphia, 1972.
NEANDER, J.A.W. *History of Christian Religion and Church*, Berlin, 1826.
OFFER, Geo. *John Bunyan*, Blackie, London 1890.
OOSTERZEE, J.J. van *Christian Dogmatics*, Eng. tr. Hodder London 1874.
PAYNE, E.A. *Out of Great Tribulation*, B.U.P. London 1974. *The Baptist Story*, B.U.P. London 1978. *The Baptist Union – A History*, Carey-Kingsgate, London 1959. *The Free Church Tradition in England*, C-K London 1944.
PHILPOT, J.H. *The Seceders*, Farncombe, London 1930/32.
PICKERING, H. *The Believers'* Blue Book, London.
RAY, D.B. *Baptist Succession*, Lexington, Kentucky, 1870.
RICHARDSON, G.C. *The Church thru the Centuries*, London; reprint New York 1983.
RIPPON, J. *Memoir of John Gill*, London.
ROBINSON, H.Wh. *Life and Faith of the Baptists*, Methuen, London 1923. *Baptist Principles*, Carey-Kingsgate, London 1938.
ROWELL, P.M. *Preaching Peace*, Zoar Publishing Trust, Ossett Yorks, 1981.
RUDEN, E. *Where is the Baptist Church?*, E.B. Fed. Copenhagen, Denmark.
RUPP, E.G. *The Patterns of Reformation*, Epworth, London 1969. *Martin Luther*, Arnold, London 1970.
RUSHBROOKE, J.H. *The Baptists in Europe*, Carey, London 1923.
RUTHERFORD, J. *Missionary Pioneers in India*, Elliot, Edinburgh 1896.
RYLAND, J. *Life and Works of Andrew Fuller*, London 1816.
SAILLENS, R. *Sur les Ailes*, Institut Biblique, Nogent-sur-Marne, 19??
SAKER, E.M. *Alfred Saker*, R.T.S. London 1908.
SCHAFF-HERZOG *Encyclopedia of Religious Knowledge*, Gd. Rapids, Mi. USA 1940.
SELBIE, W.B. *Congregationalism*, Metheun, London 1927.
SEMPLE, R.B. *The History of the Baptists in Virginia*, 1810/1894; reprinted C.H.R. & A. Lafayette, Ten. USA 1976.
SHEEHAN, Rbt. *C.H. Spurgeon & the Modern Church*, G.P.T. London 1984.
SHAKESPEARE, J.H. *The Churches at the Crossroads*, Kingsgate, London, 1918.
SHINDLER, R. *Pastor C.H. Spurgeon*, Passmore & Alabaster, London, 1892.
SKEAT, H.S. *A History of the Free Churches*, London 1891.
SMITH, C.H. *The Story of the Mennonites*, Men. Pub. Newton USA 1957.
SPURGEON, C.H. *New Park Street Pulpit*, Vol. VII Passmore, London. *Metropolitan Pulpit*, London 1881 Passmore, London. *An All-Round Ministry*, Passmore & Alabaster, London 1900.

STOVALL, C.B. *Baptist History and Succession*, Kentucky, 1945.

STOWALL, J.M. *Baptist Distinctives*, Reg. Bpt. P. Des Plaines, Ill. USA 1965.

STRONG, A.H. *Systematic Theology*, Armstrong, New York, 3rd ed. 1890.

STYLES, W.J. *A Manual of Faith & Practice*, Briscoe, London 1897.

TERRILL, E. *The Records of ... Broadmead Bristol*, London 1847.

THOMAS à KEMPIS *The Imitation of Christ*, (1390-1471) various reprints.

THORPE, John *Other Sheep of the Tamil Fold*, S.B.M. London 1961.

TODD, J.M. *Luther*, Hamish Hamilton, London 1982.

TOLAND, J. *The Life of Milton*, 1699; reprint 1761.

TOON, P. *Hypercalvinism*, Grape Vine, London 1967.

TREVELYAN, G.M. *History of England*, Longmans, London 1926. (3rd Ed. 1945).

UNDERWOOD, A.C. *A History of English Baptists*, Kingsgate, London 1947.

VALENTINE, T.F. *Concern for the Ministry*, PBF, London 1967.

VEDDER, H.C. *Short History of the Baptists*, Am. Bp. Pub. Philadelphia 1897.

VERDUIN, L. *The Reformers' Stepchildren*, Eerdmanns, Grand Rapids 1964. *The Anatomy of a Hybrid*, Eerdmann, Grand Rapids USA 1976.

VINE, W.E. *An Expository Dictionary of New Testament Words*, Oliphants, London, 1939.

WAGENSEIL, *History of Augsburg*, Augsburg 1822.

WALKER, W. *History of the Christian Church*, T & T Clark Edinburgh 1918.

WALL, Wm. *Baptism Anatomised*, Oxford 1704; *The History of Infant Baptism*, London 1703; reprint 1889.

WARNS, J. *Baptism*, Berlin 1913; Eng. tr. Paternoster, London 1957.

WENDEL, Fr *Calvin*, Paris 1950; Eng. tr. P. Mairet, Fontana London 1965.

WEST, W.M.S. *To be a Pilgrim*, Lutterworth, 1983.

WHITE, B. *Abingdon Association Records*, Bpt. Hist. Soc. London 1974. *The English Baptists of the Seventeenth Century*, Baptist Historical Society, London 1983.

WHITLEY, W.T. *A History of British Baptists*, London 1923. *The Baptists of London*, London, no date.

WILLIAMS, G.H. *The Radical Reformation*, Westminster, Philadelphia, 1962.

WILSON, W. *The Dissenting Churches in London*, London 1808.

WYLIE, J.A. *History of Protestantism*, Cassell London.

YUILLE, G. *The History of the Baptists in Scotland*, SBUP. Glasgow 1926.

ZIEGLSCHMIDT, J. *Chronicles of the Hutterite Brethren*, Eng. tr. New York 1943.